FANNY AND STELLA

*The Young Men
Who Shocked
Victorian England*

Neil McKenna

D1494441

faber

First published in 2013
by Faber & Faber Ltd
The Bindery, 51 Hatton Garden
London EC1N 8HN

This paperback edition published in 2023

Typeset by Faber & Faber Limited
Printed and bound by CPI Group (UK) Ltd, Croydon, CRO 4YY

A CIP record for this book
is available from the British Library

ISBN 978-0-571-37492-2

2 4 6 8 10 9 7 5 3 1

For
Dede Smith
companion-in-arms

Contents

List of Plates

Acknowledgements   xiii

1   Leading Ladies   1

2   The Hapless Swain   12

3   The Slap-Bum Polka   24

4   In the Dock   31

5   Foreign Bodies   42

6   Wives and Daughters   53

7   Becoming Fanny   65

8   A Tale of Two Sisters   79

9   Monstrous Erections   88

10   A Dirty Business   102

11   Getting Up Evidence   114

12   A Victorian Romance   126

13   Lord Arthur's Wife   138

14   The Toast of the Town   148

15 'Yr Affectionate Fanny'   159

16 The Dragon of Davies Street   167

17 'Come Love'   175

18 *Un Souvenir d'Amour*   187

19 The Battle of the Bottoms   198

20 He, She or It   210

21 A Bitches' Ball   223

22 The Wheels of Justice   235

23 Dead or Disappeared   246

24 This Slippery Sod   257

25 'Pestiferous and Pestilential'   269

26 The Ship of State   282

27 The Most Sensational Event   295

28 A Rout   309

29 'This Terrible Drama of Vice'   321

30 Clouds and Sunshine   336

Epilogue   353

Notes   361

Index   387

Plates

1   Fanny and Stella being led away, *The Days' Doings*
2   'Men in Women's Clothes: The Dressing Room', *The Illustrated Police News*
3   Stella Boulton, Scarborough, 1868 © Oliver Sarony/ Laurence Senelick Collection
4   Stella Boulton dressed as a man © Oliver Sarony/Laurence Senelick Collection
5   Fanny Park in white dress © Frederick Spalding/Essex Record Office
6   Fanny Park with unknown gentleman © Chelmsford, 1868, Frederick Spalding/Essex Record Office
7   Fanny Park © Frederick Spalding/Essex Record Office
8   Fanny Park, Stella Boulton and Lord Arthur Pelham-Clinton © Frederick Spalding/Essex Record Office
9   Fanny and Stella © Frederick Spalding/Essex Record Office
10 Charles Pavitt and Stella Boulton © Frederick Spalding/ Essex Record Office
11 'The Female Personators', *The Illustrated Police News*
12 The Comical Countess and Carlotta Gibbings, *The Illustrated Police News*
13 Stella Boulton © Napoleon Sarony/Laurence Senelick Collection
14 Stella Boulton © Mrs Williams of Northampton/Laurence

Senelick Collection

15   Fanny Park and Stella Boulton © Frederick Spalding/Essex
     Record Office

Acknowledgements

This book could not have been written without consulting the materials on Fanny and Stella held by the National Archives in Kew, who were unfailingly helpful. I am also grateful to the British Library and the British Newspaper Library; to the Metropolitan Police Service Archive in London; to the National Archives of Scotland; to the Parliamentary Archives; to the Wellcome Institute Library; to the library of Imperial College, London; to the libraries of the Royal College of Surgeons in London and the Royal College of Surgeons in Edinburgh; to the Flintshire Record Office who hold the Hawarden MSS; to the Library of Nottingham University who hold the Newcastle Clumber MSS; to the Post Office Museum and Archive in London; to the Essex Record Office; to Michael Hussey of the National Archives and Records Administration in the United States; to Paul Stevens, librarian and archivist at Repton School; to Elizabeth Boardman, archivist at Brasenose College, Oxford; to Rob Petre, archivist at Oriel College, Oxford; to Robin Freeman, archivist at Hampshire Archives and Local Studies; to Andrew Dowsey, archivist at Fife Council; to the *Hamilton Advertiser* and the *Hampshire Chronicle*; to Lesmahagow Central Library; to Hamilton Central Library; and to the National Railway Museum in York.

I would also like to thank the many people who have helped in ways large and small: Dawn Ades, Val Allam,

Nuria Alvarez Vazquez, Carole Angier, Hans Arnold, Ruth Atkins, Susheel Basra, Diane Bennett, Mark Booth, Jamie Buxton, Michelle Carriger, Alan Clark, Sally Cline, Hope Cooke, Ania Corless, Eleanor Crow, Jim Davies, Moris Farhi, Peter Farrer, Edward Fenton, Paul Forbes, Simon Garfield, Nick Gilbert, Christopher Golding, Allister Hardiman, Terry Heath, Alex Holroyd, Charles Hurt, Maggie Iverson, Agnes Jones, Ellen Jones, Liane Jones, Peter Jones, Sian Jones, Marina Leopardi, Jules Lubbock, Vicky Manthorpe, Naomi May, Donald Mead, Naomi Narod, Rictor Norton, Robert Palmer, Patricia Pelham-Clinton-Hope, Carl Philpott, Jonathan Pimm, Gilly Poole, Monica Porter, Keith Raffan, Eleanor Rees, George Robb, Susan Ronald, Caroline Ross Pirie, Diane Samuels, Jane Scruton, Anne Sebba, Michael Seeney, Carole Seymour-Jones, Melanie Smith, David Souden, Diana Souhami, Linda Stratmann, Ben Summerskill, Sandy Suffield, Alex Sutherland, Matthew Sweet, Simon Watney, Caspar Wintermans.

I would particularly like to thank Jonathan Ned Katz for generously sharing his research on John Safford Fiske; Peter Swaab for his insights on Fanny and Stella; Anna Swan for her many helpful suggestions; Julie Wheelwright for her continuous support; Dr Stuart Flanagan for his medical knowledge; Professor Laurence Senelick for so generously allowing me to reproduce photographs of Fanny and Stella from his collection; Sue Fox for her inspired research in the US archives; Rina Gill for her enduring friendship and encouragement; and Will Atkinson for his generosity of spirit.

Dede Smith, to whom this book is dedicated, has been a tireless researcher and an enthusiastic advocate of Fanny and Stella, reading and re-reading the manuscript and suggesting countless improvements. I am very grateful for his friendship and for his wisdom.

I would like to express my very sincere thanks to my agent, Andrew Lownie, and to Julian Loose and Kate Murray-Browne, my editors at Faber, who have been everything that editors ought to be, and more besides.

Lastly, I would like to express my profound gratitude to Robert Jones without whose love and friendship this book could not have been written.

There was an old person of Sark
Who buggered a pig in the dark;
The swine in surprise
Murmured: 'God blast your eyes,
Do you take me for Boulton and Park?'

The Pearl, 1879

1

Leading Ladies

Thursday 28th April 1870

When they were seated in the stalls,
With their low-neck'd dresses and flowing shawls,
They were admired by one and all,
This pair of He-She ladies.
The gents at them would take a peep,
And say they are Duchesses at least,
Lor! what a fascinating pair,
Especially she with the curly hair.

'The Funny He-She Ladies'

Heads turned as the two strikingly handsome women swept imperiously into the pale-green and gilded foyer of the Strand Theatre and made their way to the private box, booked under the name of Mrs Fanny Graham, where two young men – Mr Hugh Mundell and Mr Cecil Thomas were the names they had given to the boxkeeper – were already waiting for them.

In the flurry of excitement, nobody noticed the three ordinary-looking, moustachioed men who had slipped quietly into the theatre on the heels of the two women and then quickly melted away into the darker recesses of the stalls and promenade.

The boxkeeper was excited. He thought that he recognised one of these two divinities as none other than the Duchess of Manchester, the great society beauty whom the Prime Minister, Mr Gladstone, just five days earlier at a state banquet, had praised as among 'the very fairest of our land'.

But the male members of the audience at the Strand Theatre were not so easily fooled. 'The general opinion throughout the house,' one observer reported, 'was that they were two fresh stars in the firmament of the demi-monde, and that their beauty, their fascination, and their paid-for smiles would, before the London season expired, cause many a poor dupe to curse the hour in which he had been born.'

The recently rebuilt Strand Theatre was one of London's largest, and seated over a thousand people. It was famous for three things: for the quality of its air, for its burlesque productions, and for its reputation as a place of successful sexual assignations. Air quality was a prime consideration. Most theatres and music halls reeked of unwashed humanity, a hot and heady mixture of sweat, body odour, pipe and cigar smoke, cheap scent and alcohol. When it was rebuilt in 1865 the Strand was the first theatre with a purposely designed ventilation system and the first to install an industrial-sized Rimmel's Vaporiser, invented by the *parfumier* Eugene Rimmel, which released clouds of perfumed steam to sanitise and deodorise the air.

London was in the grip of a new theatrical craze for burlesques and burlettas, for light operas, comedies, farces, melodramas and pantomimes where women dressed as men and men dressed as women. The pursuit of love with all its thorny and tangled turnings, all its comic and tragi-comic complications, was the proper subject of burlesque. That young women dressed as men fell in love with young men, and young men dressed as women fell in love with young women, far from confusing the audience, seemed to add a delightful *frisson* of sexual excitement to the proceedings. And the Strand Theatre was the very epicentre of burlesque mania, mounting a never-ending succession of 'Grand Burlesque Extravaganzas' which guaranteed full houses night after night.

Above and beyond its technical marvels and its burlesque extravaganzas, the Strand was notorious as a place where men could meet women for sex, and had been patronised on many occasions by no less a personage than the Prince of Wales. It was, as the cartoonist Alfred Bryan slyly insinuated, one of London's 'Noted Shops for Tarts', and a crude but popular limerick made explicit reference to the Strand's erotic reputation:

> There was a young man of St Paul's
> Possessed of the most useless of balls,
> Till at last, at the Strand,
> He managed a stand,
> And tossed himself off in the stalls.

If there was any lingering doubt that the two strikingly handsome women in Mrs Fanny Graham's box were expensively dressed whores, their behaviour soon put paid to such notions. They nonchalantly leaned over their box, waved their fans, twirled their handkerchiefs and 'lasciviously ogled the male occupants of the stalls'. They smoked, they giggled, they nodded and they winked as they waggled their tongues at men in such a way as to leave absolutely no doubt of their sexual intentions.

And they chirruped – so loudly that at one point some members of the audience complained that it quite drowned out the performance. Chirruping was a sucking noise, made with fluttering lips and usually reserved for babies and kittens, but used by whores and their punters alike to signal sexual desire. Sometimes chirrupers were arrested for causing a public nuisance. One persistent chirruper taken up by the police excused himself at the Lambeth Police Court by claiming 'he thought there was no harm in it'.

After half an hour or so Mrs Fanny Graham and her companion, Miss Stella Boulton, stood up, smiled and curtseyed to the gentlemen of the stalls and left their box to go to the theatre's refreshment bar, squired by Mr Mundell and Mr Thomas. Again, nobody paid the least attention to the three moustachioed men who had so unobtrusively followed them into the theatre and who now reappeared in the Strand's saloon bar looking for all the world as if they were fixtures there.

It was clear that Mrs Graham and Miss Boulton had already been drinking quite heavily, and they now proceeded to consume brandies and sherries at breakneck speed. They were immediately besieged by a gang of curious and admiring swells and gallants and some dubious and not-so-dubious gentlemen eager to sample the charms of these two dazzling demi-mondaines.

Miss Stella Boulton was seemingly the younger of the pair and was resplendent in a brilliant scarlet silk evening dress trimmed with white lace and draped with a white muslin shawl. She was more than just pretty. In the glittering, flattering, faceted lights of the Strand's saloon bar she was quite beautiful. She was tall and slender, with a narrow waist and a magnificent bosom, her finely shaped head topped by raven hair fashionably dressed in the Grecian style with coils of plaited hair held in place by a crosshatch of black velvet. Her pale face was captivating, with large liquid violet-blue eyes, just a becoming blush to her cheeks, perfect full ruby lips and pearly white teeth. She seemed to scintillate and shine like a star, and the men could hardly take their eyes off her. If she was indeed a whore, she was an exceptional whore. A veritable queen among whores.

By way of contrast, Mrs Fanny Graham was (and this was putting it charitably) on the plain side and was possessed of what the *Evening Standard* called, diplomatically, 'sterner features'. She seemed older, matronly and more worldly-wise, and her cascading flaxen curls seemed to sit oddly with her dark skin and dark eyes. She wore a rather unbecoming dark-green satin crinoline trimmed with black lace and a black lace mantilla. Her eyes were a little too small and closely set together, her nose a little too large, her brows a shade too heavy, and her cheeks more than a little jowly.

But Mrs Fanny Graham was withal a fine figure of a woman with an expression of great good humour and animation. She was handsome in a mannish sort of way. Her dark eyes sparkled when she spoke to her companion, whom she addressed variously as 'Stella', 'Stell', 'Sister' and 'Dear' in a loud theatrical voice which seemed to ricochet around the refreshment bar. Stella's voice, by contrast, was sweet and musical, though equally theatrical. She called her companion 'Fanny' and 'Sister dear'.

So Fanny and Stella were, it seemed, sisters both by birth and by profession, and if the men crowding around them had paused for thought, they might have reached some bracing conclusions about the cruelty of a bestowing fate which had endowed the one sister with such beauty and the other with such decided plainness. Both women were 'painted', Stella quite subtly and effectively, Fanny with considerably more artistic licence. And both wore rather a great deal of jewellery: necklaces, lockets, rings, earrings and bracelets.

Fanny and Stella were hard to fathom. They had behaved with such lewdness in their box in the stalls as to leave not the faintest shred of doubt in even the most disinterested observer that they were a pair of hardened and shameless whores. And yet, close up, Stella was revealed as a beautiful, almost aristocratic, young woman who showed flashes of an innate, and most decidedly un-whorelike, dignity and grace. One newspaper said later that she was 'charming as a star', another christened her 'Stella, Star of the Strand'. And despite all the opprobrium that would later be heaped upon her, despite all the mud that would be slung at her and all the mud that would stick to her, she never lost the mysterious aura of a great and stellar beauty.

Mrs Fanny Graham, too, was clearly a woman of some education and breeding, and was certainly very far removed from your common-or-garden whore. Here in the saloon bar, it seemed harder to reconcile their obvious quality with the ogling, tongue-waggling, chirruping lasciviousness of the stalls.

They spent half an hour or so in the refreshment bar. Before they left, Mrs Fanny Graham, unaware that she was being watched, betook herself to the Ladies' Retiring Room and asked the attendant there to pin the lace back to the hem of her crinoline where she had trodden on it. At a quarter past ten, Mr Hugh Mundell had been despatched in ringing tones by Mrs Graham to go and call for her carriage and soon afterwards the remainder of the party made a leisurely progress to the foyer and pushed their way through the noise and confusion of an emptying theatre to the waiting conveyance.

Just as the carriage was about to depart, one of the men who had been shadowing them all that evening jumped up and swung himself in through the door.

'I'm a police officer from Bow Street,' he said, producing his warrant card, 'and I have every reason to believe that you are men in female attire and you will have to come to Bow Street with me now.'

There was a moment's pause.

'How *dare* you address a Lady in that manner, Sir,' Mrs Fanny Graham demanded with frigid hauteur. For a second it seemed as if she might slap his face as a reward for such impudence.

Then all hell broke loose as Mr Cecil Thomas frantically struggled past the policeman, leapt out of the carriage and ran for dear life, elbowing his way through the bewildered crowds. Fanny and Stella were also contemplating flight and were already quietly edging themselves towards the opposite door of the carriage. Quite how fast they could run and quite how far they imagined they would get in their crinolines was anybody's guess. But their exit was firmly blocked by another burly policeman in plain clothes who appeared seemingly from nowhere. With a smart tap on the roof, the carriage set off at a rattle and a clatter away eastwards down the Strand.

The two women sat in shocked silence for a few moments. Stella looked as if she might be about to cry. Clearing her throat noisily, Fanny spoke, only this time her voice and demeanour had changed, miraculously transmuted into the voice of a well-bred young man about town.

'Look here, old fellow,' she said, 'it'll do you no good to take us to the station and if you'll let us go we'll give you anything you want.

'*Anything*,' she repeated with a knowing look.

'Anything you like to mention,' Stella echoed meaningfully, staring directly at the two policemen, and arching her eyebrows. '*Anything* you like to mention, you can have.'

'I'll do nothing of the sort,' said Detective Sergeant Frederick Kerley, gruffly. 'I must take you to the station.' Detective Officer William Chamberlain sat there in impenetrable silence.

It took rather less than five minutes to drive to Bow Street where Fanny and Stella were marched firmly into the police station and placed in a wooden dock to be formally questioned.

A t thirty-five, Inspector James Thompson was one of the youngest and shrewdest senior police officers in London. Unlike many of his colleagues, he was an educated man, working as a clerk before joining the Metropolitan Police ten years earlier and rising quickly through the ranks to become Inspector of 'E' Division, one of the largest sections of the force, covering Holborn and the West End. Inspector Thompson's 195 police officers patrolled an exact total of forty miles and 869 yards of streets and roads and arrested around eight thousand people every year, a thousand or so of them prostitutes plying their trade on the busy thoroughfares of the West End.

Inspector Thompson had made his own way back from the Strand Theatre after giving the signal to Detective Sergeant Kerley and Detective Officer Chamberlain to arrest the two young men in women's clothes. Fanny and Stella were of course oblivious to the fact that this rather grave dark-haired policeman had been shadowing them all evening.

Under the flaring gas jets of Bow Street Police Station, they looked a pathetic pair. Stella's make-up was stained with tears, and the pearl powder that she and Fanny had so liberally applied to their *décolletages* had been shot through with sweat, revealing rather less lustrous skin beneath. Both Fanny's flaxen curls and Stella's Grecian plaits were starting to come away from the complex artificial architecture of their hair, giving them a faintly tipsy look. Inspector Thompson could see that their crinolines were long past their best, the antique lace borders grimy and torn. The flounces of their petticoats peeping out from under the crinolines were stained and decidedly grubby. He noticed that their hands were a shade too large, and their feet, encased in white kid boots, looked a shade too masculine. And beneath the peeling make-up, was that the merest shadow of a beard?

'Your name and address?' Inspector Thompson asked, looking at Stella severely. There was no reply. 'Your name and address?' he repeated.

'My name is Cecil Graham,' mumbled Stella, 'and I live at number 2 Bruton Crescent.' There was silence as Thompson wrote this down, the sound of his metal nib scraping the paper.

Stella suddenly decided that there was no point in lying to the police.

'Actually,' she interrupted quickly, 'my name is Ernest Boulton. I'm the son of a stockbroker and I live with my father at 23 Shirland Road, Maida Vale.' Thompson calmly scratched out 'Cecil Graham'.

'And I've just come back from Edinburgh,' Stella added lamely by way of an afterthought.

Inspector Thompson turned quizzically to Fanny.

'My name is Frederick William Park,' said Fanny wretchedly. 'I'm a law student and I lodge at number 13 Bruton Street, Berkeley Square.'

There was a long silence as Inspector Thompson slowly surveyed the pair, taking in every detail of their appearance.

'It seems a very extraordinary thing to me,' Thompson said quietly and deliberately, 'and I don't quite understand it. Will you give me some explanation for appearing in this dress?'

Fanny and Stella shifted about uncomfortably.

'We *are* men,' they mumbled miserably in unison. It had all been just 'a lark', 'a spree' that had got out of hand.

'And we are very, very sorry.'

A few minutes later Fanny and Stella found themselves in one of the chilly outdoor cells in the yard behind Bow Street. Detective Officer Chamberlain had ordered them to strip in the glare of the gas jets. The nightmare had started to unfold. They undressed slowly, reluctantly and awkwardly as Chamberlain and a crowd of other policemen watched with fascination and horror. There were jeers, whistles and sneers, followed by gasps as Fanny and Stella's crinolines fell to the floor revealing their undergarments.

'There were flannel petticoats,' Chamberlain testified later, 'and I believe calico petticoats; there were stays, a short white skirt, very short under the stays', and both of them had bosoms padded with wadding to make them appear 'very full'.

There was some confusion over whether or not Stella was wearing any drawers. Chamberlain was sure that she was not, a fact that he could only have ascertained by making Stella strip until she was completely naked and revealed as a slender young man with the face of a beautiful young woman.

Mr Hugh Mundell was not under arrest but he had insisted upon coming to the station. 'One of the police said he did not want me, that I could go,' Mundell said later. 'I said I had done nothing wrong.' He felt compelled, he said, to accompany Fanny and Stella to Bow Street. 'I did not want to desert them,' he said nobly. 'I wished to go and get bail for them. I thought they had been out on a lark, and that I might get bail for them.'

When Hugh Mundell joined them in the cell a little later, arrested for refusing to give his name and address, he found them very 'downspirited' and tried 'to keep them up'. It was hard work. Fanny and Stella were shivering and crying, their hair awry, their painted faces smudged with tears. They had been allowed to keep their underwear and were desperately trying to dress themselves and rearrange the wadding in their bosoms into some semblance of normality.

> Oh, was it not a cruel sell,
> That night they must remember well,
> When they had to pig in Bow Street cell,
> What a change for them he-she ladies.

It was the first of many public and not-so-public humiliations that Fanny and Stella would have to endure, and even the hard-nosed and even harder-hearted Detective Officer Chamberlain had to concede that Fanny and Stella were being 'so brave'.

2

The Hapless Swain

These young men appear to be very unfortunate,
for whenever they dressed in men's clothes they
were always taken for women, and when they were
attired in the dress of the fair sex they were always
taken for men. Under such unfortunate circumstances what were they to do?

Extraordinary Revelations, 1870

Mr Hugh Alexander Mundell was the ardent, if hapless, swain of Fanny and Stella, but his devotion had only re- cently been minted. He had met them just six days earlier, having made his way to the Surrey Theatre, of low repute, in the Blackfriars Road, in the hope of finding some female com- pany. It was a regular haunt of his and, for just a shilling's entrance, he could pass a pleasant evening in the companion- able fug of humanity that thronged the theatre.

Though it aspired to be 'the nightly resort of all the Rank and Fashion in London', the Surrey's fortunes had been in decline for the last fifteen years and now its clientele was a motley assemblage of working people from Lambeth and Ken- nington sprinkled, according to Charles Dickens, with 'a few pilgrims from the West End'. It was a rowdy, blowsy, familiar sort of place, where the noise made by the audience frequently drowned out the performance. It could be decidedly rough both in and around the theatre.

Hugh Mundell was by his own reckoning exactly '23 years and a half old'. He was a remarkably naive, not to say gauche, young man, who later confessed in court that he had had 'very little experience' when it came to the ladies. He had never even corresponded with a lady, he admitted with a stammer and a blush. He described himself as a gentleman, but this was stretching the truth. He had no occupation and lived with his widowed father, a barrister of modest means, in Pimlico, a far from salubrious area. By his own admission he was leading an 'idle' sort of a life.

At the Surrey, Hugh Mundell wandered aimlessly around for an hour or so, then gravitated to the saloon bar, a glittering gilded temple of glass and mirrors. He was lounging against the long bar drinking a bumper of sherry with the theatre manager, a Mr Shelly, when he saw two extremely effeminate young men enter the saloon bar with perfect self-possession. They looked about the same age as himself, perhaps even a little younger. Their hair was rather longer than was usual and had the appearance of having been frizzed and teased into a mass of tight curls, perched upon which at a jaunty angle were tiny top hats of the sort fine ladies wore when riding to hounds. Both were clean-shaven, in an age when the absence of whiskers, moustaches and beards gave rise to the most terrible suspicions.

Their smooth skins seemed to shine and shimmer in the flaring gaslight of the buffet and Hugh Mundell wondered if they were wearing paint. Their jackets had astonishingly exaggerated revers and looked to have been specially nipped in to accentuate the smallness of their waists. Both young men wore large and exquisite flowers in their buttonholes and had small feet which seemed perfectly suited to the tiny, tottering, sashaying steps they took. They seemed to sway and ripple like reeds in the wind. And as they walked they talked in loud, affected, brittle voices and waved their beautifully manicured hands in elaborate gestures.

Hugh Mundell could hardly take his eyes off them.

Mr Shelly nudged him sharply. 'Those two are women dressed as men,' he said with a knowing wink and a leer, 'two gay women dressed up in men's clothes.' Hugh Mundell could well believe it. They were certainly unlike any men he had ever encountered. They had to be women. Women dressed as men. They walked like women and they talked like women. Their gestures were dainty and womanish. Their hair was curled like women's hair and surely only women wore paint.

'I took them to be women, and so did everyone else who was there,' Hugh Mundell said lamely. 'I was led blindfolded on. I was led away.'

Hugh Mundell could be forgiven for being so led away. It was not unusual for spirited young women to dress as fashionable young men about town and go on a spree. It gave them a thrill to penetrate the stag resorts, the traditional preserves of male privilege like the gentlemen's clubs and cigar divans, or go slumming to low taverns, to attend dog fights and cock fights, and bet on bare-knuckle pugilists.

After parading grandly around the saloon, the two young men swept out, announcing in loud and braying tones that they were going to a nearby public house. The dazzled Hugh Mundell felt himself compelled to follow, and in the pub he stared at them fixedly for twenty minutes, until they blushed.

'We think you're following us,' one of the young men observed 'in a joking manner'.

'I – I think I am,' Mundell managed to stammer and blush in reply.

The ice had been broken, and Hugh Mundell found himself talking to two of the most delightful people he had ever encountered. There was more than a little confusion about names. The young men introduced themselves as 'Ernest' and 'Frederick' but within minutes were addressing each other as 'Stella' and 'Fanny'. Hugh Mundell was thoroughly bewildered and gallantly started to call them 'Miss Stella' and 'Mrs Fanny', after Fanny announced that she was a married lady, a fact confirmed by the gold wedding band she wore.

Fanny and Stella clearly liked Hugh Mundell. He was tall and dark and moderately handsome. He was a puppy, to be sure, but a likeable puppy nevertheless. And, when he was not blushing and stammering with embarrassment, he was well-mannered and charming in a shy, spaniel-like way. Fanny and Stella had assumed that he was one of the many 'so' young men who hung around the theatres and music halls in the hopes of picking up other 'so' young men to have sex with. And his dogging of their footsteps and staring them out of countenance only strengthened their conviction that he was in hot – if mute – pursuit.

The problem of men looking for other men to have sex with had reached almost monstrous proportions in some London theatres. According to the pseudonymous author of *The Yokel's Preceptor*, a guide to the sexual pitfalls of London, 'these monsters in the shape of men, commonly designated Margeries, Pooffs, &c . . . flock to the Saloons and boxes of the theatres'. It was a particular problem in theatres like the Surrey, the Strand and the Lyceum which embraced burlesque and where every night 'so' young men could experience the erotic *frisson* of watching young men on stage apparently falling head over heels in love with each other and making passionate love to each other.

The evening passed in a kind of dream for Hugh Mundell. Before the show was over there were more drinks, more slow and stately promenades around the dress circle, and more intoxicating *badinage*. Everyone seemed to be looking wonderingly at this extraordinary pair of young men, and Mundell swelled with pride that he, beyond all others, was the object of their kindest attentions. As they left the Surrey Theatre, he gave an arm each to Fanny and Stella and escorted them to Waterloo Bridge, still convinced they were women.

'I talked to them as women,' Mundell recalled. 'I chaffed them in a quiet way about being women dressed in men's clothes. I did not carry it very far, though. I told them, when they walked, they ought to swing their arms a little more, like men when they walk.'

They parted on the friendliest of terms. Fanny and Stella extracted a promise that Hugh Mundell would meet them again at the Surrey on the following Tuesday evening so that they could watch the performance from beginning to end. 'I shall only be too happy,' he replied. And he meant it.

Hugh Mundell was walking on air as he made his way home to Pimlico. He had fallen suddenly and spectacularly in love with the beautiful and beguiling Miss Stella. And, amazingly, the beautiful and beguiling Miss Stella had accepted his advances, even going so far as to encourage them. But she had behaved that first evening with absolute propriety. 'There was never anything improper in her conduct,' he maintained stoutly. 'I thought her conduct was natural. I thought it was *womanly*.'

The next four days passed in an agony of anticipation for Hugh Mundell. He got to the Surrey Theatre early and had to wait over an hour, pacing up and down the dress circle, before the ladies arrived. He was clutching two red roses – one for Miss Stella and one for Mrs Fanny. This time they were dressed as women, resplendent in their finest crinolines, their hair elaborately coiffured, and dripping in glittering gaudy jewellery. They were quite dazzling. Pleasantries were exchanged.

'Will you come into our private box, Mr Mundell?' said Fanny, smilingly.

'Yes, I should be delighted,' he replied with a short bow, presenting each lady with a rose before rushing to get pins from the box attendant.

'While they were pinning the flowers, Miss Stella gave me a letter,' Mundell remembered. It was quite short and to the point. 'Dear Mr Mundell,' it began:

> You were telling us some stories the other night about a man dressing up as a woman. We are men, and we have put on women's dresses now to see what you think of our get up!

Hugh Mundell smiled to himself. 'It's a good joke,' he told them, 'but I don't for an instant believe it!'

'But it's quite true. We *are* men!' Fanny and Stella exclaimed in unison.

Mundell laughed. 'It's a good joke,' he repeated. 'A very good joke!'

Fanny and Stella shrugged. They had done their best. Their lovesick puppy was convinced they were women. Try as hard as they might to persuade him that they were in truth men, their adoring swain could not countenance it. It was a joke, it was a lark. Nothing more.

To almost everyone in the auditorium that night, it was clear that Fanny and Stella were, to put it bluntly, a pair of beautiful and dangerous young whores. But to the love-struck Hugh Mundell they represented something rather more complex, a strange and contradictory amalgam of the sacred and the profane; of pure love and impure lust.

Later in court, Mundell was asked about his behaviour towards Miss Stella on that evening.

'In what way did you treat her,' counsel for the prosecution demanded, 'as a lady or as a woman of the town?'

Mundell hesitated. He did not know how to answer. The truth was that he had treated Miss Stella as both a lady and as a whore. He was in love with her *and* in lust with her.

'Stella kept me from making any advances,' he mumbled at last, flushing scarlet. 'Whenever I made any advances, she kept me off. She resisted.'

'Describe what kind of advances you made to her,' counsel demanded.

'I put my arm round her neck once.' Mundell's reply was drowned out by laughter in the court, most loudly from Stella and Fanny. 'I might have gone further,' he said, provoking even more laughter. 'But we were not alone. A gentleman coming into the box stopped me.'

The evening ended with an invitation – almost an instruction – to call upon Fanny and Stella the day after next. Fanny handed him a card with the name of 'Frederick Park, 13 Bruton Street, Mayfair' engraved upon it.

'I shall ask for Mrs Park then,' Mundell said doubtfully to Fanny.

'You will not be let in if you do,' replied Fanny tartly.

'Well, if that's the case, I'll ask for *Mr* Park,' Mundell answered, and they all laughed.

Stella's feelings towards Hugh Mundell were, like his for her, a curious amalgam of lust and love. She wanted Hugh Mundell. She wanted to be loved by him, she wanted to be desired by him. She wanted to charm him and channel his love and his lust for her until he became her devoted slave, and she his coy, mercurial mistress. He was good-looking in a coltish sort of way, and his boyish naïveté and enthusiasm made a charming change from the usual run of men who fell in love with her.

There was, of course, the obvious hurdle that Stella was in truth a man. But that was a small matter and could usually be managed. Stella had, over the years, become very adept – an expert, in fact – at managing it. The trick was to make Hugh Mundell fall so deeply in love with her, so deeply in lust with her, to key him up to such a pitch of sexual desire that her surrender – when it finally came – was so looked for and so longed for that her gender became merely a matter of geography. Of course, when she was drunk and whoring, which was frequently, her drunken and whoring punters rarely noticed the difference. After all, most whores hardly ever took their clothes off, instead pulling up their skirts and using strategic slits in their drawers to allow entry.

And even on those rare occasions when the punters suspected she was a man dressed as a woman, or – even more rarely – when she had told them on a whim, or out of caprice, or from a desire to shock, that she was a man, when it came down to it, down to the nitty-gritty, down to the bump and grind of it, the offer of 'a bit of brown' or some 'back-door work', as it was called, was rarely refused and, truth be told, more often eagerly claimed as a prize beyond rubies and pearls.

Yes, Stella thought to herself, it most certainly could be managed.

Hugh Mundell deliberated long and hard on what exactly he should wear to pay a morning call on Miss Stella and Mrs Fanny. He arrived in Bruton Street promptly at eleven o'clock and rang the doorbell of number 13. It was answered by a small girl who took his proffered card and invited him to wait.

The gentlemen were at home, the small girl informed him, and he was shown into a spacious first-floor front. Fanny and Stella were playing the piano and singing a charming duet as he entered the room. If Hugh Mundell was a little disconcerted to find them dressed once again as young men, he did not show it. He noticed that the men's clothes they were wearing were identical to those they had worn six days earlier when he had first met them in the Surrey, and that the collars were none too clean.

To begin with, the conversation was a little stilted. Unlubricated by beer, sherry or other intoxicants, Hugh Mundell was more than usually tongue-tied and embarrassed. But Stella and Fanny's high spirits soon lifted the atmosphere, and before too long there were gales of laughter. Had he, by the bye, still got that letter they had given him the night before last at the Surrey Theatre, enquired Stella in her most playful tone.

'I said I had,' Mundell recalled. 'I took it out of my pocket and had it in my hand. They asked me to give it to them. I said I wouldn't. Then we had a little tussle for it.

'They both tried to get it from me,' he continued. 'They did not succeed. Afterwards I gave it to them and they returned it to me torn. I said, "I don't want it." I did not accept the pieces.'

Hugh Mundell's refusal to accept the fragments of the letter was a symbolic repudiation of an unwelcome truth. Deep down, in his heart of hearts, he may have suspected, may even have known, that Fanny and Stella were telling the truth when they said they were men. But how could he reconcile this with his powerful yearnings for Miss Stella? And if he could admit – did admit – that he loved Stella *and* that she was a man, he exposed a truth about himself too awful to contemplate.

Doubts were already beginning to assail him. If Mrs Fanny was really a woman, why did she have a card with the name Frederick Park engraved upon it? And why did the girl who answered the door talk about 'the gentlemen' being at home? Surely Miss Stella and Mrs Fanny only dressed up as men occasionally as a lark. It was all becoming very confusing.

Fortunately, there were more duets at the piano to take his mind away from such unwelcome contemplations. Stella gave her heart-rending version of 'Fading Away', a syrupy lament about the transience of life, quickly followed by a series of comic, not to say downright bawdy songs.

'They were talking constantly about performing and playing,' Mundell said later. An album was produced with photographs of their theatrical triumphs. Stella seemed to always play the young tragic heroine, the beautiful widow, the friendless girl cast adrift in a cruel world, while Fanny for the most part seemed to play old women, and 'principally dowagers'.

When it was decided that the party should go out to lunch, Fanny and Stella disappeared into a bedroom for the best part of an hour and came out dressed as ladies. It was like two butterflies emerging from their drab chrysalises, Hugh Mundell thought in a sudden flight of poetic fancy, though rather more prosaically he did notice that, in the unforgiving light of day, Fanny and Stella's frocks were worn and stained, and that the flounces of their petticoats were quite obviously in need of laundering.

Luncheon was a long and decidedly drunken affair during

which Fanny and Stella declared that if they did not go to the Strand Theatre to see the new Easter burlesque *St George and a Dragon* that evening, they would quite simply fade away and die.

At eight o'clock that evening Hugh Mundell found himself in a box at the Strand Theatre. Fanny and Stella were late and there was only one other gentleman to talk to. His name was Mr Amos Westropp Gibbings, a wealthy if rather effeminate young man with a pronounced lisp, who clearly knew Fanny and Stella very well.

'Who *are* they?' Hugh Mundell asked plaintively. 'I am quite in a myth about it. I sometimes think they are men, and sometimes that they are women.'

Mr Gibbings's reply was emphatic. Both Fanny and Stella were men, men who enjoyed dressing up as women.

'I have my doubts very much about Mrs Fanny,' Hugh Mundell retorted, 'but I am certain that Miss Stella is a woman.'

Much to his dismay, Fanny and Stella were clearly the worse for drink when they finally arrived, and their behaviour was considerably less than ladylike. It was not merely coarse, it was downright obscene. Hugh Mundell blushed and flushed and stammered and stuttered more than ever. The more he looked at Mrs Fanny, the more his doubts resolved themselves into certainties. Mrs Fanny *was* a man dressed as a woman. He felt sick.

And if Mrs Fanny was a man, where did that leave Miss Stella? Was it possible that this beautiful young woman really was, as she herself had consistently, insistently proclaimed, really a man? 'I am not a lady. I am a man,' she had kept repeating. 'I am not a lady. I am a man.'

In the gaudy, mirrored saloon bar of the Strand Theatre,

Hugh Mundell felt as if he had wandered into a waking nightmare, the distorted reflections of Fanny and Stella crowding in upon him, reproaching him, mocking him. He did not know what to do. He gulped his brandy and watched and waited while a gaggle of admirers surrounded Fanny and Stella. When Mrs Fanny commanded him in ringing tones to go and call a cab, it was a relief to get out into the chilly night air and try to clear his befuddled wits.

A few moments later all hell broke loose.

'There was a great deal of confusion,' Mundell recalled, 'and I hardly know what occurred, but I found myself in a cab on the road to Bow-street. I was very flurried. I don't know how it was.'

'I don't know how it was' was a metaphor for poor Hugh Mundell's life. He found it hard to make sense of the world. He was constantly in a quandary: confused and perplexed – 'quite in a myth', as he put it – about everything to do with Fanny and Stella. It was as if the world had connived and conspired against him, to mislead him and to misdirect him. Again and again his complaint was that he had been 'led on', 'led away', 'sold', told or otherwise persuaded that Fanny and Stella were really women when it was he and he alone who had convinced himself that they were women. No wonder he was flurried.

Barely a quarter of an hour later he was sharing a cell with two young men in female undergarments, trying to make some sense of the awful calamity that had overwhelmed him.

3

The Slap-Bum Polka

One day a cute detective chap,
Who of their game had smelt a rat.
Declared he would get on the track,
Of those two He-She ladies.
So he bolted up to Regent Square,
And soon espied this worthy pair.
They hailed a cab, who took his fare,
Says the police, 'I am after you my dear'.

'The Funny He-She Ladies'

At ten o'clock on the morning after the arrest of Fanny and Stella, in the first-floor front of an inconspicuous lodging house in Wakefield Street, Bloomsbury, Mr Amos Westropp Gibbings (known as Carlotta to all of her many friends) and Mr Martin Luther Cumming (or the Comical Countess) were in the middle of an extremely agitated conference with their land-lady, Miss Martha Stacey, when they heard a loud and prolonged knocking on the front door.

They froze and looked at each other. Carlotta Gibbings tip-toed to the window and carefully peered out to see a man standing on the doorstep. She guessed he was a detective in plain clothes. She knew the type. Tallish, shabby, sharp-eyed and shifty with a self-important, bullying air about him. A nasty piece of work and, nine times out of ten, corrupt and corrupting.

'Police,' she mouthed silently.

There was an agonising wait while old Mrs Stacey, Martha's arthritic mother, shuffled up from the basement kitchen and fumbled awkwardly with the locks on the front door. When she finally managed to open the door she found a grim-faced man planted firmly on the doorstep who said he was a policeman. Before she knew it and with hardly so much as a beg-your-pardon or a by-your-leave, he had unceremoniously pushed his way past her into the narrow hallway and begun firing off a series of questions to which old Mrs Stacey, flustered and agitated as she was, could give no coherent answers.

Upstairs, Carlotta Gibbings and Martha Stacey looked at each other. The muffled exchanges from below were getting louder and more heated. Something had to be done. Martha Stacey nodded and, putting her finger to her lips, closed the door very quietly and went down the stairs to see what all the commotion was about.

Detective Officer Chamberlain curtly introduced himself to Martha Stacey. He had no time to waste, he said. There was urgent business, police business, that needed attending to.

'He asked whether two gentlemen lived there who dressed in female attire. He said they were in custody,' Martha Stacey recalled a week later. 'I forget the answer I gave but I said I was astonished.'

'What were they taken for?' she asked him.

'Either it was a freak or a lark,' Chamberlain replied shortly. 'Which room do they occupy?'

'I said they dressed in the one adjoining the ground floor,' recalled Martha Stacey. 'He went into the room and commenced searching it.

'Chamberlain did not show me any warrant, and I did not ask him for it,' she added. 'I was too confused.'

Once inside, Chamberlain began methodically opening boxes and portmanteaux, pulling out dresses and bonnets and boots, tipping out drawers, leafing through piles of papers and rummaging through boxes of jewellery.

'My mother remonstrated with him about it,' Martha Stacey testified. But Chamberlain merely shrugged his shoulders contemptuously. 'He said he had a right to do it and that he would take them away with him and *sell* them if he thought proper.

'He also took away some letters,' she continued. 'I can't say how many. Chamberlain looked at an album and took what portraits he thought proper out of it. He also took some more from another album. I should think about twenty in all.'

Clutching a pile of papers and photographs, Chamberlain locked the door and pocketed the key. No one, not a soul, was to enter those rooms under *any* circumstances, he said. There was important evidence which needed to be taken into custody. He would return in an hour or two.

Martha Stacey was in trouble and she knew it. 'Houses of accommodation' like hers were common in London and came in all shapes and sizes. They were not exactly brothels but they were places where people went to have sex, away from prying eyes and with no awkward questions asked. On the very lowest rung of the erotic ladder, they were places where for a shilling, sixpence or even less, streetwalkers could take their punters to a room where there would be a bed with filthy sheets, a verminous mattress and a bucket for the punters to wash in before and after doing the business. But at least there would be privacy. At the upper end of the scale, sumptuously appointed rooms or suites catered for wealthy gentlemen to pass an hour or two with a high-class whore.

Martha Stacey's house of accommodation was somewhere in the middle range. Though there was a problem with the whores in nearby Brunswick Square, Wakefield Street was, by and large, a respectable and quiet residential street, the ideal street for a respectable and quiet house of accommodation. The houses were very often owned and run by former prostitutes who in sharp contrast to the prevailing notion of the natural history of the profession – seduction, ruin, degradation, disease and premature death – had often saved a comfortable little nest egg from the game and wanted to invest it. Running a house of accommodation was a safe bet. They knew the business; they knew the girls; and they knew there would always be a demand for rooms from everyone from the poorest streetwalker to the grandest concubine.

Martha Stacey was most likely a former prostitute herself. She was certainly not the shy, retiring or easily shocked type. Quite the opposite. Even old Mrs Stacey may have been in the business once. Prostitution ran in families, and successful prostitutes would teach their daughters the tricks of the trade. Even Frances Stacey, Martha Stacey's niece, who came in to help with the chores at Wakefield Street, may have been on the game some of the time.

Martha Stacey's establishment was, as far as she knew, unique in London, and its very uniqueness made it vulnerable and made it dangerous. It was a house of accommodation for young men who liked to dress up as young women and go out on the spree, for young men who liked to get themselves up 'in drag' – as Mr Gibbings used to call it, though for the life of her she couldn't see why.

Running her house for the 'so' young gentlemen who liked to drag themselves up had seemed like a good idea to Martha Stacey. They were certainly a cut above the professional Mary-Anns, or male whores, she had met. There was Mr Gibbings, Mr Thomas, Mr Boulton, Mr Park, Mr Cumming and Lord knows how many other young gentlemen who used to come to her house. They were clean, always polite to her, and ever so friendly. She liked her boys when they were boys and she liked her boys even more when they were girls. What a lark it all was! She had often joined in the 'laughing, chaffing and joking' when her boys were getting dragged up, and in the mornings when they recounted their adventures of the night before.

Besides, it was good business, very good business. They always paid on the nail. She charged five shillings a night, and a bit more besides if one of the young men entertained a gentleman – or two – overnight. She didn't know and she couldn't say, she was sure, how often this happened or if the young 'ladies' ever took money from their gentlemen callers. Her boys had their latchkeys and what they did in or out of their rooms was no concern of hers. She never saw anything – well, not much anyway. Mind you, she was quite ready to admit, you'd have to be deaf, dumb and blind not to have an inkling of what went on. Some nights there was an awful lot of to-ing and fro-ing; doors banging; moans and groans and giggles and screams. Judging from the state of the sheets, she had her suspicions – certainties, more like. Those boys certainly knew how to dance the 'Slap-Bum Polka'!

And for a modest charge of a few shillings a week she looked after the frocks, the wigs, the pots of paint, the unmentionables, the what-have-yous, the thingamajigs – and all the rest of the paraphernalia – and my goodness me there was enough of it; enough to open a shop nearly; enough to fill two rooms at Wakefield Street so tight you could barely squeeze your arse in. And for a few shillings more she wasn't averse to doing the odd bit of laundry if Frances was there to help her out. But now the police were involved and what a to-do it had all turned out to be. It was all ruined and spoilt and if she was not very careful, she would find herself in hot water, very hot water, and no mistake.

After twenty minutes or so of waiting, the stomping, thumping and banging from the room below stopped. Carlotta and the Comical Countess heard Chamberlain's muffled voice and then the thud of the front door shutting. He was gone and there was silence. Cautiously, Carlotta crept downstairs. Old Mrs Stacey and Martha were staring at the door of Fanny and Stella's room. They were plainly terrified. Chamberlain had locked it and he was coming back – and soon – with reinforcements.

Miss Carlotta Gibbings did not hesitate. Despite her 'very effeminate appearance' and her girlish lisp, Carlotta was determined and resourceful. She was the only person present not completely paralysed by fear. She guessed that Chamberlain had found plenty of material that would incriminate Fanny and Stella and might perhaps incriminate them all. But if there was anything that Chamberlain hadn't already grabbed, anything that he'd missed, anything that he'd overlooked, now was the time to remove it out of harm's way. She put her shoulder to the door and pushed hard; the lock burst open, and with a girlish shriek of surprise, Carlotta almost fell into the room.

It was a mess. Carlotta and the Comical Countess worked furiously. They could not be sure how long it would take Chamberlain to return. He might be back in an hour or two, as he had threatened; equally, he could be back in fifteen minutes or less with a couple of police constables requisitioned from the beat. Where should they start? Letters, papers, photographs, money and any jewellery of any value that Chamberlain hadn't already squeezed into his capacious pockets – anything that could incriminate them, anything that might incriminate others. It was all stuffed furiously into a carpet bag and a small portmanteau, together with two or three of Carlotta's 'handsomest frocks', some chignons, a bit of slap and two pairs of her favourite stays. And then they were gone, as if the devil himself were at their heels, the door left swinging open.

4

In the Dock

When first before the magistrate
Oh, what a crowd did them await,
It was a lark and no mistake,
To look at them He-She ladies.
Lor! how the people did go on,
With, 'I say I'll have your fine chignon,'
Another cried out, 'Stella dear,
Pull off those togs, and breeches wear.'

'The Funny He-She Ladies'

A night in the cells had done little to improve Fanny and Stella's bedraggled appearance. They had barely slept in the freezing cold, and spent most of the night crying and whimpering. They were very frightened, weak with hunger, and their heads ached with exhaustion and the effects of the numerous brandies and sherries they had knocked back the night before. A tin mug of weak tea and a hunk of cheap black bread made them feel only a little better.

Their dresses were returned to them at first light and they were gruffly instructed to make themselves decent, ready for their appearance before the beak. Fanny and Stella looked at each other in dismay. They had hoped and prayed that somehow or other a suit of men's clothes might be procured for them, that they would not have to appear in court wearing last night's frocks.

Although they did not know it, Carlotta Gibbings had already rushed to Bow Street Police Station early that morning with a change of clothes, calculating that they would stand more chance of getting off with a caution or a small fine if they appeared as respectably dressed young men rather than as two young men dressed as ladies of the night. But the officers had curtly turned Carlotta away.

Somehow or another, with a great deal of grumbling and a great deal of ingenuity, Fanny and Stella managed to tidy themselves up and recreate some faint echo of last night's finery. A handkerchief and some cold water from the ewer helped wipe away the dark tracks of their tears and the worst smudges of paint. Dressing themselves and repairing their toilette as best they could helped to lift their spirits. They looked very far from perfect but they were once again Mrs Fanny Graham and Miss Stella Boulton, stars of stage and street, and whatever the day might bring they hoped they would conduct themselves like ladies.

As Fanny and Stella waited in their cell, they could already hear the muffled hoots and yells of a mob swarming outside, and it took them some little time to realise that the mob was almost certainly assembled in their honour. They turned white with fear. When they left the police station, they would have to run the gauntlet as they crossed Bow Street to the courtroom opposite.

A loud roar went up as Fanny and Stella, followed by Hugh Mundell a few steps behind, came out of Bow Street Police Station flanked by half a dozen uniformed policemen. The diamanté star in Fanny's hair glinted in the thin April sunshine. Fanny and Stella seemed dazzled by the light and dazed by the mob of several hundred which milled and swirled around them trying to catch a glimpse of 'the Funny He-She Ladies'.

There were hoots, hisses, catcalls, whistles and a few ragged cheers. Where had they all come from? Fanny and Stella had been arrested at around eleven o'clock the night before, too late for the morning papers to carry the story. Who were these people? How had they found out? And why were they here? They heard their names, 'Fanny', 'Stella', shouted out in thin, raucous voices that seemed to float momentarily above the roar of the crowd. Voices that sounded familiar. Turning round they caught a few blurred glimpses of the smiling faces of friends and acquaintances frantically waving. They were not entirely friendless.

It took five minutes or more for the police to clear a path. Fanny and Stella were pushed and shoved and pinched and propelled forwards, backwards, sideways. Greedy, greasy fingers grabbed at their dresses and tried to touch and pull their hair. At first Fanny and Stella faltered, stumbled and al-most fell. But they went on. And as they went on, they grew visibly taller, visibly stronger, more dignified. By the time they had crossed the road they were carrying themselves like a pair of duchesses attending a ball. They mounted the steps to the court, paused and turned to face the crowd, which had for a moment fallen silent. Fanny and Stella smiled gravely and – with the merest ghost of a curtsey – turned smartly on their heels and swept inside. The jeers and catcalls broke out again. But this time they were drowned out by a fusillade of cheers and whistles.

Mr James Flowers, Stipendiary Magistrate at Bow Street, had a reputation as one of the kindest men on the Bench. The tiny courtroom measured just thirty feet by twenty feet and 'was crowded with people eager to hear the charge', the

Illustrated Police News reported; 'crammed to suffocation' was the verdict of the *Evening News*. All eyes were on Fanny and Stella as they stepped into the wooden dock, followed by a rather sheepish Hugh Mundell, 'and great surprise was manifested at the admirable manner in which Boulton and Park had "made up" '. Fanny and Stella stood impassively, almost proudly, in the dock, as they surveyed the scene. Hugh Mundell looked anxious and fidgety as he stood alongside them.

Had this been a theatre rather than a court of law, a stage rather than a dock, Fanny and Stella would have been only too delighted to tread its hallowed boards. They liked nothing better than a house full to bursting and a rumbustious, restless and expectant audience ready to be quelled, ready to be charmed, ready to be dazzled by their performance. They could so easily have been appearing in *Retained for the Defence*, or one of the dozen or so other comediettas and one-act melodramas they had performed so often, together and separately, in which the beautiful and wronged young woman – invariably more convincingly played by Stella than by Fanny – would stand up before a jury of her peers and by the sheer power of her beauty and by the sheer force and passion of her rhetoric be declared innocent by acclamation. And even though Bow Street was a court and not a stage, Fanny and Stella felt a little of the familiar theatrical glamour stealing over them. They were dressed and they were ready. All they had to do now was to give the performance of their lives.

In the best traditions of burlesque there was not a little confusion and much laughter from the audience over the use of the personal pronoun. Were Fanny and Stella 'he's' or 'she's'? It was a vexed question. Clearly they were men dressed up as women and should, by rights, be referred to as 'he', but somehow it came more naturally to call them 'she'. The clerks who recorded the proceedings got into a terrible muddle, littering their transcripts with crossings-out and corrections, turning 'he's' into 'she's' – and vice versa. The witnesses were equally confused, stumbling and tying themselves in linguistic knots, usually ending up calling Fanny and Stella both 'she' and 'he' in the same sentence. Reporters for the *Daily Telegraph* and the *Illustrated London News* explained delicately to their readers that, though the defendants were emphatically young men, for the purposes of reporting the proceedings they had adopted the preponderant pronoun used in court – in this case 'she'. And Mr Flowers, the magistrate, got round the problem by referring to Fanny and Stella as 'these two women, as I may call them'.

The charges were read out by the Clerk of the Court to loud gasps from the crowded courtroom. Ernest Boulton and Frederick William Park were charged that they 'did with each and one another feloniously commit the abominable crime of buggery':

> further that they did unlawfully conspire together, and with divers other persons, feloniously, to commit the said crimes
>
> further that they did unlawfully conspire together, and with divers other persons to induce and incite other persons feloniously with them to commit the said crime
>
> and further that they being men, did unlawfully conspire together, and with divers others, to disguise themselves as women and to frequent places of public resort, so disguised, and to thereby openly and scandalously outrage public decency and corrupt public morals.

It was an extraordinary set of charges. Fanny and Stella paled and visibly trembled as they were read out. Only the last charge, that of disguising themselves as women and frequenting public places with the intention of outraging public decency and corrupting public morals, held any water. Although there was no statute in English law which specifically made it a criminal offence for men to dress up as women, by dressing up as women and behaving in an undeniably and extremely lewd manner at the Strand Theatre, Fanny and Stella had outraged public decency. On the substance of that charge and that charge alone, they were incontrovertibly guilty. It was a fair cop.

Crimes were divided into two categories: misdemeanours – less serious crimes usually dealt with by the stipendiary magistrates – and felonies, which were much more serious and were tried before a judge and a jury. Outraging public decency was a misdemeanour. If this were the only charge, Fanny and Stella would be well advised to plead guilty, throw themselves upon the mercy of the court and hope they could escape with a hefty fine and a good talking-to from Mr Flowers.

But the charge of buggery was much, much more serious. Until 1861, only nine years earlier, buggery had carried the death penalty. As it was, buggery still carried a prison sentence of penal servitude for life. Penal servitude meant, for murderers, rapists and sodomites, long hours of hard labour picking oakum, walking the treadmill, or working the dreaded crank, back-breaking work turning a handle to push a paddle through a vat of sand. No wonder Fanny and Stella turned pale.

Not only were they charged with buggery, they were charged with a catch-all *conspiracy* to commit buggery. In other words, the police were saying that not only had Fanny buggered Stella, and Stella buggered Fanny, but both of them had also buggered and been buggered by any number of 'divers persons'. Furthermore, they had each conspired with the other, and with any number of unknown, unnamed others 'to induce and incite' yet more men to commit buggery. It all conjured up an image of a vast, ever-spreading sodomitical spider's web with Fanny and Stella at its dark heart, controlling and directing, combining and confederating, to entrap and ensnare any and all men.

Seen through the prism of this conspiracy charge, Fanny and Stella's drunken double act in their box at the Strand Theatre, their ogling, tongue-waggling, chirruping invitations to the gentlemen in the stalls, took on an altogether darker and more menacing aspect. It could quite easily be construed as a conspiracy to incite and induce men to feloniously commit 'the abominable crime of buggery'.

There were only four witnesses produced for this preliminary hearing – all of them policemen. The evidence of Inspector Thompson and the evidence of Sergeant Kerley merely rehashed the events of the night before. Fanny and Stella listened, even smiled occasionally, but seemed largely uninterested in what they had to say. 'Both conducted themselves decorously,' the *Daily Telegraph* reported. 'While listening to the evidence, Boulton rested her head on her right hand but did not pay very particular attention.'

But everything changed when Detective Officer Chamberlain started to give his evidence.

'Last evening, about twenty minutes past eight, I saw the two prisoners dressed in female attire at 13, Wakefield-street, Regent-square.'

'You had followed them?' the Clerk of the Court asked.

'Yes,' Chamberlain replied simply.

Fanny and Stella looked at each other uneasily. This was a complete shock. Until now, they had assumed, perhaps naturally, that they had been arrested almost by accident, that the manager or some other dull functionary at the Strand Theatre had summoned the police when he saw what he suspected were two men dressed as women behaving obscenely and 'lasciviously ogling' the male occupants of the stalls.

Chamberlain's evidence changed everything. Neither Fanny nor Stella had breathed a word about 13 Wakefield Street to anyone. Not to Hugh Mundell, and certainly not to the police. Fanny had given her address as Bruton Street, and Stella had given the address of her mother and father in Maida Vale. Wakefield Street was a secret, their secret. So how did the police know about it? How was it that Chamberlain had been there last night, outside, watching for them, waiting for them, following them?

Chamberlain's next piece of evidence was even more alarming.

'I have been to 13, Wakefield Street, Regent-square this morning, and searched the parlours occupied by the prisoners Boulton and Park, and some other gentlemen,' he announced.

Fanny and Stella listened with increasing horror. Not only did Chamberlain know about their secret place, he had entered it, penetrated it, violated it. Their secret place, their place of safety.

'I found the photographs in the front parlour,' Chamberlain continued, using both hands to pass a tottering pile of photographs to the Clerk, who in turn handed them to Mr Flowers. 'They represent the two prisoners both in male and female attire.'

'Do you detect a likeness with either of the two prisoners

in female attire now, dressed both as male and female?' Mr Flowers asked.

Chamberlain squinted almost leeringly at Fanny and Stella in the dock.

'I do, Your Worship,' he said.

Chamberlain went on to reveal that he had been watching Fanny and Stella 'for a year past'. A whole year. And Police Constable Charles Walker, the fourth and last policeman from 'E' Division to give evidence that day, testified that he had been on constant surveillance duty outside Wakefield Street for the past fortnight and 'had seen both the prisoners go in and out at all hours of the night, repeatedly'. The neighbours, he said, had started to complain.

Fanny and Stella were in a state of shock. Their arrest, far from being almost accidental, far from being a bit of bad luck, now looked much more sinister. It had clearly been planned down to the last detail. Both by day and by night they had been watched, they had been followed, and their comings and goings recorded by a phalanx of policemen. And it had been going on for more than a year. Their sanctum in Wakefield Street had been discovered and turned over. Their photographs had already been produced in court, and they knew that there was more, much more, to come.

For a start there were the letters. Stella, in particular, wished that she could remember exactly which letters she had so carelessly strewn around Wakefield Street, and wished that she had been a little more careful, a little more discreet. Some of the letters – in truth, most of the letters – were in one way or another compromising, certainly to her, and more than likely to her friends. Those letters told the story of her life, and now that story was in the hands of the police.

Mr Abrams, the solicitor hired by Carlotta Gibbings to speak for Fanny and Stella in court, did his best, but he was clearly out of his depth. He was under the impression that he was to plead for two young men who had been caught out in a lark, a frolic, a call-it-what-you-will, but now he was confronted by something far more serious.

'Much of the evidence brought forward has taken me somewhat by surprise,' he told Mr Flowers, quite truthfully. 'But, so far as it goes, I respectfully submit that unless it can be clearly shown that these two persons were engaged on this evening in some unlawful purpose, no offence against the statute has been committed.'

It was a brave try but Mr Flowers was having none of it. 'The onus is rather thrown on them to allow that there was no unlawful purpose,' he retorted.

'I am not going to uphold their act, but I submit that it was . . .' and here Mr Abrams faltered, ' . . . that it was an act of folly.'

'This act of folly has been going on for a long time,' said Mr Flowers severely, and proceeded to remand Fanny and Stella in custody for seven days.

Fanny gave a start and Stella swayed a little. They both gripped the rail of the dock to support themselves. Stella looked as if she might faint. They were numb with shock. There seemed to be no end to the charges against them, nothing the police did not already know. The curtain had fallen on their first appearance and now there was a veil of darkness between them and the world they had once so joyously inhabited.

With their elbows firmly gripped by the court gaoler, they were forced to put one foot in front of the other and stagger out of the dock on their way to heaven-knows-where.

A prison or a scaffold. At that precise moment it was all the same to Fanny and Stella.

5

Foreign Bodies

EXAMINATION OF PEDERASTS: Place the
suspect in a well-lit room and bend him forwards in
such a way until his head is almost touching the
floor. Part his buttocks with your hands and note
the appearance of the anus. Then slowly insert a
finger into the orifice to test fully the resistance of
the sphincter.

Charles Vibert, *Précis de médicine légale*, 1893

Dr Paul never was able to give a convincing explanation as
to why he was loitering in the street immediately outside
Bow Street Magistrates' Court just as the hearing inside was
coming to an end. It was almost exactly one o'clock and he
looked as if he were waiting for someone or something.

Though he later tried to suggest that it was a mere coincidence that he happened to be in Bow Street on that particular
day, at that particular time – that he just happened to be passing
– Dr Paul did not seem in the least surprised when a police
constable touched him on the arm. In fact, he seemed almost
to be expecting it: 'I was in the street,' Dr Paul said, 'and the
policeman came and told me that Inspector Thompson wanted
me.'

Dr James Thomas Paul was Divisional Surgeon to 'E' Division of the Metropolitan Police. He had been appointed in
January 1864, and the salary the job afforded was a useful ad-

dition to the meagre income he earned from his practice as a surgeon. The work was repetitive rather than onerous. His job was to look after any and all of the medical needs of the 195 police officers of 'E' Division: their aches and pains, their cuts and bruises, their coughs and sneezes and wheezes, Dr Paul dealt with them all. If they were injured, he patched them up; if they were ill, he physicked them; and if they had the clap – and many of them did – he tried to cure them.

It was Dr Paul's job, too, to do what he could for the eight thousand or so dregs of humanity who washed up on the shores of Bow Street Police Station every year: the drunks and the whores; the thieves and the pickpockets; the mendicants and the mendacious; the mad, the sad and the bad. There were cuts and contusions to attend to, split lips and split heads to join together, the odd fracture, and all the accumulated and interacting diseases of poverty, overcrowding, poor air and even poorer diet. Dr Paul was not a bad man, and he did what little he could.

The constable guided Dr Paul through a warren of stairs and corridors to a small bare room at the back of the court building, lit only by a grimy skylight. It was a forlorn, out-of-the-way place, and it looked as if it had not been used for many a year. It smelt musty and stale. There was a desk, a stool and a tall screen. Inspector Thompson and two of his detectives, Chamberlain and Kerley, were waiting for him.

The door opened and Fanny and Stella were ushered in by the court gaoler. That they were badly frightened was only too evident from their chalk-white faces and the uncontrolled trembling of their bodies. It was barely ten minutes since Mr Flowers had remanded them in custody for seven days. Instead of being taken to the Black Maria to be transported to the

House of Detention, they had been herded along corridors and up and down stairs and now found themselves in this bleak place where the three policemen from the night before and an unknown fourth man were waiting for them, looking very grave.

Fanny and Stella thought they were in for a terrible beating – or even worse. They had heard about such things. It was common knowledge that some policemen liked to administer their punishments privately. It was common knowledge, too, that some policemen liked to take their pleasures privately. And sometimes they liked to do both at the same time.

Fanny and Stella stood in the dark and dingy little room shivering and trembling and imagining the worst when Dr Paul abruptly addressed Stella.

'Step inside here,' he said, pointing to the screen. 'Unfasten your things and drop them down, please to step out of them,' he ordered gruffly, clearing his throat. Stella started to undress: off came the dress and the petticoats, and lastly a curious arrangement: a pair of drawers with silk stockings sewn to them.

Dr Paul took a desk stool and pointed to it.

'Put yourself over that stool,' he said coldly.

'Without saying a word he did so,' Dr Paul said later when questioned in court. 'I did not use my hand with any violence. The prisoners did not offer any opposition to my examining them.'

This was bending the truth. Stella had been reluctant, fearful until Chamberlain or Kerley, one or the other, had said that if she did not comply, 'force would be used'.

Dr Paul claimed that he had been instructed by Inspector Thompson to examine Fanny and Stella to discover whether they were men or women. 'I examined them for the purposes of ascertaining their sex,' he declared baldly.

It was a lie, and not a very clever lie. There was no longer any possible doubt over Fanny and Stella's gender. The whole world knew that Fanny and Stella were men – except, apparently, Dr Paul. Inspector Thompson already knew for a fact that Fanny and Stella were men. They had told him so in no uncertain terms the night before. Ditto Detective Sergeant Kerley and Detective Officer Chamberlain. (It was Chamberlain who had watched, fascinated, as Fanny and Stella slowly stripped off their feminine finery the night before to reveal the shivering, slender bodies of two frightened young men.) The mob that had filled Bow Street that morning knew that they were men, the mob that was still milling around outside the court while Dr Paul was waiting, the mob that had chanted and cheered and jeered, the mob that had screamed filthy and lewd suggestions at Fanny and Stella. Every person present that sunny morning in Mr Flowers's courtroom knew that Fanny and Stella were men. The whole world knew that Fanny and Stella were men – except, apparently, Dr Paul. It was not the first lie that Dr Paul told, and it would not be the last.

When asked again, Dr Paul stuck to his guns.

'I examined them for the purposes of ascertaining their sex,' he answered, but this time adding one crucial qualification. 'I examined them for the purposes of ascertaining their sex, but not that only. I wished to ascertain something more, that was of my own accord, and my own idea.'

Something more. Dr Paul's career as a surgeon had hardly been glittering. He was hard-working enough, a belt-and-braces, run-of-the-mill surgeon with a barely adequate private practice and just his police work to keep the creditors at bay.

What set Dr Paul apart from the legions of other middle-aged, middle-of-the-road surgeons was that Dr Paul had an unusual hobby. He was interested – very interested – in sodomy and in sodomites. Dr Paul had been interested in sodomy and sodomites ever since he was a student, twenty years ago, when he had been taught by Dr Alfred Swaine Taylor, the celebrated and sometimes controversial father of English forensic medicine.

In one of his lectures to students at Guy's Hospital in 1850, Dr Taylor had spoken about a bizarre and disturbing case he had been involved in as a young doctor nearly twenty years earlier. It concerned the death of one Miss Eliza Edwards. On 23rd January 1833, Miss Eliza Edwards had roused her 'sister', seventeen-year-old Maria Edwards, who was sharing her bed, and complained of 'a wheezing in the throat'. It was clear to Maria and to the landlady of the 'house of doubtful repute' in Westminster that Eliza was very poorly indeed.

'Maria, I am dying,' Eliza whispered, gasping for every breath. 'It has pleased God to call me.'

Five minutes later Eliza Edwards was dead. She was just twenty-four, and the probable cause of death was consumption, though some were convinced that it was syphilis. For many years Eliza Edwards had made a name for herself as an actress of some repute, specialising in playing tragic young heroines. But the parts had dried up and, for the past three years, Eliza and Maria had been forced to work as prostitutes.

At an inquest held two days later no one claimed Eliza's body and the corpse was, in consequence, sold to Guy's Hospital for dissection. The dissection was to be carried out by Dr Alfred Swaine Taylor and was expected to be a routine affair, but when Eliza's nightclothes were removed, Dr Taylor discovered to his shock and amazement that the body of this young woman was in fact the body of a young man with a normal set of male organs strapped up with a bandage tied around the abdomen.

Outwardly, Eliza Edwards looked like a young woman.

'There was no appearance of a beard or whiskers,' Dr Taylor reported. 'The hairs on the face seemed to have been plucked out with tweezers. The hair was upwards of two feet in length, of a soft glossy texture. The features were of a feminine character.'

No one had suspected that Eliza was a man: not Maria, Eliza's supposed sister, who had lived with her since she was seven and who had worked with her as a prostitute; not Dr Somerville and not Dr Clutterbuck, both of whom had attended Eliza during her last illness; not the proprietress of the brothel in which Eliza and Maria lived and worked; and not, most of all, the succession of gentlemen callers who came, and came again, to pass an hour or so with the beautiful and talented Miss Edwards.

Pressing on with his examination, Dr Taylor noted that Eliza Edwards's anus was deformed. 'The state of the rectum left no doubt of the abominable practices to which this individual had been addicted,' he wrote. 'It was noticed by all present that the aperture of the anus was much wider and larger than natural.' Dr Taylor was also shocked to discover that 'the *rugae* or folds of skin which give the puckered appearance to the anal aperture had quite disappeared' – so much so, indeed, 'that this part resembled the labia of the female organs'.

Not only had Eliza Edwards dressed as a woman, acted as a woman, passed as a woman, she had, by the mysterious alchemy of sodomy, effectively *become* a woman.

This strange story of Eliza Edwards had fired the imagination of the young student doctor James Thomas Paul, and he had maintained an interest – verging on the obsessional – in sodomy and sodomites ever since. There was, he found, precious little information on the topic, but what there was Dr Paul had read. There was Dr Taylor's cautious and short section on the forensic aspects of sodomy in his book *The Principles and Practice of Medical Jurisprudence*. Then there was George Drysdale's hugely popular *The Elements of Social Science, or Physical, Sexual and Natural Religion*, first published in 1854 and running to no fewer than thirty-five editions, which was remarkably frank about the extent of sodomy in England, its causes and its cures.

Dr Paul's most recent and highly prized acquisition was a copy of Professor Ambroise Tardieu's *Étude médico-légale sur les attentats aux mœurs*, first published in Paris in 1857 and running into many editions. It was an astonishing work of urban anthropology, a physiological and psychological primer in sodomy. It professed to be a textbook telling the police, the medical profession and the legislature everything they had ever wanted to know about sodomy and sodomites, and much more besides. In it, Tardieu made a series of sensational claims about how the signs of sodomy were forensically written upon the body, indelibly inscribed, especially upon the anus and upon the penis.

Now, for the first time in his career, Dr Paul was about to examine two real-life sodomites. Dr Paul did not know what – if anything – he would find. Perhaps there would be nothing. The anuses of these two young men might prove to be no different from the hundreds, nay thousands, he had examined during his medical career. And in all these thousands of anuses never once had he seen any signs of sodomy – though it was, it must be said, *not* for the want of looking.

It was true that on a few occasions – several occasions, in fact – he had examined the anuses of women who had been buggered or 'abused by men', as he carefully and cautiously phrased it, and he had even given evidence in some of these cases. Dr Paul knew very well, as did every doctor worthy of the name, that buggery between men and women was much more common than most people dared to imagine.

Many men thought that having anal sex with a woman protected them in some way from syphilis and gonorrhoea – contagions and contaminations indissolubly associated with the spasms and miasmas of the vagina and its secretions. And there was a persistent folk belief that buggery with a woman would even effect a cure for clap, any sort of clap. Anal intercourse with a woman might be considered by some a 'special continental vice', an imported speciality of the swarms of decadent French whores who had flooded into London in the past twenty years, but in reality it was a widespread practice – not just a convenient form of birth control, but also a pleasurable end in itself.

Of course, as Dr Paul knew only too well, buggering a woman was – on paper at least – a serious crime: 'unnatural connexion with a woman' was the way the charge was usually, euphemistically, phrased. But was it not woman's ordained role in nature to be penetrated, to be a receptacle, for man? Anal sex was an unspoken part of that ordained role, unless, of course, there were special circumstances, like anal rape, which brought the crime to the attention of the police. Buggering a woman might be illegal, but the law more often than not turned a blind eye. Buggering a woman might be unnatural, but at least it was *naturally* unnatural – utterly unlike a man buggering another man or, God forbid, allowing himself to be buggered by a man.

That was quite another order of crime, an *unnaturally* unnatural connexion, a crime, an outrage upon Nature and an affront to God, an inversion, a blaspheming of the divinely ordained order of things.

Male and female created He them.

Only when he came to sum up his findings did Dr Paul betray the least emotion.

'I had never seen *anything* like it before,' he said in a shocked tone of voice. 'I have been in practice sixteen years, seven years out of that at the St Pancras General Dispensary, and I have on very many occasions examined the anuses of persons. I do not in my practice *ever* remember to have seen such an appearance of the anus, as those of the prisoners presented.

'I examined Boulton, and found him to be a man,' Dr Paul testified. 'The anus was dilated, and more dilatable, and the muscles surrounding the anus easily opened.'

Then it was Fanny's turn.

'Boulton was then removed, and the prisoner Park came behind the screen,' Dr Paul deposed. 'I said to him the same I had said to Boulton.'

Fanny stripped herself naked and bent herself over the same desk stool.

'The anus was *very* much dilated,' Dr Paul recounted almost by rote in court, 'and dilatable to a very great extent. The rectum was large, and there was some discoloration around the edge of the anus, caused probably by sores.'

The small puckering folds of skin around Fanny's anus – the *rugae* – he noticed were abnormal: 'I found them loose, and not in their normal state. I should say they were rough.'

There could, he said, be one – and only one – explanation

for the slackness of Fanny and Stella's bottoms. 'The insertion of a foreign body numerous times would account for those appearances,' he said.

Dr Paul was pressed as to exactly what he meant by 'the insertion of a foreign body numerous times'.

'The insertion of a man's person would cause the appearances I have described,' he replied. A 'man's person', a man's penis, or rather, men's penises – lots of men's penises – were the cause of the extraordinary state of Fanny and Stella's bottoms. They had, in Dr Paul's opinion, been so repeatedly sodomised by men that the anus had lost much if not most of its natural elasticity.

There was more. Dr Paul also examined Fanny and Stella's penises. Again he was shocked by what he found. Stella's penis and scrotum were 'of an inordinate length' and Fanny's 'private parts were elongated'. What, he was asked, might cause such an elongation of the penis?

'Traction,' Dr Paul replied solemnly. 'Traction might produce elongation of the penis and the testicles.'

It was an alarming comment, conjuring up an image of Fanny and Stella's penises physically distorted and elongated by the rigours of anal penetration. One of Dr Paul's treasured authorities on sodomy claimed that very often 'the dimensions of the penis of active pederasts were excessive in one way or another', that they were 'pointed and moulded to the funnel shape of the passive anus'. And sometimes they were 'twisted' – a consequence of 'the corkscrew motion required during anal sex'.

There was no doubt in Dr Paul's mind that the bodies of the two young men he had just examined bore all the hallmarks of sodomy. They might protest their innocence until they were blue in the face, but their sins were engraved in scarlet upon their flesh. It was proof, indisputable and unarguable scientific proof, of the charges against them that they 'did with each and one another and with divers other persons feloniously commit the abominable crime of buggery'.

6

Wives and Daughters

Say, Stella, was Prometheus blind,
And, forming you, mistook your kind?
No; 'twas for you alone he stole
The fire that forms a manly soul;
Then, to complete it every way,
He moulded it with female clay:
To that you owe the nobler flame,
To this the beauty of your frame.

Jonathan Swift,
'To Stella, Visiting Me in My Sickness', 1720

Mrs Mary Ann Boulton was a devoted wife and an indulgent mother and she did not mind who knew it. Whatever adversity and misfortune they had as a family experienced (and, really, they had endured more than their fair share of adversity and misfortune), they were, she always maintained, a happy family. A very happy family.

Whatever sneers and snide asides there might be from those ignorant souls who looked down upon them because Mr Boulton was engaged in trade, she knew that she was every inch a lady. Her Papa had been a gentleman of 'independent means' and when they were in Dalston Terrace they had lived in quite some style. They were respected and respectable.

And her Papa had not ceased to be a gentleman just because the family had fallen on difficult times and had gone into manufacturing in a small way. Just as she had not ceased to be a lady because she had sought suitable employment as a governess, though she had never 'lived in'. She had been quite emphatic on that point. It was very hard for governesses who lived in not to be made to feel like servants.

Whatever people said about Tottenham, she had always found it most genteel. Indeed, it was her decided opinion that Tottenham, at one remove from the noise and the bustle of the metropolis, with its hedgerows and quaint cottages, was rather more genteel, more truly genteel, than many other parts of London famed for their gentility.

It was in Tottenham that she had been introduced to Mr Boulton. He was handsome, kindly and worldly-wise and six years older than herself – a perfect gap, she maintained. And he was called Thomas, which was her Uncle's name, and the coincidence had struck her as propitious. There seemed to be so many coincidences, so many good omens and portents: Thomas's Papa was a gentleman living in reduced circumstances (though perhaps not quite as gentlemanly as her own Papa), and Thomas, like herself, had cheerfully adapted to his altered condition and was making his way in the world. She knew little about stockbroking, but Thomas had assured her that it was a gentlemanly sort of occupation and that the prospects were excellent.

Thomas Boulton had paid his attentions to her very properly. They had quickly fallen in love, and when he proposed marriage she had accepted with alacrity. He had been undeterred by the absence of any fortune on her part, which, she must confess, had been something of a stumbling block on the road to matrimony. There had been times when she almost despaired of meeting a suitable husband. So on that blessed day when her Papa walked her down the aisle, she had been filled with an overwhelming sense of joy, not unmingled with relief.

Ernest was such a delicate boy from the very start. He was born in the bitterly cold December of 1848 and she worried that her baby, so small and pale and delicate and perfect, would not survive. He had a cough that would not go away, and she would lie awake at night, her heart in her mouth, listening out for him. There was consumption in Thomas's family and he had lost three brothers to it. So she fretted and nursed and prayed and coddled her darling baby boy, and by some miracle he survived that first harsh winter and she was grateful.

She remained grateful, even when her second baby son was called to God just days after he was born. She still had Ernest, her darling Ernest, and he was a joy and a comfort. He was such a lovely little boy, so pretty with his blue-violet eyes, large as saucers in his pale face, and his dark hair cascading in baby curls. People often mistook him for a baby girl.

By the time Gerard was born, when Ernest was four, Mr Boulton had left the stockbroking business and entered the wine trade, which was, by all accounts, a most gentlemanly profession and one in which he was bound to prosper, as it stood to reason that people would always want to drink wine. Mr B did indeed prosper – at least at first – and they moved to Greenwich, to a house in Queen Elizabeth Row.

Ernest was an extraordinary little boy. Extraordinary. He could sing before he could speak, with such a beautiful clear soprano voice. 'And Ernest was so fond of dressing up,' she recalled. 'From the age of six, before he could well speak, he was fond of dressing up and acting female parts.' He could play a maidservant or a little girl with ringlets and a lisp, or he could suddenly assume the airs and graces of a grand lady and then change, in the twinkling of an eye, to a rude, rough, drunken woman of the type they averted their eyes from in the streets. Nothing was lost on Ernest. He saw it all, he stored it all up.

She always remembered the time when her Mamma was staying with them in Queen Elizabeth Row and they were dining. Ernest came in, dressed to perfection as the parlourmaid, and waited upon her Mamma at table. He served the food and poured the wine and the water beautifully.

'Mamma did not recognise him in the least,' Mrs Mary Ann Boulton smiled indulgently at the memory. Indeed, her Mamma had been more than usually stern upon the subject. 'I wonder that, having sons, you have so flippant a girl about you,' she had said, after Ernest went out of the room.

Ernest was not what you might call a boyish boy, and had never exhibited the least interest in the sports and games that most boys liked to play. Mr Boulton had even gone so far as to suggest that Ernest was a trifle effeminate, something of a mollycoddle. They had had words. She would not dignify such an accusation with argument. Suffice it to say that Ernest had always been extremely delicate, and was extremely delicate still, and what mother worthy of the name would not cosset and coddle such a rare and delicate bloom?

It was, perhaps, a little unusual for a boy to make such a convincing girl and sing with such a beautiful soprano voice, but then Ernest was an unusual and talented boy. *She* had never worried about him dressing up as a woman to act and sing. *She* was not narrow. Was it not the rule in the Elizabethan theatre for beardless boys to act the parts of Shakespeare's heroines? If it was good enough for the Bard, it was surely good enough for her. When it came down to it, it was just dressing up and make-believe and, really, she did not see any harm in it then, and she still could not see any harm in it now – even though there had been all this unpleasantness, all these complications.

Dressing up and make-believe. Stella knew – she had always known, ever since she was a little girlish boy – exactly what she wanted for herself. She was to be an actress – a *great* actress, it went without saying – in musical comedies and in burlesque extravaganzas. She would be a dazzling dramatic actress, too, and men and women alike – but in her mind's eye, mostly men – would swoon and thrill as she sang sad songs of love in her perfect soprano voice and weep with pity and wonder at the pathos and power of her performances.

She was to be a queen of the stage: regal, gracious and greatly loved. She would hold her audiences in the palm of her hand. Night after night they would offer their loyalty and their devotion, and in return she would give herself to them, body and soul. Every time she made an entrance a tidal wave of applause would sweep through the auditorium and she would bathe in a rosy hue of love and adoration.

She would be a star. A star shining brightly and beautifully in the magical firmament of the stage. Her image would be etched and reproduced a million times in grainy black printer's ink in the popular newspapers. And theatregoers, from wealthy young sprigs of the aristocracy to spoony young men and rude shop boys, would queue up and pay two shillings and sixpence for a photographic portrait of her looking beautiful and soulful.

Then there would be her beaux, an endless line of love-struck admirers, those selfsame sprigs of the aristocracy, wealthy gentlemen and young officers in full dress uniform, all of them darkly, devastatingly handsome. They would send her lovesick notes written on thick creamy vellum and pretty gifts of hothouse flowers in boxes tied up with golden ribands. She would be duly grateful and duly gracious and send charming little notes of thanks written on delicate lace-edged paper scented with orange-flower water. She would try to be kind and try to be loving to each and every one of them. It was the very least she could do.

She had made her public debut at the age of fourteen playing Maria, the beautiful and tragic young heroine of *The Brigand*, where she sang very prettily and swooned very convincingly as she was abducted by swarthy moustachioed bandits who threatened to rob her of her virtue. She had been loudly applauded and there had been shouts of '*Brava! Brava!*' from the young men in the audience, and some of them even waved and smiled at her when she made her curtsey at the end, blushing very prettily under her greasepaint.

Life, alas, did not run smooth for Mrs Mary Ann Boulton. The wine trade fell rather short of its early promise and the family was forced to retrench and to move to a smaller house in Peckham Rye.

With careful housekeeping, with much scrimping and scraping, with a great deal of ingenuity, and a few small godsends of gifts of money from her family, Mrs Mary Ann Boulton had just about managed to keep up appearances and ensure that Ernest and Gerard had 'everything they required', everything that two young men from a good family would expect and might be expected to have.

'I never allowed any cloud to fall upon my children,' she declared proudly. 'Whatever troubles we have had, I have always shielded them from everything.'

Things went from bad to worse. Mr Boulton continued to suffer 'reverses' – in truth, 'great reverses' – in business, so much so that he was obliged to cut his losses and look about him for a new opportunity. Only a small legacy from her departed Grandpapa kept the family afloat. The vexed question of Ernest's profession could not be put off for much longer. Ernest was nearly eighteen and had done very little since leaving school except act and sing and mope around the house. With things as they were, they could not afford articles for a profession, so what was Ernest to do with himself?

Ernest was adamant that he did not want to enter a dreary profession. He wanted to sing and to act. But his father was equally adamant that no son of his would ever work in the theatre. Dressing up and make-believe were no life for a boy, he said. Private theatricals were one thing. But he could not, would not, countenance the theatre as a profession. It was not a fit place for a young man starting out in the world.

Quite apart from the unsuitability of the theatre, it was a question of money. Ernest would always have a home with them, but a boy of his age needed money of his own.

'If he asked his father for anything, he always gave it,' Mrs Mary Ann Boulton said. 'I daresay he had upon an average, a pound a week pocket money and sometimes more.' It was a not inconsiderable sum, and it pressed hard upon their slender and straitened means. Mr Boulton said Ernest needed to earn his living, and the sooner he started work, the better.

As Ernest's mother, she found herself in a difficult position. Of course she agreed – she always agreed – with Mr Boulton. She had the greatest respect for his judgement. He knew the world and its manifold snares for the unwary and the naive. But it was hard to see Ernest so unhappy and so pale. There had been scenes and tears, and it was all very upsetting.

The London and County Bank in Islington was a very long way from Peckham, and each morning Stella would have to rise shortly after six to make the tiresome journey. Sometimes she would take the train from Lower Knights Hill to Victoria and then catch an omnibus, or when the weather was kind she would walk some of the way and pocket the money.

She had agreed, with the greatest reluctance, to become a clerk at the London and County Bank at a salary of £50 a year. Papa had arranged it. The prospects, her fellow clerks assured her, were excellent. In due course, Stella would become a fully fledged counter clerk and might eventually rise to the dizzy heights of a senior clerk. Stella could barely repress her yawns. If Mr Lewis, the chief clerk at the Islington branch, was anything to go by, she would rather die, she was sure, before turning into such a fussy, fiddling, pernickety dried-up stick of a man. She was bored and exhausted by the time she arrived in the morning, and she could hardly wait for the majestic mahogany timepiece to chime six times and let her make good her escape from the terrible clockwork monotony of the bank.

Mrs Mary Ann Boulton blamed herself for Ernest's illness. It was really very extraordinary that Ernest's ill-health should have so exactly coincided with his work at the bank. The hours were far too long, and there was that terrible journey, there and back, five – sometimes six – days a week, and in all seasons. It was all too much for him. He was delicate. 'He was consumptive – three doctors had said he was consumptive – and he had a constant cough,' she said. It was no wonder that

Ernest was so continually absent from the bank. And if the cough and the colds and the weakness of his chest were not enough, he developed that terrible abscess, that fistula, in such an unfortunate and indelicate area, which caused her poor boy so much pain and discomfort, so bravely borne.

In the end she put her foot down and insisted that Ernest could not continue. Which was just as well, because Mr Lewis had written a very serious letter to Mr Boulton about Ernest's absences and even suggested, none too tactfully, that he might be temperamentally unsuited to the London and County Bank. From the very moment he resigned, Ernest's spirits soared and he declared that he would devote his life to the theatre. There was little they could do to dissuade him.

'I was always rather opposed to his acting,' Mrs Mary Ann Boulton said later, her voice thin and querulous. 'But I did not forbid it. I would rather he would have done anything else, but he always had such a penchant for it that I was almost compelled to give my sanction.'

For as long as Stella could remember men had always taken notice of her. In school and out of school, at the theatre and at concerts, in church on a Sunday, on the streets, out shopping with Mamma, sitting on the omnibus and walking in the park, she had felt the hungry eyes of men of all types and all conditions upon her. There were the usual sniggerings, catcalls and whistles, and a quite bewildering array of lewd and shocking suggestions and gestures from the army of coarse and common young men thronging the streets as she made her way to and from the London and County Bank. She had been mortified at first and had cried into her pillow at night, but her Mamma had comforted her, smoothed her brow and lulled her into sleep.

And then she had started answering the rude men back, and sometimes she made them laugh. It did not take long to learn the difference between the hostile men and those whose suggestive banter was nothing more nor less than flirtation. She could see and feel the shiver and ache of desire in the flashing eyes of these young men. And some of them were quite handsome, really *very* handsome, in a common sort of way, and she was sometimes surprised to find that they provoked an answering shiver, an answering ache within herself.

Then there were the respectable men, mostly married, who would fall quite naturally into polite conversation with her at the bank and on the bus and in the park and at the concert hall. One thing would lead to another, and she would accept their invitation to luncheon, to tea or to supper. She would be modest and polite and smile boyishly or girlishly and sometimes look at them intensely from the depths of her blue-violet eyes and, when she saw them tremble, she knew what it was that they wanted.

And often, quite often – in fact, more often than not – she gave them what they wanted, in small, strange hotel rooms; in little out-of-the-way lodgings; in small houses where wives and children and maids-of-all-work were out; in parks and garden squares, after dark, behind trees and bushes; down alleyways, along towpaths; in closes, courtyards and crooked ways; in urinals and cubicles and public conveniences; in the dark, always hiding, always hidden; always watching, always fearing; always ready to fly when danger threatened.

Sometimes they told her that they loved her and they wanted her. Sometimes they said nothing. Only a few ever kissed her. Which disappointed her. Most only wanted one thing. They would hug and hold and squeeze her and then fumble clumsily with her trousers until they were down and off and then the deed was quickly accomplished. They would spend in her mouth or in her hand, and sometimes between her buttocks. If she felt like it, if she had that curious feeling, like an itch but not quite an itch, if they were not too big – or even if they were – she would let them penetrate her and spend in her bottom.

Afterwards they would wipe themselves and wash themselves vigorously, as if they were ashamed of what they had done. She was surprised at how many would start to cry. Sometimes they would kneel and pray for forgiveness from God. And sometimes they would hand her a golden sovereign and beg *her* forgiveness. Stella never knew what she had to forgive. But she said she forgave them nonetheless because it made them feel happier, and she always pocketed the golden sovereign.

Thankfully they were not all like that. Some men wanted to stay, to talk, to kiss, to embrace. And a few, more than a few, said they wanted to see her again and seemed to mean it. Such ardent swains could be very persistent and very cloying. Some of them begged her to share their lives, begged her, with tears in their eyes, for her love. But such love affairs were doomed, Stella concluded. They did not so much want to love her as to possess her, to own her as their plaything, as a china doll to be dressed up prettily in a suit or a satin gown.

Some of the coarse young men from the uncharted erotic swamp of nameless streets and alleyways, the working men, the soldiers and sailors and dark-skinned foreign men, just wanted to fuck her again and again until she could hardly bear the pain. She would leave drenched in the smell of their sweat and their seed and she would feel different. She would feel replete. And again and again she found herself drawn back to these men, drawn back by their feral bodies and their feral smells and, through the strange alchemy of lust, find rest and repose.

Stella loved them all. She knew that she could saunter on to the streets – in drag or out of drag, as Stella, Star of the Strand, or as plain Ernest Boulton – and that sooner or later a man, or several men, would proposition her. She drew notice. She compelled notice. They told her she was beautiful and that they desired her. They wanted her, they needed her. And Stella knew that it was within her power to make them happy.

In her mind, Stella compared going with men – for love or for money – with her life as a great actress. Were the two things *really* so very different? She was kind to men, she gave pleasure to men, to many men, to lonely and unhappy men. She brought joy to their lives, and they returned the favour with pretty gifts. She gave everything she had. She gave herself, body and soul. She performed – consummately – for each and every one. Each encounter was magical and memorable, and until the time came when she would find fame and fortune and marry the younger son of a Duke, she lived in a rosy hue of love and adulation.

7

Becoming Fanny

And all that's madly wild, or oddly gay,
We call it only pretty Fanny's way.

Thomas Parnell,
'An Elegy, to an Old Beauty', 1773

Number 35 Wimpole Street was a house of sorrow, and the early years and youth of Master Frederick William Park, or Miss Fanny Winifred Park as she invariably thought of herself, were tinged and tainted with grief.

Sometimes Fanny would sit quietly in the drawing room and solemnly turn the stiff, gilded leaves of the album of family photographs, and she would feel a lump in her throat and tears pricking at her eyes when she came to the photographs of those three of her brothers and two of her sisters who had died in their infancy. As the youngest of twelve children, she had not known these early departed brothers and sisters and she would often wonder how they would have been had they lived.

But Fanny had known her brother Atherton for all her short life. She was seven when the news of his death was received, and she could still recall how 35 Wimpole Street was plunged into a dark and terrible passage of grief, and how her Papa turned suddenly into a frail old man. Lieutenant Atherton Allan Park, so handsome in the full dress uniform of the 24th Bombay Native Infantry, so proud to serve his Queen and country, so cruelly cut down – hacked to death – at Jhansi under the burning Indian sun. Fanny shivered and shuddered at the thought.

Her tears would flow even more strongly when she looked at those precious few photographs of her poor Mamma, taken from them when Fanny was not yet three. Fanny herself could only remember her Mamma in fragments and feelings, as if from a half-waking dream. But Lucy, Sissy and Atherton (until he was so cruelly taken), and Alexander and Georgina – even Harry (though he was only seven at the time) – could all remember Mamma and could all tell Fanny about her and the way she was.

And then there was Mary Batson, who had nursed all twelve of them and had been her Mamma's nurse when *she* was a little girl. Mary Batson was still with them after all these years, and Mary knew everything there was to know about Mamma. Fanny would sit and listen to Mary's stories about the old days, about life in Merton Grove, when Wimbledon was a charming small village, about the balls, the parties and the love affairs, and about the time Papa and Mamma got married.

Everybody, from Mary Batson to Papa, to Lucy and Sissy and Georgina, agreed that her Mamma had been sweet-tempered and kind, with never a harsh word to say about anybody or anything.

She was also very devout, and it was she, Mary Batson said, who had introduced morning and evening prayers into the house. Even after Mamma's early departure from this world, the tradition had continued, though now only in the mornings, and for as long as she could remember Fanny had knelt in the crowded drawing room for what seemed like an age as Papa led the household in prayers of exhortation and supplication. (Not that any of it had done much good, Fanny reflected, given the catalogue of griefs and sorrows that had been inflicted upon them.)

Number 35 Wimpole Street was a house of women. Counting the servants, there were no fewer than thirteen women to three men and two boys. When he was at home, Papa was usually in his study. Atherton was away with the Army in India, and Alexander, who was eleven years older than Fanny, was away at school. Which left only herself and Harry in a houseful of women.

Lucy, who was nineteen when Mamma departed this life, had brought up the two boys, with the assistance of Mary Batson and the kindly interference of two elderly aunts. As the baby of the family, Fanny was showered with love and attention and was frankly a little spoilt. Indeed, both boys were spoilt. Harry was tall and handsome. He could charm the birds from the trees, a talent he used to talk his way out of hot water, in which commodity he frequently found himself immersed. Trouble followed Harry like a shadow, and Papa used to despair of him.

Frederick William, or Fanny Winifred, was altogether a different kettle of fish. He – or she – was quite unlike any of his siblings in looks or personality or demeanour. Mary Batson would nod and shake her head sagely over Freddy. It would often turn out this way, she was fond of saying, when the twelfth child was the last child and a boy-child. A changeling. A child of the fairy folk. And, indeed, for those with eyes to see there was something Puckish, something very sprite-like about Fanny, whose mischievous, joyous and playful nature made him into a regular Robin Goodfellow.

It was hard to be angry with Freddy for very long. He was an appealing if curious child, with large, fluid eyes, a mouth that seemed too big for his face, and an abundance of protruding teeth. He was slight and pale, altogether sickly-looking, and was disinclined to sports or exercise – other than walking the streets and promenading in Regent's Park – and he looked as if he needed a good dose of sunshine and fresh country air.

Most of all, Freddy liked to sing and to act and to dance. He liked to dress up as a soldier or a sailor or, better still, a lady, and would caper about the house as a Duchess or a drab and make jokes until the servants' sides ached with laughter. Or he and Harry would write plays and perform them for Lucy and for Papa and Mary Batson. Harry made a dashingly handsome hero, while Freddy would play the imperilled and lovesick heroine, and play her with such conviction and such verve that Lucy and Papa and Mary Batson would sometimes forget for more than a moment that Freddy was a little boy.

Quite when it was that Freddy became Fanny, she could not recollect. Suffice it to say that *she* had not changed. There had been no great or sudden revelation on the road to Damascus for *her* (always a favourite parable of Papa's). The Temple curtain was not rent asunder and nor had the scales fallen suddenly from *her* eyes. No. Becoming Fanny was a process of realisation, rather than revelation. For as long as she could remember, from before she had words to express it or explain it – before she had words at all – she had always been Fanny in her heart, she had always sensed she was different from other boys – but thankfully not from Harry. Never from Harry.

Fanny could not even remember when Harry stopped calling her Fred or Freddy and started to call her Fanny or Fan. It seemed just to happen, and once or twice Harry forgot himself and let it slip before Lucy, who frowned, and Papa who would turn pale and angry. And all the time Mary Batson would chuckle to herself and shake her head and talk nonsensically of changelings and fairy folk.

B ecoming Fanny was a slow and painful process, and as she grew older, she became more and more aware that the world as currently constituted did not always look kindly upon those who were different, upon those who did not conform.

To this uncomprehending and uncaring world she was, she realised, an effeminate youth – an effeminate youth unrelieved by any conventional saving graces of beauty. Her head was too big for her body and her teeth were too big for her mouth; her skin was blotchy and inclined to pustules; her hair was wild and wiry; her eyes rather too close-set; her brows too dark; her nose decidedly too emphatic.

Fanny could not help it. She had tried and tried and tried to change, to become more manly, to be more like Atherton and Alexander. But however hard she tried, she always failed. She was never in step with the merry dance of manliness. It was like chasing her own shadow. It eluded her. It evaded her. However hard she sought it, she was destined and doomed never to find it – in this life at least – and there were many nights and many days over many months and many years when Fanny would weep with frustration, shame and misery, and wonder why it was that she had ever been born.

Why could she not be more like Harry, Fanny would often wonder in angry and bitter retrospects. They were cut from the same cloth, coined from the same mint. They were the same, but different. Harry passed. Nobody noticed and nobody guessed. He was just Harry, charming, handsome Harry, who fitted into the jigsaw of his life perfectly. Well, almost perfectly.

But when it came to herself, everybody noticed, everybody

guessed. Fanny could never pass, could never deceive, could never fit in. She was the odd one out, the ugly duckling, the cuckoo in the nest that nobody really wanted or knew what to do with. Nobody except Harry. And then she would weep afresh, with gratitude and love for Harry, and with sorrow that her Mamma was dead.

When the time came, Papa decided not to send Fanny to school. He insisted that she should be a scholar-at-home, taught by Lucy and by Miss Isabella Norris, the governess who had taught all the girls, and though Fanny could not at first fully understand why Papa did not send her away to board at school like Alexander, or be a day boy at a school like Harry, she began to apprehend that her Papa's decision was a strange amalgam of the best and worst of motives: best because he sought to spare her from the taunts and jibes of cruel boys who could not and would not understand her; and worst, because he wanted to hide her away from the world, to save himself and his family from owning to the shame of having Fanny as his child.

It was a dark day when Fanny finally realised that she was an affront to the world, that her very being offended the world in ways small and large. She was not entirely a man and not entirely a woman. To be sure, she had the body of a man. Harry, who seemed to know everything about the bodies of men, had assured her she was a man. There was no doubt about it, he said. But Fanny craved the company of women and she liked womanish things, like dresses and dances and beaux. She could sew, she could knit, and she was at her happiest at home with her sisters, sitting quietly together, or down in the basement with Mary Batson, listening to the reassuring drone of the servants' chitter-chatter.

There were times, however, when Fanny was obliged to venture beyond the grand portico of 35 Wimpole Street and go into the world that she so affronted. It was hard. Eyebrows would be raised, gazes averted, backs abruptly turned. Sometimes she would be stared out of countenance, stared at like an exhibit in a museum, or like shoddy goods in a shop window. Glared at with looks of such hatred that she trembled and felt fearful. There would be muttered comments, whispered threats and imprecations. Sometimes she was unceremoniously pushed or shoved aside, spat upon. Or stones were thrown at her. Urchins would hurl abuse, and furious red-faced gentlemen would come up to her and deliver foul-mouthed volleys about who she was and what she was and the terrible fate that would soon befall her – from the noose to the fires of Hell. And she would turn pale and tremble but stand her ground.

Thank goodness for Harry. It was Harry, of course, who so patiently explained everything to her, though where and how he found it all out, God only knew. If she was being truthful, it was not so much of a shock, or even a surprise. Harry's disclosures only served to confirm what she already more than halfway knew. Fanny knew that she liked men in ways that other boys could not conceive of, and she knew that her feelings were like those of her sisters. And she knew that Harry was the same.

Harry's disclosures made her feel she might, after all, have some purpose in life, that she might eventually meet and fall in love with a gentleman and live happily ever after. But in the meantime, Harry told her, there were any number of men in London – and not all of them gentlemen – who would want to go with her. He would take her. He would show her. Fanny listened with bright eyes. She felt a shiver of excitement and anticipation at the prospect.

Even though she and Harry both loved and desired men,

Harry was different. He had never evinced the least inclination to dress up as a lady or a serving wench or a fallen woman of the streets (and you did not have to venture very far from the front door of 35 Wimpole Street before stumbling across whores by the dozen plying their trade). Lucy, who had inherited her Mamma's compassion, called them sad creatures, though even she was discomfited by the more brazen types. The elderly spinster aunts merely stuck their noses in the air and hurried past as if to avoid a noxious emission.

But Fanny was fascinated and dazzled by the gaudy peacock colours of these women, by their blowsy ease and raucous laughter, by their painted faces and their billowing, untidy hair, by the smell of sweat and cheap scent which seemed to cling about them, and by other, strangely compulsive smells, which she would have thought she shouldn't like, but she did. And the whores were, by and large, nice to her. They would call her 'Dearie' or 'Margery' or 'Mary-Ann' or 'Miss Nancy', and most of the time it was not in a nasty way. Sometimes she would talk to them, and she found – to her surprise – that she was drawn to them and liked them more than she thought she would. They did not judge her like the others. They did not look down upon her. They would curse and cuss her in a friendly way, and then she would answer back with a haughty toss of her head and they would laugh uproariously.

That it was all wrong in the eyes of God, Fanny of course knew. Between those endless prayers and Bible readings at home and the droning, drowsy sermons in church on a Sunday, Fanny had come to understand the meaning of Sodom and Gomorrah. Harry had told her she was a sodomite (or she would be when the deed was accomplished). Fanny did not altogether care for the word. Sticks and stones, she said to herself, may break my bones, but names can never hurt me.

That it was all wrong under the laws of the land, she quickly discovered, and then wished that she had not. She was eleven or twelve when Harry first got into trouble with the police. The angry conversations went on for days behind the closed mahogany doors of 35 Wimpole Street. But Fanny heard enough about the wretched Italian boy, and Harry filled in the rest, swearing her to secrecy. Harry had been foolish and had fallen in love with a boy who abused his trust. Money was demanded and when no more was forthcoming, the boy carried out his threat. Harry was arrested and taken before the magistrate. It was all a pack of lies, he claimed, his handsome, honest face shining bright with righteous indignation. Fortunately his handsome, honest face carried the day and the case was dismissed.

And then, two or three years later, when Fanny was fifteen or sixteen – she could not properly recall – Harry was arrested in Weymouth Mews in the middle of the night and there was a great to-do and much weeping and wailing and talk of prisons and hard labour. It was a great and terrible scandal, made even worse by the fact that Papa was a very distinguished judge. Harry had shamed himself, shamed his family and shamed his Papa.

Harry was to go away, to disappear, and no one was supposed to know anything about it. And no one was ever to see him again, save for Papa, and perhaps Lucy (and Mary Batson, of course, as she was so old and it was thought that a permanent separation from her darling Harry would hasten her demise).

But as the months and years passed, Papa relented a little, and Harry the prodigal son would sometimes return from exile in Scotland to the bosom of his family, and the blood of fatted calves would be spilt. But only at the small villa in Isleworth, and never, ever in Wimpole Street, for fear of discovery. And through all the long years, despite the separation, the bond between herself and Harry was unbroken, and even strengthened.

What was to become of her? There were two, and only two, professions for the Parks: soldiering and the law. But the idea of Fanny going for a soldier was patently ludicrous. Even Papa had smiled at the idea. So law was the only option. Papa had decided that the best and most profitable – by which he meant morally profitable – course was for Fanny to be articled to a solicitor. He had a gentleman in mind, Mr Gepp of Chelmsford. A steady, slow, solid gentleman with a steady, slow, solid county-town practice.

Judge Alexander Park fervently hoped and prayed that a few steady, slow and solid years under the watchful eye of Mr Gepp would rub off on Frederick, that his enthusiasms would be curbed, that his manner would become graver and more manly, that he would grow some sense – and perhaps even some whiskers.

But the months and years passed and Frederick did not seem to be growing any sense at all. Quite the reverse. The older he got, the less manly, the more effeminate, the more extreme he became. There he would stand, a cigarette in his gloved left hand, his right leg bent slightly forwards, his hips tilted like a woman of the street. His hair would be teased and shined and curled, and he would reek of strong perfume. His face in repose was disdainful, but his eyes were like a lizard's, dark and glittering and restless. He did not have to speak. He did not have to act. His very being, his very presence proclaimed and declared to all the world the sodomite that he was.

It was a strange thing, but it was hard to imagine where Frederick had come from, or who he took after. Rack his brains as hard as he could, Judge Park could not recollect any family member on either side who bore even the remotest resemblance to Frederick. It was as if his son were undergoing a species of transformation from caterpillar to chrysalis to brilliant, gaudy butterfly, and there were times when he found himself half-believing Mary Batson's nonsense about changelings and fairy folk.

Frederick was now a gabbling, good-natured, prattling, gossiping, charming young man who seemed older – much older – and more worldly than his nineteen years, who caused heads to turn for all the wrong reasons whenever he entered a room. He was loud and lewd, and laughed uproariously at his own jokes. Ladies adored him, and he invariably had them in fits of hysterics. Men were either bewildered by him, or made uneasy or hostile by his otherness, by his difference (though a few, surprisingly, were flattered by his violent flirtatiousness).

'Theatrical' was the word, perhaps the only word (or at least the only decent word), to describe the young man that Frederick had turned into. He lived for the theatre. The theatre was his day and his night; his sun and moon and stars; his darkening storms and sunlit passages. There was little or no division between the dressing up and make-believe of the theatre and the dressing up and make-believe of his daily life. They were one and the same. All the world was his stage, and Frederick seemed to ricochet between melodrama, tragedy and comedy – especially comedy of the low and vulgar variety.

There were times when Judge Park had to pinch himself to

make sure that he was not dreaming, that he had not strayed into a fairy realm, or fallen down a rabbit hole and found himself in Wonderland, like the young heroine of Mr Lewis Carroll's story. Frederick's world – or that small portion of Frederick's world of which he had caught glimpses – struck him as decidedly odd. It was a grotesquerie where the men were more like women and the women, though seemingly rarer than unicorns, behaved like men. Nothing was straightforward. Nothing was serious. All was surface. Nothing was substance. It was amorphous, ephemeral and inconsequential and yet, for its denizens, at least, it seemed compelling and all-absorbing.

Of those denizens, from the few that he had met, Judge Park had formed a low opinion, a very low opinion. There was Mr Charles Pavitt, a plump miller's son from Chelmsford who was some sort of professional actor. Then there was the fat and florid Mr Martin Luther Cumming who giggled constantly. Mr Cumming was an Oxford man, supposedly, though he had yet to hear an intelligent remark from him. There was Mr Amos Westropp Gibbings, with a girlish lisp and more money than sense. And finally there was Mr Ernest Boulton, a delicately beautiful young man with sad eyes and a startlingly lovely soprano voice. Mr Boulton was apparently Frederick's best friend and boon companion and they spent hours closeted together, though how they had first met was a mystery that had never been satisfactorily unravelled. There were others, too, who came and went and went and came so often that they seemed to blur into one long, lingering shriek of effeminacy.

Frederick's passion for burlesque had led him into the deplorable habit, in Judge Park's view, of dressing up in women's attire and acting the parts of women. But even Judge Park had to concede that sometimes he did this with consummate skill, having a natural bent for playing domineering duchesses and dowagers of a certain age with great flair and an eye for comic detail that made his audiences laugh out loud.

What could he hope for, what hope was there, for this strange hybrid child, for his changeling son? He was under no illusions. His elder son Harry was tainted with sodomy. There could be no doubt about that and, however much Harry's version of the incident in Weymouth Mews differed from that of Police Constable George White, it was clear to everyone that sodomy was at the very heart of the transaction. And if Harry was so tainted, so stained with sodomy, then Judge Park feared that there could be very little doubt that Frederick was equally tainted, equally stained with the sins of the Cities of the Plain.

Judge Alexander Park was a devout Christian, 'sound in principles, firmly and zealously attached to the sound orthodox doctrines of the Church of England, and pure and correct in his morals'. But devout though he was, devout as his dear departed wife had been, neither of them were Christians of the hellfire and brimstone variety. With half of those children born to him already dead and buried, Judge Park loved and valued those still left to him. He sorrowed and grieved and prayed for Frederick, just as he sorrowed and grieved and prayed for Harry. He could not but despise and loathe the sin, but he could not help loving the sinners. How could he not love his sinful sons? They were the flesh of his flesh, the fruit of his loins. And if that fruit was rotten, then he must shoulder some of the blame and some of the burden and he must do whatever he had to do, whatever could be done, to help and protect them.

What could he hope for – what hope was there – for his errant sons? He could not bear to see them punished. The gravest penalty for sodomy had only been abolished a year or two ago, but ten years to life with hard labour was equally a sentence of certain death. Such a sentence would crush and break them within weeks, and their decline and death would be agonising and inevitable, and every night as he lay sleepless in bed he trembled at the prospect of the terrible fates that might befall his two sodomitic sons.

8

A Tale of Two Sisters

A SISTER'S LOVE : There is no holier feeling
than a sister's love – no affection purer and more
enduring than hers.

The Family Treasury, 1854

W hat could she say about Fanny? That she was a formidable actress? That she was funny? That she was
courageous? That she was loyal? That she drank too much,
spoke too much and laughed too loudly? That she was wise
beyond her years? That she looked older than her years? (And
Stella was sure that she was not being unkind when she said
this, as it was universally agreed that Fanny, with what might be
called her 'sterner features', certainly did look older, very much
older, than her years.) That she knew everything there was to
know about Mary-Anns (as well as knowing every Mary-Ann
on the pad in London)? That she was steeped, not to say
pickled, in the ancient mysteries and rituals of drag? That she
was generous, more than generous – generous to a fault, in fact
– with her favours? That despite the disadvantages of person
she laboured under, Fanny had, more often than not, snatched
erotic victory from the jaws of defeat by a combination of
charm, determination, guile and utter ruthlessness? That she
was a true friend? That she was a loyal sister, if not by ties of
consanguinity then by the most secret and the most sacred
bonds of sorority and of sodomy?

Miss Fanny Winifred Park was one of those young ladies who had blossomed into womanhood early. By the age of sixteen, when most well brought-up girls had but a dim apprehension of distant marriage and motherhood, Miss Fanny Winifred Park was already well schooled in the dark arts of seduction and sodomy. She was certainly no stranger to those thronged thoroughfares around Coventry Street and the Haymarket where the gay ladies of London plied their trade so vigorously. Indeed, Miss Fanny Winifred Park had made her professional debut, so to speak, on this particular West End stage, not far short of her seventeenth birthday, and by dint of assiduous application and hard practice had risen rapidly through the ranks of her chosen profession.

It was a curious thing, but she soon discovered that she was considerably more successful in selling herself when she was in drag than when she was out of drag. While it was certainly true that there were some men to whom a painted and effeminate youth strongly appealed, there were a great many more who were interested in her when she was dressed as a woman.

Miss Fanny Winifred Park was nothing if not a realist. Nature had not endowed her with an abundance of personal advantages. In matters of face, figure, complexion, teeth and hair, Nature had been less than generous (if not downright stingy), and she was only too well aware that in the hierarchy of painted effeminate youths working the streets, she barely reached the middle rank. Though there were some who had left their youth far behind them and now relied on paint slapped on like stucco, equally there were plenty of other, prettier boys who skimmed off the choicest punters and steamers. Not that she was complaining. After all, they were all God's creatures.

Fanny, however, when she was dressed in silk and suitably padded with a bustle and false bubbies, bewigged and with a generous application of paint, was transformed into what was generally termed a handsome woman. Not beautiful, certainly, but then not plain. Nor was there any of the blushing virgin nonsense about her. She was, she liked to think, very much a 'Girl of the Period', as the *Saturday Review* had so memorably phrased it: a fast girl, a girl who lived her life to the full, who drank and smoked, who went about and abroad and was curious about the world. A girl not trepidatious about life; a girl not startled by her own shadow; a girl not hidebound by convention and propriety and all those other suffocating corsets of the mind.

In her short span upon this mortal coil, Miss Fanny Winifred Park had certainly savoured life, and drunk deeply from the cup of Venus. She held her head high and was not ashamed to look men boldly in the eye and to give them what they wanted. Miss Fanny Winifred Park's favours usually came at a price, but she could be soft-hearted and sentimental. There were occasions when she felt it her duty to do what she could to console lonely men, especially soldiers and sailors in the service of the Queen – for whom she felt a particular *tendresse*.

Whatever her faults and virtues, Miss Fanny Winifred Park understood men. Like the best whores, she knew instinctively what men needed. She had the knack of making them happy. She was a good sport. She would dance with them and drink with them. She would listen to them and make them feel wanted. She understood, only too well, the intensity of the erotic abyss men so constantly struggled against and yet so constantly sought. She was their guide. She would take their trembling hands in hers and lead them to the dark side of the moon to assuage the desires that raged like a torrent within them till the pale dawn came and they would be released.

Most, if not all, of her customers laboured under the illusion that Miss Fanny Winifred Park was a woman, and why should they think otherwise? With her generous embonpoint, tweezered eyebrows, painted face and luxurious curls, she looked every inch the successful gay lady. Those gentlemen fortunate enough to enjoy her favours were generally more than satisfied with their purchase and left satiated and entirely unaware that she was not quite what she seemed. And for the most part, the few who were entrusted with her secret, far from running away from her, seemed all the more excited by the idea. There would always be one or two who would recoil in horror, lash out with their fists or threaten her with the police. It was an occupational hazard, and Fanny was far from blind to the risks (look at her poor brother Harry, exiled to the wilds of Scotland). But she knew she could not live her life in any other way. She was young, she was strong and she was resourceful. She was more than a match for those who would try to do her harm.

Miss Fanny Winifred Park was all things to all men, switching in the twinkling of an eye from the commonest of common whores to the grandest of *grandes dames*. One minute she could wallow and rejoice in filthy talk like a streetwalker, and the next she could delight and charm with small talk which would not disgrace the most refined London drawing rooms. She was welcoming, warm and funny, but when the occasion demanded it, could wither with one fell look. Though she still harboured hopes of a life in the theatre, fame and fortune on the London stage had so far eluded her. She had notched up some considerable successes in the provinces, playing principally dowagers, and her performance as Agatha De Windsor, a wronged woman of a certain age in *Retained for the Defence*, had astonished and delighted the audience in Chelmsford at a benefit for the Infirmary. It had been the high-water mark of her stage career. Never before (and sadly never since) had she experienced such storms of applause; never before (and sadly never since) had she so scaled the heights of Histronia; and never before (and sadly never since) had she been the recipient of one or two admiring letters and bouquets from gentlemen.

Not infrequently Fanny would sally forth dressed in the most impenetrable black with a stricken look upon her face. On such occasions she would be Mrs Fanny Winifred Graham (*née* Park). From the weeds she wore and the expression upon her face, it was assumed by her friends and acquaintances that Mrs Fanny Winifred Graham (*née* Park) was the worthy and dutiful relict of Mr Graham. But none of them could be certain. It was the one subject – in truth, the only subject – upon which Fanny never spoke. Her lips were sealed and if anyone was sufficiently unwise or unfeeling to attempt to resurrect – Lazarus-like – the memory of Mr Graham, Fanny's face would assume a tender expression. Dabbing a handkerchief to her eyes and clearing her throat noisily, she would beg her interrogator's pardon and swiftly change the subject to the latest fashions from Paris, the shocking price of bombazine, or the scandalous antics of the new French girls in Coventry Street.

There were those in Fanny's circle of candid friends, needless to say, who pooh-poohed the very idea of Mr Graham, who said that he was a figment of Fanny Park's fevered imagination, amiably remarking that she had never yet managed to keep a man for more than a night, let alone for long enough to lead him to the altar. These friends were further of the opinion that if Fanny Park really had got herself married, then the gentleman in question must have been very much advanced in years. He was probably senile, quite possibly blind, perhaps even crippled, or a combination of all three. There were many other such pleasantries. Through all these slings and arrows, Fanny would sail serenely on, tightly clasping the truth about the mysterious Mr Graham to her ample and womanly bosom.

'A Tale of Two Sisters'. It might have formed the plot of a burlesque melodrama; or been a story in an illustrated penny magazine; or even a front-page report in one of the more sensational weekly newspapers: by a terrible twist of Fate two sisters are separated at birth and grow to womanhood, each unaware of the existence of the other. Both sisters are sweet, kind and beautiful, and both of them are the object of many handsome and rich beaux. But both sisters are inexplicably sad; they feel a curious sense of being incomplete, of being one half of a whole; they sense a lack, an absence, a void in their lives. Something is missing, or is it *someone*?

Both sisters live useful, busy and fashionable lives in London, filling their time with society, shopping and good works. As they go about their daily business and as their paths inevitably cross (London society is, after all is said and done, not much more than a large, gossipy village), they sometimes have the strangest feeling of having met before. Fanny, the elder of the sisters, who speaks perfect French, uses the phrase *déjà vu*. Stella, who is musical, feels something similar, like a heard, familiar melody from the dim and distant past that she cannot quite place. After many vicissitudes, hair-raising escapades and improbable adventures, after some songs and dances and a few comic interludes, the scales fall from their eyes and a benignant

Fate reunites the two sisters who fall weeping upon each other's necks and vow never again to be parted on Earth or in Heaven.

So it was for the sistering of Fanny and Stella. The heavenly spheres were aligned, and Fanny and Stella had come together as sisters. Fate had brought them together, two halves of a whole, now united, now conjoined in joy. And having found each other, Fanny and Stella were loath to be parted.

By night and by day they did everything together and went everywhere together. To the theatre, to the halls; to the Boat Race, to Bond Street and to the Burlington Arcade; to parks and pleasure gardens; to dives and divans; to balls and cheap dances. Up and down, and down and up, they promenaded and paraded the streets of London, sometimes in drag and sometimes out of drag (and sometimes half-in and half-out, which confused and confounded everybody and meant that no one could be quite sure who or what they were). They hunted and searched and scoured the streets looking for men for love or for money, sometimes finding neither and sometimes finding both.

They wore the same clothes, the same paint and the same *coiffures*. They stood in the same way, their slender feet neatly pointing outwards like a ballet dancer's, their heads slightly thrown back, their gloved hands invariably holding a cigarette or a glass of champagne or a bumper of sherry. They walked arm-in-arm and alike: adopting a rapid, tittuping walk, with their noses stuck in the air, when they wished to have no truck with the world ('your mincing and theatrical walk', Louis Hurt, another of Stella's ardent swains, had once disparagingly and despairingly called it); or a slow, bottom-rolling, leering and lascivious royal progress which caused everyone – foes and friends alike – to stop and stare with a look of horror or delight, or a mixture of the two, upon their faces. Many, if not most, of those who encountered them thought they were either whores or actresses, or both, as – in the minds of most people – the two professions were indivisible. Their life was a performance. London was their stage. The world was their audience. They were exotic, extraordinary and quite magnificent.

'They always said the same thing,' was the hapless Hugh Mundell's attempt to explain the extraordinary manner in which Fanny and Stella spoke in concert. They said the same things at the same time. One would begin and the other would finish. Fanny would echo Stella, and Stella would echo Fanny. And when they spoke, they spoke with the same inflections, intonations and affectations. They used the same gestures, the same mannerisms and the same facial expressions. They laughed in the same way at the same jokes, and the same things displeased them, their brows contracting darkly in the same way. And though they spoke the Queen's English in loud and well-bred tones of command, they were also masters – or rather, mistresses – of common slang, of the argot of whores and the backslang of thieves and trampers and gypsies.

Above and beyond that, they had their own special language, a language into which only they and their confederates – the sodomites, the hermaphrodites and the God-only-knows-what-else-ites – had been initiated. It was called 'the Female Dialect' (or so Fanny, the fount of all wisdom on matters sodomitical, had informed Stella), and it was as old as time, or nearly so. It was a strange and secret language; an upside-down, inside-out sort of dialect where 'she' meant 'he', and 'he' meant 'she'; where men were called by women's names, where Frederick was Fanny, Ernest was Stella, Amos was Carlotta, and Cecil was Cecilia, or Sissy for short. Most of the men styled themselves just plain Miss and Mistress, but there was no shortage of those who liked to call themselves Lady This, the Countess of That or the Dowager Duchess of So and So. There was a positive glut of Princesses, and more Queens in the few square miles of London than there were kingdoms in the wide world for them to rule over.

They were sisters. Side by side and shoulder to shoulder. Sisters for better or for worse. Sisters in sickness and in health. Sisters in drag and sisters out of drag. They made a formidable and fearless pair. London stood before them, waiting to be conquered, ready to fall at their feet in a swoon.

9

Monstrous Erections

At Wakefield Street, near Regent Square,
There lived this rummy he-she pair,
And such a stock of togs was there,
To suit those he-she ladies.
There was bonnets & shawls, & pork pie hats,
Chignons and paints, and Jenny Lind caps.
False calves and drawers, to come out slap,
To tog them out, it is a fact.

'The Funny He-She Ladies'

Aweek to the day after their first appearance in Bow Street,
Fanny and Stella were due in court again. 'The crowd
outside was immense,' *Reynolds's Newspaper* reported, and
'completely blockaded the thoroughfares.' The police
struggled to control the excited mob of a thousand or more
who had come to gawp, to jeer and to cheer. Every window that
commanded a view of the court was crowded with spectators,
and dozens of people clung precariously to the roofs of cabs to
try and catch a glimpse of these extraordinary men-women.
Inspector Thompson and several detachments of his officers
were hard-pressed to clear a way through the noisy, seething
mass to allow the prison van to make its slow progress to the
entrance of the court.

If the mob had expected Fanny and Stella to appear in all
their feminine finery, they were disappointed. Instead of the

gaudy, painted creatures they had hoped to see, two neatly dressed, clean-shaven young men stepped out nervously, evidently bewildered by the size and the noise of this largely good-natured crowd. Without paint and after a grim week on remand in the House of Detention in Coldbath Fields, they looked pale, frail and fragile. Even though they were out of drag, their plucked and tweezered eyebrows and their tightly fitting suits with nipped-in waists and exaggerated revers gave them a decidedly arch and feminine air.

The arrest of 'the Young Men Personating Women', 'the Hermaphrodite Gang', 'the Funny He-She Ladies', as they were called variously by the newspapers, had caused an unparalleled sensation. Every aspect of Fanny and Stella's lives – their arrest, their appearance, their clothes, their backgrounds – had been lovingly and lasciviously dilated upon and speculated over and, where facts were in short supply, cheerfully invented. 'It is suspected,' the *Daily Telegraph* breathlessly reported, 'that there are others, besides those in custody, who have for some time past been personating females in London. In fact it is stated that an association exists which numbers nearly thirty of these foolish young men.'

The *Illustrated Police News* went further and stated as a fact that a number of 'these foolish if not unnatural young men' had recently given a drag ball 'at a well-known hotel in the Strand, at which twelve of the party represented females and twenty of their companions the opposite sex'. There were rumblings and rumours too of important people – politicians and peers of the realm – who were implicated in the growing scandal, and heavy hints that mass arrests were imminent.

Every newspaper in the country had carried the story, and it would soon be making headlines in Europe and in the United

States. An enterprising publisher had already rushed out a penny pamphlet – *The Lives of Boulton and Park: Extraordinary Revelations* – which told the story so far, rehashing the testimony of Hugh Mundell and expressing many pious disapprovals of Fanny and Stella.

Of all the crimes Fanny and Stella were purported to have committed, by far the most heinous was Fanny's 'violation' of the Ladies' Retiring Room at the Strand Theatre on the night they were arrested. 'Nothing', the anonymous author of the penny pamphlet declared, more plainly showed 'the base and prurient natures which these misguided youths possess' than the 'unblushing impudence' of Fanny's application to the female attendant to pin up the gathers of her skirt which had become unfastened.

It was standing room only inside Bow Street and the courtroom was stiflingly hot. Some spectators had queued for five hours to see Fanny and Stella and to hear 'the filthy details' of the case. There was an unexpected air of jocularity and expectation, quite at odds with the severely moralising tone of the newspapers. One 'noble lord' spent the greater part of his day in Bow Street surveying Fanny and Stella through an opera glass. Many of those present were, as the newspapers reported, gentlemen belonging to the theatrical profession, and one of them, the manager of a popular theatre in the Strand, was heard to remark that if this sort of attraction was likely to last, it would be desirable to add another row of stalls to the court and 'allow seats to be booked a fortnight in advance'.

It was clear, too, that some friends of Fanny and Stella had queued for hours to get into court. 'Theatrical' covered a multitude of sins, and in addition to such leading comic actors as

Edward Askew Sothern and J. L. Toole, who had come to witness and wonder at the sport in Bow Street, there was an odd group of spectators who came to the court day in and day out. They were allsorts: young and old, tall and short, fat and thin – and all conditions in between. Some were well dressed, some sloppily dressed, and some were quite clearly mutton dressed up as lamb, wearing clothes that were too young, too fashionable or too tight. Some were decidedly effeminate with perfectly arched eyebrows that made them look permanently surprised, and some were sporting subtly dyed or not-so-subtly dyed curling locks. Many seemed to know one another and despite their very obvious differences there seemed to be a common weal between them. They were the very disparate parts of a curious whole, and there was a distinctly tribal quality about them.

As the case went on, this clique or claque of men formed a strange chorus, greeting much of the evidence – especially the evidence that favoured Fanny and Stella – with 'a most indecent manifestation of applause expressed by stamping and cheering' – much to the dismay of the magistrate, Mr Flowers, who entreated, most ineffectually, that 'such ebullitions of feeling should be restrained'. In the days that followed, as the witnesses for the prosecution took their turn in the box, many of them denounced these ardent supporters as sodomites, Mary-Anns and fellow he-she ladies.

Commencing proceedings, Mr Poland, the prosecuting attorney, stood up and brandished theatrically the detailed inventory of items seized at Wakefield Street by Detective Officer Chamberlain. Clearing his throat he proceeded to read it aloud to the accompaniment of much raucous laughter. Fanny and Stella could hardly repress their smiles. 'The list of articles included the following,' Mr Poland said, drawing a deep breath before plunging in:

Dresses:

Mauve satin, trimmed with black lace
White corded rep silk, trimmed with white lace
Pink satin, and tulle
White glacé, trimmed with blue satin and lace
White Japanese silk, pink stripe, trimmed with white lace
    and swansdown
Green cord silk
Violet glacé silk and white lace
Black satin, trimmed with mauve satin
Blue and white satin, piped with white satin
Mauve rep silk and green satin
Blue satin tunic
Pink tartalan
Muslin
Camlet costume
Cambric evening
Grey moiré antique
&c.

Here Mr Poland paused for breath. The list was exhaustive and exhausting. 'Also,' he continued:

a number of skirts and petticoats, in tulle, tartalan, white frilled cambric, white book muslin; frilled, check, plain and coloured petticoats, crinolines, &c; cloaks, jackets and bodices, opera cloaks, shawls, ermine jackets and

muff; crimson velvet and tunic; about a dozen pairs of
ladies' kid boots, shoes, &c; seven chignons (of various
kinds and colours), two long curls, ten plaits, and one
grey beard.

'The grey beard can hardly be called part of a woman's
costume,' a bemused Mr Flowers interjected.

'It may be part of a disguise,' Mr Poland snapped, clearly
irritated by the interruption. 'Curling irons, sunshades, six
pairs of stays,' he went on, 'one face press-over, two tulle falls,
chemisettes, garters, drawers, four boxes of violet powder, one
of bloom of roses, silk stockings, eight pairs of gloves, one
bottle of chloroform, artificial flowers and a great quantity of
wadding – used apparently for padding.'

D rag was not for the faint-hearted. It required discipline,
stamina and a great deal of ingenuity. Money helped, as
did plenty of space to store it all – which is where Martha Stacey's ground-floor dragging-up rooms came in so useful. The
sheer volume and complexity of the wardrobe of even the moderately well dressed young lady-about-town required a great
deal of time and attention.

Fanny and Stella's extensive drag wardrobe mirrored the
garish artificiality that was the fashionable order of the day.
Women of fashion laboured long and hard to present to the
world a brilliantly enamelled exterior of wasp-waists, heaving
bosoms and large bustling behinds. Nature was not enough.
It could be improved upon, altered, faked and falsified. Wasp-
waists required the tightest of tight-lacing, causing ladies
young and old to faint frequently and doctors repeatedly to
warn that prolonged tight-lacing could lead to permanent in-

ternal damage; bosoms were pushed and prodded and padded until they heaved; and the largest or smallest of behinds could be made to bustle by the use of a steel frame and half a dozen layers of flounced horsehair. An arsenal of false hair, false teeth, false bottoms, false breasts – and on at least one occasion, a false leg – was strategically deployed, along with a formidable battery of dyes and paints and an artillery of chemical processes to create the perfect woman. Beauty was made, not born. It was a commodity, manufactured, measured, sold and, above all, bought.

Acquiring the frocks, the petticoats, the stays, the undergarments, the shoes and all the other female accoutrements was no mean feat. It was hard, but not impossible, for men to buy dresses without arousing suspicion and hostility. Fanny and Stella had made daring trips in drag to the new emporia of Regent Street and Oxford Street where they had bought gloves and other accessories. Such was their airy disregard of convention, and so convincing their disguise, that Fanny and Stella could easily sweep into almost any gown shop in London and try on as many frocks and petticoats and cloaks and coats as they liked. Shopkeepers would naturally assume that they were a pair of soiled doves – extremely soiled doves – but then, many of their best customers were ladies of that sort, and morals rarely, if ever, got in the way of business.

Even if the doors of some of the most refined shops were firmly closed to Fanny and Stella, there were always alternatives. Like the irrepressibly cheerful young hero of the burlesque farce *A Sneaking Regard*, who breezily declares that he's off to 'a Theatrical Wardrobe Shop in Cross Street, to borrow the toggery, and equip myself well out in tip-top feminine style', Fanny and Stella would visit theatrical costumiers for wigs, for make-up, and, importantly, for boots and shoes which were hard to find in their sizes.

And if the need arose, there were any number of skilled needle-women in London – milliners, dressmakers, stay-makers, bonnet-makers and assorted lowly stitchers – who could barely support themselves and who had, more often than not, to turn to prostitution when times were hard. Many would happily turn a blind eye to measuring up and making up frocks and garments of a more intimate nature for young men for their 'private theatricals'.

Then there were the countless fripperers' shops, selling second-, third- and even fourth-hand finery, where a young man might purchase a dress for his wife or for his sweetheart – or for himself. And like thousands of women, Fanny and Stella may have taken advantage of the offer of sending '42 stamps' to Isabella and Samuel Beeton's *The Englishwoman's Domestic Magazine*, receiving in return a paper dress pattern of the latest French fashions. With a sewing machine and a little common sense, they could run up their own exquisite creations.

Since the 1850s there had been an explosion in the number of newspapers and magazines – and a corresponding explosion in advertising and mail order. By 1870, ladies and gentlemen could buy almost anything by mail order, particularly products the mere mention of which might bring an unbecoming blush to their cheeks. Publications groaned with advertisements for quack cures – pills, balms, cordials, panaceas, elixirs, specifics and tonics – for every ailment, real or imagined. Pages were crammed with advertisements for every kind of corset, stay, busk or truss; for undergarments of all conceivable varieties; for hair removers and hair improvers; for breast enlargers and breast re-ducers; and for a bewildering variety of cosmetics, creams and lotions to allow gentlemen and ladies – and would-be ladies – to transform themselves from ugly ducklings into fully fledged swans. Mail order was a godsend for Fanny and Stella, and no doubt a steady stream of packages addressed to Mrs Fanny Graham or Miss Stella Boulton would arrive at Wakefield Street or wherever else they happened to pitch their camp.

Hair was another vexed question. Hairstyles were heroic: towering, complex architectural follies involving one, two and sometimes as many as three chignons, hairpieces attached to a substructure called a frisette. Chignons and frisettes – these 'monstrous erections of dyed and false hair' – were heavy, often weighing two or three pounds. They were said to 'impose such a weight on the heads of these martyrs that they deserve pity rather than reproof', and the notorious procuress Madame Rachel wore such 'a whopper' of a chignon, ''twas said she was quite bandy-legged through the weight of her head'.

In the hysteria generated by Fanny and Stella's arrest, the *Graphic* claimed that there were 'hair-dressing establishments at the West End where a young gentleman, although previously bearded like the pard, may emerge within an hour's time so disguised by chignon, rouge and pearl-powder that his own mother would fail to recognise him'.

When she could afford to, in the days of plenty in 1868, Stella used to insist on twice-daily visits from a hairdresser in Brydges Street, Covent Garden. 'The hairdresser used to come in of a morning to clean Boulton's hair,' Maria Duffin, a maid, recounted, 'and if he was going to an evening party or to the theatre, the hairdresser used to come and arrange the chignon and the hair.'

But most of the time Fanny and Stella had to rely on their own resources. On the night of their arrest, Fanny and Stella had dressed each other's hair expertly. Stella wore hers *à la grecque*, with at least one – and probably two – chignons of elaborately curled and braided hair, while Fanny's was a profusion of tiny flaxen curls dressed with a diamanté star. Fanny, with her 'sterner features', also wore a Eugénie bandelette, a popular style of chignon, a fringe of curls worn across the forehead in the manner of the Empress Eugénie. It was said to soften the face.

Judging from the 'great quantity of wadding' found at Wakefield Street it was clear that Fanny and Stella used to pad their busts. They might as easily have resorted to 'The Registered Bust Improver', patented in 1849, which claimed to do away with the 'evident defects of pads made of Cotton and Wool'. Improvers were made from an 'air-proof' inflatable material, sold in boxes of half a dozen and available by post from Mr White of Gresham Street.

Fanny and Stella may have also followed the practice of French male prostitutes in drag, who wore false bosoms made from boiled sheep's lights – or lungs – cut to shape and then inflated. 'One of the prostitutes complained to me the other day,' the Parisian doctor François-Auguste Veyne reported, 'that a cat had eaten one of his breasts which he had left to cool down in his attic.' Stella had visited Paris in 1868 to perform in drag and would have met some of the city's formidable brigade of men who dressed as women and carried back to London the latest tips and fashions.

Facial hair was another headache. They could shave it, they could pluck it, or they could try to remove it permanently. Close shaving was effective but short-lived. However closely they shaved, a shadow of stubble would appear within hours, making kissing a little risky. This was a bigger problem for

Fanny, who was more hirsute than Stella. Plucking was painful, time-consuming and likely to lead to irritation. Some men swore by a weak solution of arsenic for removing facial hair or by hydrogen peroxide to inhibit beard growth.

Make-up was a vexed question too. There were those who saw any kind of 'paint' as an affront to Society, and the first vicious step on the road to ruin. Women who wore paint were no better than actresses or whores. But the fashion for paint grew steadily in popularity and by 1871 a ladies' magazine observed that 'no one who goes much into Society can fail to notice how common the use of paints, powders and cosmetics has become of late years.' Mrs H. R. Haweis was rather more forthright. 'If a girl has the trial of a complexion so bad that the sight of it gives one a turn,' she wrote in *The Art of Beauty*:

> it is a simple duty for her either not to go into Society at all, or, if she does, to conceal it, as she would not scruple to conceal lameness or leanness. You have no right to inflict your misfortune on everybody – it is an unpardonable offence against good taste.

The liberal application of paint helped cover a multitude of sins. Nearly all the witnesses who queued up to testify against Fanny and Stella spoke of them being heavily painted, though much of their make-up must have been hastily thrown into Carlotta Gibbings's carpet bag and spirited away from Wakefield Street. Detective Officer Chamberlain had only found a box of Bloom of Roses – liquid rouge made from the shell of the cochineal beetle – and four packs of violet powder. The writer and 'Practical Artist in Hair' Edwin Creer recommended violet powder as 'one of the most innocent and best preparations for whitening the skin' but warned against the plethora of 'pernicious compounds done up in a packet and labelled "Violet Powder"' which could be extremely injurious to health and sometimes cause death.

Among ladies, violet powder was widely used to dry out and deodorise the moister, more secret parts of the body – so much so that the *Pearl, a Monthly Journal of Facetiae and Voluptuous Reading* felt itself obliged to issue a 'CAUTION TO LADIES':

> A contributor wishes to remonstrate against the practice of a very nice young lady friend of his, who treats her quim as if it were a baby's arse. He says, 'a nice cunt is a delicious thing to suck, but damn the violet powder, which dries up all the natural juiciness'.

Then there was the mysterious bottle of chloroform found in Wakefield Street. By 1870, chloroform was in common use as a general anaesthetic and as a way of relieving pain. It was famously administered to Queen Victoria during the birth of Prince Leopold in 1853, and again at the birth of Princess Beatrice in 1857, creating outrage among many in the medical establishment who believed that the pangs of childbirth were divinely ordained and a painful but necessary rite of passage.

Chloroform also induced euphoria. Like laudanum, it was readily available without prescription from chemists' shops, and there were hundreds if not thousands of addicts who sought and found oblivion through inhalation of its sweet-smelling vapours. But it was highly addictive and too much could prove fatal.

Rather more alarmingly, chloroform was said to induce uncontrolled libidinous feelings. Mild inhalation had a strong aphrodisiac effect. When asleep under its influence both women and men reported dreams so vivid and so powerfully erotic that they felt as if they were real. There were in consequence many accusations of seduction and rape made by women against doctors and dentists who had administered the drug. Chloroform became inextricably bound up with the great moral panic over the white slave trade, stories of which had respectable young women travelling alone being waylaid, rendered unconscious, raped and then sold into sexual slavery in the far-flung corners of Empire.

Stella had been suffering for years from fistula, a painful abscess in the rectum, which by February 1869 had become so severe that surgery was the only solution. Chloroform was administered as an anaesthetic during this operation and Stella may well have been tempted to continue to use it as an effective analgesic. Chloroform vapours injected directly into the rectum were said to be highly efficacious for a variety of anal disorders.

Additionally, chloroform may have been a useful means of relieving pain and discomfort during anal sex, especially for Stella for whom it must have been a sore trial. Like amyl nitrite, which was discovered in 1844, chloroform dilated the blood vessels causing the involuntary muscles – especially the anal sphincter – to relax, making anal penetration much easier and rather less painful.

Chloroform's combined qualities as analgesic, aphrodisiac and anal dilator rendered it the drug of choice for Fanny and Stella. It might rouse the dormant passions of hesitant or reluctant lovers into vigorous life, at the same time as its vapours loosened and widened the sodomitic passages. And if it was used for nothing else, chloroform was the remedy of last resort for drunken, difficult or violent punters. They could be swiftly knocked out cold and dumped comatose in a back street or alleyway to wake up with a sore head and only a hazy recollection of the erotic misadventures of the night before.

A Dirty Business

Amenities of Leicester Square

Girl to Ponce: 'Go along, you bloody Mary-Ann, and tighten your arsehole with alum.'

English Whore to French Woman: 'Yah, you foreign bitches can only get a man by promising them a bottom-fuck!'

French Woman: 'Yes, I do let the English gentlemen have my arsehole, but my cunt I do keep for my husband.'

The Pearl, 1880

T he dramatic arrest at the Strand Theatre was not the first time that Stella had been in trouble with the police. In 1867, when she was just eighteen, Stella had been arrested on at least two occasions in the Haymarket, the London thoroughfare synonymous with the very worst excesses of prostitution.

On the first occasion, Stella and her friend Martin Luther Cumming were both in drag, almost certainly drunk and plainly soliciting men – much to the indignation of half a dozen battle-scarred female streetwalkers who, as the *Daily Telegraph* delicately phrased it, 'considered they were interfering with their calling'.

A brawl quickly broke out between Stella and Cumming and the formidable old whores into whose tramp, or territory, they had dared to trespass. The altercation began with name-calling and threats and quickly escalated into violence. Stella and Cumming were promptly arrested by Police Constable Thomas Shillingford, as much for their own safety as for the offence of soliciting men.

Stella had met Martin Luther Cumming a year earlier, in June 1866, when she was invited to Oxford to perform in drag with 'The Shooting Stars', the university amateur theatrical troupe, in a burlesque double bill, *The Comical Countess* and *Lalla Rookh*. Though he was a little on the stout side, Cumming made an engagingly comic dowager, and *The Times* praised his 'admirable' performance as the Countess.

Stella and the Comical Countess became firm friends. They made a slightly ridiculous drag duet: Stella, beautiful, slender, soulful and, above all, a convincing girl; and Cumming the Comical Countess, plump and well-bred, comically camp, and quite clearly a man dressed in women's clothes.

In their drunken forays into the Haymarket, Stella would have stood more chance of getting away with soliciting had she been alone, though the whores of the Haymarket were notoriously protective of their patches and it was not uncommon for new girls to be badly beaten up, scratched and bitten, and sometimes scarred for life when they tried to muscle in on the best tramps. But the Comical Countess was so obviously a drunken toff in comic drag, that the whores straight away spotted him and Stella as a pair of interlopers.

Quite apart from the attempted trespass onto their hallowed tramps, the whores considered Stella and the Comical Countess unfair competition. It was one thing to compete against all the other girls on the street. The whores were used to that. They were even used to gaggles of Mary-Anns waggling their scrawny arses up and down the street. They didn't mind that so much because the steamers, or punters, that went with the Mary-Anns would hardly want a real woman. It stood to reason. But when it came to Mary-Anns dressed as women, and one of them properly beautiful, that was too much. It was downright deceitful. It wasn't right; it wasn't proper and it wasn't fair. It was taking the bread out of their mouths.

Though it hardly mattered to the Comical Countess, the money to be earned from whoring was no small matter for Stella. She needed it. She had just a pound a week for pocket money – and even that was not always assured, as Papa seemed to be forever in difficulties. She needed more than a paltry pound a week. She needed a wardrobe of silk and satins, of day gowns and evening gowns. She needed wigs and chignons. She needed stockings and shoes and boots and slippers. She needed powder and paint, muffs and capes, and hats and gloves and handkerchiefs. And more – much more – besides.

Stella could never remember if – let alone when – she had decided that going with men for money was the solution to her problems. It had somehow just happened. It had crept up on her. It had taken her from behind, you might almost say. Little and not-so-little gifts; half-a-sovereign here and a sovereign there; money pressed upon her whether she had asked for it or not; money baldly offered for sex; and money boldly taken for sex. Easy money. The easiest money. And she could take her pick. They were queuing up for her. It was a pleasure. Leastways, most of the time.

A few weeks after the incident with the Comical Countess, Stella was arrested in drag in the Haymarket again, this time in the company of a man named Campbell, better known as Lady Jane Grey, a notorious male prostitute in drag who was 'well-known to the police'. This time the case ended up in Marlborough Street Magistrates' Court, and Stella and Lady Jane Grey were fined and had their knuckles firmly rapped.

The courts dealt with a surprisingly large number of men who were arrested dressed as women. Usually they were charged with a breach of the Queen's peace, with creating a public nuisance, or with being drunk and disorderly, and let off with a small fine and a good talking-to. It was only if there was compelling evidence of some 'unlawful purpose' – of sodomy or prostitution, or both – that matters were treated more seriously.

Twenty years earlier, in the early hours of Saturday, 21st September 1850, Mr Bennett Martin, a clerk to a glass works, was on his way home from a party when he was accosted by a young woman dressed in a light cotton gown with stripes and wearing a straw bonnet and a veil.

'Are you good-natured, dear?' she enquired. It was the traditional opening gambit of London's whores. Mr Martin noticed that her voice was unusually husky and she had a strange sing-song accent which for the life of him he was unable to place. But he was certainly very willing for a bit of slap and tickle, for a thrupenny stand-up, as it was called.

'I of course thought she was a woman,' Martin recalled. 'She certainly had a most feminine appearance and we walked together.'

But when the woman lifted her veil, Martin received two shocks. 'I observed to my utter astonishment that the face was that of a person of colour,' he said, 'and I soon suspected, from the growth of the beard, that I was speaking to a man.'

Martin seized hold of this 'woman' and dragged her along the street looking for a policeman.

An intimate examination at the police station confirmed that the woman, who gave her name as Eliza Scott, was in fact a man. In court, Eliza – or Elijah – Scott, speaking 'in a very mincing effeminate tone of voice', told the extraordinary story of her life. She claimed she had been sold by her aunt for a slave, escaped and, after many adventures, fetched up in the West Indies where she 'got her living by washing, ironing and cleaning, and attending people who are ill, more particularly those afflicted with rheumatism', whom she cured with the application of Indian herbs.

Many, if not most, arrests were accidental. When the routine nightly quotas of streetwalkers were rounded up, every so often one of them would turn out to be a man dressed as a woman. The police were at a loss as to how to deal with these strange apparitions. More often than not they were released with a caution. Willy Somerville, one of Stella's many admirers, wrote to her anxiously in 1868: 'Did you see a fellow had been taken up for being in drag but he was let off?' he enquired. 'Did you know him by name?'

Though politicians and preachers were quick to angrily deny its existence, male prostitution, especially among boys and young men, was widespread, not to say rife in London. 'There is a considerable amount of sodomy practised in London,' Howard Vincent, Director of the Criminal Investigation Department of the Metropolitan Police, told a Select Committee of the House of Lords in 1881. 'It is a fact, and it is an indisputable fact, there are boys and youths soliciting in the streets.'

'A great many brothel keepers lure young boys to their establishments,' Mr Talbot, Secretary of the London Society for the Prevention of Juvenile Prostitution, told the French socialist Flora Tristan. 'I believe I am correct in estimating that 2,000 out of 5,000 brothels encourage the prostitution of young boys.'

There was a veritable 'army' of male prostitutes in London, according to another observer. There were, he said,

> thousands of boys of precocious debauchery, either in the pay of mature male procurers and patrons, or 'working' by themselves, idle and corrupt youths in their late teens, young men in their twenties and thirties, older types (often of repulsive maturity), catamites of all ages, complexions, physiques, grades of cleanliness and decency.

And not only in London. When Inspector Silas Anniss of the Metropolitan Police raided brothels and bawdy houses in 1868 in the naval town of Devonport, he 'found seven or eight notorious houses specially the resort of boys and girls, from 12 to 17'. In just one house he found twenty-five boys available for sex. Different houses specialised in different sorts of boys. 'One house was frequented by butcher boys and errand boys; another by sailor boys; and another by drummer boys.'

Prostitution in drag was far less common but was still to be found on the streets of London. According to one observer, 'such types haunt the parks, public thoroughfares and so on, after nightfall', or could commonly be met with at the lowest cafés, bars and ballrooms.

A young man could make enormous sums of money, sometimes as much as £10, for sex with a man. But a sovereign or less, much less, sometimes as little as a shilling or two, was more usual. When the young male prostitute Jack Saul first came to London from Dublin in 1879 he was earning 'often-times as much as £8 and £9 a week' from selling himself. The work was easy and the punters plentiful.

Despite drunken disputes and brawls, relations between women on the game and the Mary-Anns, the men on the game, were usually cordial, often very cordial. After all, they were all in the same line of business. They were all in it together. Some-times they fell in love and lived together and even got married. A male prostitute nicknamed Fair Eliza kept a 'fancy woman' in Westminster who did 'not scruple to live upon the fruits of his monstrous avocation'. Another 'notorious and shame-less poof', known only as Betsey H—, married and fathered two sons, both of whom followed their father into male prostitution.

Charles Hammond, the lover and pimp of Jack Saul, lived very happily with a whore called Emily Barker for nearly three years before he met and married Madame Caroline, a buxom French whore with whom he set up a male brothel in Cleveland Street. Hammond was, by all accounts, a loving and consider-ate husband, though his affection for Madame Caroline did not prevent him taking one Frank Hewitt to his bed as his 'spooney boy'.

Lots of whores were quite happy to procure boys for men who occasionally fancied a bit of the other. 'Walter', the pseud-onymous author of the autobiographical *My Secret Life*, recounts how a whore called Betsy Johnston easily procured an ageing and enthusiastic sodomite for his pleasure. Many years later, an-other of his favourite whores, Sarah, agreed to procure a boy for him. 'One man's prick stands and spends much like another, play with your own,' she had told him gruffly when he first mooted the idea. 'But if you want, I can get one easily enough, and I'll let him come here for you.' Sarah kept her promise and procured a young house decorator who had not been in employment for two months, who was desperate for money and prepared to have sex with a gentleman for a golden sovereign.

Relations between the police and the Mary-Anns were fraught with dangers – and sometimes with possibilities. On the night of their arrest outside the Strand Theatre, Fanny and Stella had arched their eyebrows and stared suggestively at Detective Sergeant Frederick Kerley and Detective Officer William Chamberlain. 'If you'll let us go we'll give you anything you want. *Anything*,' they had said, like a Greek chorus. 'Anything you like to mention. *Anything* you like to mention, you can have.' Money or sex or both.

Fanny and Stella were acting exactly as they had acted dozens of times before, as every whore – male or female – had acted countless times before. Whores would be arrested and, nine times out of ten, would be released after favours, financial or physical – or both – were forthcoming. As Fanny and Stella knew from experience, lots of policemen wanted to be gamahuched, to have their cocks sucked, while they were out on the beat, and they were never too particular about who did the sucking. Some of them wanted a bottom-fuck as well.

'I have been in the hands of the police (don't be frightened) or rather the other way round, the police have been in my hands so many times lately that my lily white hands have been trembling, and I am *utterly* fucked out,' wrote Malcolm Johnston joyously to his 'Pa' in Dublin. It was, he said, 'Such Camp!'

Malcolm Johnston was a Mary-Ann, who also liked to drag up. He was known to his friends and fellow Mary-Anns as 'The Maid of Athens'. Johnston was visiting London in the late

1870s and was making hay while the sun shone. 'Nearly all the police about here have been up in the evenings,' he confided to his Pa. 'Some I have done, others I have only kissed, a kissing one was up last night, and a fucking one two nights previous.'

After his arrest, Johnston helpfully amplified the meaning of certain phrases in his letter. 'Camp means amusement,' he explained to the police who were puzzled by the word. 'It might mean proper amusement or it might mean improper amusement,' he told them. 'The meaning of "some that I have done" is frigged off.'

But there was a darker side to this erotic moon. As Johnston's injunction – 'don't be frightened' – to his Pa suggested, there were some decidedly less 'camp' sides to relations between the Mary-Anns and the police. For the past twenty years the police had been arresting a steadily increasing quota of men for having sex with other men. Many hundreds, perhaps even thousands, were arrested and charged every year. The charges, most of them falling short of sodomy, were haphazardly and euphemistically reported as 'abominable offences', 'unnatural crimes', 'uncleanness' or 'unspeakable conduct' in the myriad local and national newspapers.

Some arrests resulted from tip-offs, others from complaints from men claiming they had been indecently assaulted by other men. Often these complaints were a ploy in the growing trade in blackmail and extortion. It was good business. Men who had sex with other men were usually too terrified to go to the police if they were being blackmailed. They reasoned, probably rightly, that once the police got wind of their proclivities, they themselves would be charged with a sexual offence. It was better to pay, and pay again and again and again, rather than face prosecution, prison and social ignominy.

A Dirty Business

Every man, no matter who he was, was potentially the target of blackmail and extortion. One fine Sunday evening in June 1868, Anthony Daly, a retired and highly respectable grocer from Walthamstow, went into the urinal at Mansion House Place to relieve himself. It was just after six o'clock in the evening and the only other person there was a snappily dressed youth, James Kean, who was just sixteen years old.

According to Daly, Kean behaved 'in a very extraordinary manner', attempting to touch his private parts. As they left the urinal, Kean asked Daly for sixpence and threatened him with an accusation of indecent assault if he did not pay up. But Anthony Daly was not going to allow himself to be blackmailed by a young male prostitute. He saw a police constable on the other side of the road and summoned him. After a chase, James Kean was arrested and it emerged that other gentlemen had made complaints about both his disgusting behaviour and his attempts at blackmail.

Anthony Daly was either very brave or very foolhardy. Mud stuck and many men in similar situations simply paid up. As the magistrate observed at Kean's trial, a charge of indecent assault was 'a charge which it was most difficult to rebut'. A few pence, a few shillings, a few pounds were nothing to the spectre of public ruin if the case came to court.

Increasingly, men were being arrested and charged as a direct consequence of police surveillance. By the 1860s, London's urinals and public water closets had become magnets for men who wanted to meet other men for sex. They had also become a target for the police. It was already an established and increasingly common practice to use policemen – sometimes in uniform and sometimes not – to keep watch in public lavatories for men loitering with sexual intent or for men actually committing indecent acts in the lavatory.

When a twenty-two-year-old carpenter, Benjamin Kersey, was charged with indecent exposure in a urinal in Hyde Park on 1st March 1871, the evidence was provided by Police Constable Farrier, A 289, who testified that he had 'been specially employed for the purpose of checking indecent practices in urinals' for the past eighteen months. After remarking on the frequency of such unpleasant cases, and on the difficulty of dealing with them, Mr Tyrwhitt, the magistrate, addressed some stern observations on the practice of using dedicated police constables to spy on men in public lavatories. 'The system is injurious to the public interest,' he said, 'and bad for the constables themselves, as after a time their minds become, as it were, diseased by being bent on the same point.'

But the practice continued unabated. Men who wanted to have sex with other men, men who loitered in parks and lavatories, were easy prey. They were usually too scared or too ashamed to resist arrest, most of them pleading guilty in the hope of landing a lighter sentence.

There were acquittals but many men charged with unnatural crimes or abominable offences were convicted. Sentences varied wildly, ranging from three months with hard labour to fifteen years' penal servitude. Some men chose to commit suicide rather than face the shame and ignominy of a conviction for a sexual offence with another man.

There was another side to relations between the police and men who wanted to have sex with men. It was a common practice for police constables on the beat to invite men to gamahuche them or to offer to bottom-fuck them down a dark alley. Once the deed was done, the constable would demand money. If it was not forthcoming – and even when it was – the constable would arrest the man and charge him with attempting to indecently assault a police officer.

The practice had become so common that learned tomes on medical jurisprudence urged caution.

> There cannot be the slightest doubt that false charges of this crime are more numerous than those of rape, and that this is too often a very successful mode of extortion. This is rather a legal than a medical question, but it is especially deserving of attention that these accusations are most frequently made by soldiers and policemen.

Fanny and Stella were only too well acquainted with this particular trick. Eight years earlier, in 1862, Fanny's older brother Harry had been arrested and charged with attempting to indecently assault Police Constable George White down a dark alleyway in the early hours of April Fool's Day. Harry appeared before the magistrate the next morning. As the eldest son of the respected and respectable Judge Alexander Park, Harry was granted bail set at a hefty £600, a small fortune. But once released from police custody, he disappeared for eight long years until, by a cruel twist of fate, Fanny and Stella's arrest would bring him face to face with Police Constable George White once again.

Getting Up Evidence

That if any witness or witnesses who shall be
examined by or before any justice or justices or
otherwise, upon oath, shall wilfully and corruptly
give false evidence, he, she, or they so giving false
evidence shall be subject to the same punishment
as if convicted of wilful and corrupt perjury.

A Compendious Abstract, 1823

Inspector Thompson was struggling to keep his head above water amidst the deluge of information about the two young men in women's clothes that had quickly started to flood in after the arrest of Fanny and Stella and showed no sign of abatement. The police had been 'literally inundated with communication regarding this case from all parts of the country', *Reynolds's Newspaper* revealed.

'I have had a great deal of hard working on this case, and six other officers with me,' Thompson remarked feelingly towards the end of May, a month to the day after the sensational arrest of Fanny and Stella. 'I have had fifty or sixty letters sent to me about this case,' he continued. 'I have also had many letters, not only affecting these prisoners, but other persons as well.'

It was a tidal wave of letters: letters of all shapes and sizes; letters written in all hands from the most elegant to the barely decipherable; misspelt, fulminating, incoherent, menacing, damning, defending, and dark; letters expressing indignation, outrage and horror; letters demanding severe – indeed, the severest – penalties to be inflicted; aimless, rambling, ranting letters on every subject from sodomy to prostitution to private theatricals; letters lamenting the sad decline in the standards of behaviour of young persons; letters with reported sightings of Fanny and Stella from the four corners of the world; letters enclosing smudgy clippings from newspapers with accounts of concerts and performances given by Fanny or Stella, in places as far apart as Chelmsford, Scarborough and Edinburgh; letters – many of them anonymous – voicing dark suspicions about alleged confederates of Fanny and Stella; and letters of accusation about countless other young men given over to this vice.

All these letters had to be read (and in some cases deciphered), understood, digested and acted upon – or not, as the case may be. New enquiries had to be initiated: leads followed, journeys undertaken, witnesses interviewed, statements taken, records kept. Almost every day there was a new development, and often more than one. Almost every day the net seemed to widen and another young man – and sometimes more than one – was implicated.

And then there were the personal callers at Bow Street Police Station: a steady stream of men and women from all stations and conditions of life, hesitant, apologetic, indignant, apoplectic, who had something to say or something to tell and felt compelled to do so in person. It really was no wonder that Inspector Thompson and the six officers helping him were beginning to feel the strain of such a long and complex investigation which seemed to be growing daily ever larger.

Most of those who called at Bow Street in person could add very little to the substance of the investigation. They were there because they wanted to call the attention of the police to supposed sightings of Fanny or Stella going back years; to reported cases of importuning by gay ladies who were, in the indignant opinion of the importuned, not ladies at all, but men; and to every kind of suspicious behaviour by young men, including some direct and not so direct allegations of effeminacy, sodomy and other dark crimes, not to be named among Christians.

Most could be safely ignored. Some might provide useful intelligence. A few were more promising. And one or two were crucial. One of the most important witnesses to come forward was Mr John Reeve, Staff Supervisor at the Royal Alhambra Palace in Leicester Square. And then there was Mr George Smith, Beadle of the Burlington Arcade, who was an entirely different kettle of fish.

Mr John Reeve was a tall, well-made man in his middle years. He was a man of few words, and what words he spoke were spoken gravely and chosen with great care. Reeve had been most reluctant to put pen to paper, as he was more than a little ashamed of his sprawling and ill-formed – almost childish – handwriting, and he would go to any lengths to avoid writing letters. He much preferred to call in person at Bow Street and tell Inspector Thompson what he knew about this dirty business.

In the five years and five months he had been at the Alhambra, Reeve said, he had fought a running battle with these painted young men who, no matter how many times they were turned out, forbidden to return or threatened with the police, nevertheless fetched up again and again like a bagful of bad pennies. Boulton and Park were two of the worst offenders; two of the most persistent, two of the most badly behaved.

'I have known Park three years, and Boulton nearly as long,

upwards of two,' Reeve told the court in Bow Street.

> I have seen them at the Alhambra many, many times – at
> least twenty times. My attention was first called to them
> about two years ago. I saw them walking about as
> women, looking over their shoulders at men as if enticing
> them. I went to them and desired them to leave.

Fanny and Stella would not give up. They were soon back, this time dressed as men, though, as Reeve reported, it was a very strange form of male attire. 'They were walking about together, their faces painted up, their necks powdered, their shirt collars much lower than they are now, and their waistcoats were very open.' They were openly flirting with gentlemen, John Reeve spluttered. 'They looked at people as they passed and their mannerisms were more feminine than masculine. People round them were saying they are two women dressed in men's clothes. I had observed them looking at a gentleman in a manner that I thought highly improper.'

In fact, Fanny and Stella had been at the Alhambra within the last six weeks. 'They were in a Private Box, and dressed as men. They were painted up. They wore pink coloured flowers and hung their pink gloves over the box.'

> I saw the people looking up at the box they were in and
> rising from their seats to get a better view of them. I saw
> that they were playing all sorts of frivolous games with
> each other: they were looking down in front of the box,
> handing cigarettes backwards and forwards to each other
> and lighting them by the gaslight. I went to the box and
> told them they must leave.

Fanny and Stella were decidedly the worse for wear.

'They asked to have more soda and brandy,' John Reeve remembered. '"No," I said, "I've told you to keep out of the place many times," and I marched them out. I told the Box Keeper to be very particular about admitting them again.'

The worst part of it, Reeve said, was that they came in company with a great gaggle, a great tribe of similar young men. 'I have seen about twenty young men at the Alhambra with their faces powdered in company with Boulton and Park.' Painted and powdered and perfumed young men, with shrieking voices and tweezered eyebrows and curled hair. It was bewildering and confusing, and John Reeve did not mind admitting it. Sometimes they came dressed as women, and sometimes they were dressed as men, or rather as young women might look if they had dressed themselves as men.

'I could not tell whether they were men or women,' he said. 'Sometimes I thought they were women, and sometimes I thought they were men.'

The very thought of what these young men had in mind for the gentlemen they ogled and chirruped at turned his stomach. Despite his best endeavours, these young men continued to plague the Alhambra, seemingly in greater numbers and with more perseverance than any other music hall or theatre that he knew of. Nothing seemed to deter them. They were more than a nuisance. They were a veritable plague. He had made 'frequent complaints to the Police about these men'. Nobody had seemed interested. Nothing was done. And then, to his very great surprise, there in the newspapers, were the two worst offenders, caught red-handed in wickedness.

He had of course gone to see Inspector Thompson at Bow Street as soon as he found out about the arrest of Park and

Boulton, as he discovered they were called. He had only ever heard them referred to by foolish girls' names – Jane and Fanny and Stella and a whole host of other pretty names. Inspector Thompson was very interested. He told him he was to go and quietly observe them in the Magistrates' Court in Bow Street to confirm that they were the very same young men who had so plagued the Alhambra. If they were indeed one and the same then John Reeve was to go straight away to Whitehall, to the offices of the Treasury Solicitor who, since 1661, had been in charge of all serious public prosecutions, and tell Mr John Greenwood himself everything he knew.

Whether Inspector Thompson was always strictly truthful about what went on behind the scenes of the investigation into the Young Men in Women's Clothes was thrown into some doubt by the testimony of Mr George Smith, the genial and beaming Beadle of the Burlington Arcade. A former constable with eight years of more or less unblemished service in the Metropolitan Police, Mr George Smith had, according to Thompson, been most eager to offer every assistance to the police.

Mr George Smith knew a great deal about Fanny and Stella and about the Mary-Anns that walked the Burlington Arcade, the hollow-eyed, hungry young and not-so-young men with their tawdry, gaudy, cheap clothes and their oh-so-tight trousers, marching and mincing up and down the Arcade and glaring and staring at every man who walked by. Some of them were painted like women, and some of them were even dressed like women.

One of the worst offenders was, according to Mr George Smith, the youth called Boulton. A pretty fellow, to be sure, in every sense of the word. Sometimes he was dressed as a man (or rather how a lady might look dressed as a man), and at other times he would be dressed as a gay lady, looking every inch the part, from the wig on his head to the kid boots on his feet. Mr George Smith had kept a particular and close eye on this one, who would come on his own or in company with one or two others. 'I noticed his face,' Smith declared in Bow Street Magistrates' Court.

> It was painted very thickly with rouge and everything else on. He always caused such a commotion when he came into the Arcade. Everybody was looking at him . . . I saw him *wink* at a gentleman and turn his head in a sly manner. He winked his eye and put his face on one side, and did like *that*, the same as a lady would do, the same as a woman would do.

And here George Smith paused and, to much laughter, made a passable stab at contorting his manly visage into the lascivious come-hither nods and winks he had witnessed. He was rather less successful when it came to attempting to reproduce chirruping, that particular and peculiar sound made by the most depraved and desperate of streetwalkers and common prostitutes when they were enticing passing gentlemen to buy their jaded wares.

'I dare say I do not do it so well as they can,' was his rueful verdict.

Mr George Smith could speak to one infamous afternoon, in 1868 or thereabouts, when Boulton had come up close to him, so close that he could see the paint thickly caked upon his phiz, and actually tried it on with him.

'Oh, you sweet little dear!' said Boulton, leaning forward and lisping and whispering in his ear. 'Oh, you nice little dear!'

Mr George Smith was, he was quite ready to admit, quite taken aback. He was surprised and he was shocked. Such a thing had never happened to him before, and he was obliged to stop and pause. It had been quite a facer for him, and no mistake. Of course, the youth was drunk or deranged, or both. By the time Mr George Smith had recovered himself and found out Constable Holden, Boulton was nowhere to be seen. He had scarpered.

A few days, or even a few weeks, later, Boulton was back in the Burlington Arcade in company with a plump and florid youth prone to fits of giggling. 'I saw Boulton turn his head to two gentleman, smile at them, and again make a noise with his mouth, the same as a woman would for enticement.'

Mr George Smith did not hesitate. He marched straight up to them and said, 'I've received several complaints about you, and you remember what you said to me a week or two ago. I've seen enough of your conduct to consider you to be an improper person to be in the Arcade. You must leave at once.'

'Take no notice of that fellow,' Boulton told his companion, in 'a feminine manner'. The pair of them tried to push past the solid and majestic bulk of Mr George Smith. But that gentleman was having none of it. He took hold of Boulton and frogmarched him to the gates at the Piccadilly end. 'You're as bad as the other,' he told him, 'you leave the Arcade at once,' before grabbing him and flinging him down on the pavement outside.

Just three days after this episode, Boulton was back, this time with a flint-faced Mary-Ann called Park with whom Smith was already acquainted, having seen him a dozen or so times before, alone and in company with various other Mary-Anns.

'They used to walk the Arcade arm-in-arm with such an effeminate walk that it used to cause the notice of everyone,' Smith recalled. 'On seeing me they directly walked into a hosier's shop kept by Mr Lord.'

Mr George Smith waited outside Mr Lord's hosiery shop. And he waited and he waited, for an hour or more, until at last the pair of them emerged with their noses stuck in the air as if they were fine ladies out for an afternoon's shopping.

'I've cautioned you not to come here,' he said to Boulton. 'You'll leave the Arcade at once.'

'I shall go where I like,' Boulton haughtily replied.

'You'll do nothing of the sort. You'll go out.' They tried to walk on, but Mr George Smith seized the pair of them by the scruffs of their necks and violently ejected them onto the pavement.

And so the skirmishing went on. There was no rhyme or reason to this siege of the Burlington Arcade. Sometimes they were there, and sometimes there was no sign of them. A week or a month might pass and Mr George Smith would not see a Mary-Ann from one day's end or one week's end to the next. But on other days, in other weeks, they were ever present, an army of angry, buzzing flies. Swat as many as he liked (and Mr George Smith did like), it made no difference. They came back, again and again and again. They would try and catch him off his guard, watching and waiting for him to go off for his dinner or for a refresher in the tavern next door. Then they would sail in, bold as brass, and when he got back he would have to chase them out all over again.

This happy state of antagonism might have continued indefinitely had it not been brought to an end by Mr George Smith's abrupt dismissal for the trivial offence of accepting tips from some of the gay ladies who patronised the Arcade.

Out on his ear and out on his arse. No warning, no notice, nothing. Nothing but his wages to date and barely the price of a glass of beer in his pocket. As Beadle, he received a wage of a guinea a week, but that was nothing compared to the tips he collected. In a good week he could easily expect to make £5, and he had been known, on high days and holy days, to pocket that much in a day if business was brisk.

'I don't think it a disgrace to have taken money for drink,' Smith declared. 'Everyone does it. I am not ashamed of it. If a lady offered you half-a-crown, wouldn't you take it?'

Stripped of his Beadle's rank and denuded of his Beadle's blue frogged greatcoat and shiny top hat, Mr George Smith made a less than impressive witness for the prosecution when he went into the box at Bow Street. Matters were not at all helped by the fact that it was obvious to everyone that he had been drinking and it was not yet even noon.

'Have you been drinking today?' counsel for the defence demanded.

'Yes I have,' replied Smith defiantly. 'I have had two or three half-pints of ale.' But judging from Mr George Smith's florid complexion and his 'flippant and impertinent' manner, which seemed to verge on insolence, it was clear to one and all that he had imbibed at least double that quantity, and perhaps a tot or two of brandy as well.

That same drink which made Mr George Smith so combative, so flippant and so impertinent in court also made him loquacious and incautious. He had a great deal to say about the circumstances of the investigation into the young men in women's clothes, a great deal too much to say.

Smith claimed he went to see Inspector Thompson in a

positive frenzy of public-spiritedness. But then he let slip a shocking admission.

'I have been getting up evidence for the police in this little affair,' he boasted. 'They asked me to do so on Sunday, 24th April. I told Inspector Thompson what I knew about the defendants.'

Mr George Smith's revelations caused rather more than a murmur or a ripple of surprise in Bow Street. They caused a minor sensation. After all, Miss Stella Boulton and Miss Fanny Park had been arrested only on 28th April, fully four days *after* Mr George Smith's meeting with Inspector Thompson. And though he corrected himself later on – 'I see now I have made a mistake as to the date' – it was hard for anyone present in Bow Street Magistrates' Court to believe that there was any conceivable confusion or ambiguity concerning Sunday 24th April, about which Mr George Smith had been so emphatic.

Not only that. Smith's choice of words was particularly unfortunate. 'Getting up evidence' was a phrase commonly understood to mean contriving and fabricating evidence to incriminate the innocent. It sounded rather as if Mr George Smith had been toiling away, poking his reddened nose into dark corners, sniffing out odds and sods of information, putting two and two together and making ten.

'I have been seen at the Treasury-office,' he continued in a bragging sort of way. 'I gave the same evidence as I gave to Thompson, with one or two corrects caused by thinking over the matter again –' and here Mr George Smith abruptly paused, as he caught sight of Inspector Thompson's darkening, thunderous face. 'I – I mean additions,' he added lamely.

'I *may* be paid by Mr Thompson for attending this court,' Mr George Smith added injudiciously. 'He said I should be paid for my trouble in giving evidence and I shall not object. I should not object to a situation if the Treasury should give me one.'

Taken all in all, the testimony of Mr George Smith was disastrous for the prosecution. He was like a bull in a china shop, a drunken, blundering, crashing, self-serving oaf. He was vain, greedy and corruptible. He freely admitted to helping the police gather evidence against Fanny and Stella in return for money or for help with a situation, or both, and he appeared to give the impression that at least some, if not all, of the evidence against them was 'got up'. With his various 'additions', 'corrects' and contradictions, it was clear to everyone that Mr George Smith was a liar, and a bad liar at that.

But out of this treacherous swamp of lies, certain truths began to emerge vaporously. The arrest of the two young men in women's clothes was not as haphazard or accidental as the police and the prosecution liked to make out. Taken together with the evidence of Police Constable Charles Walker, who said he had been covertly watching the movements of Fanny and Stella in and out of Wakefield Street for a fortnight before their arrest, and the evidence of Detective Officer Chamberlain, who said he had been keeping his beady eye on them for a year past, the arrest of the young men in women's clothes took on a very different complexion. Clearly, it had been planned and schemed over and thought about for some time in advance, and things were not quite so simple, not quite so cut and dried as first they might appear.

12

A Victorian Romance

At length I am a bride! Lord Arthur was so pathetic, and appealed so earnestly to every sentiment of
my love, that I could not do otherwise than entrust
my happiness to his keeping, and agree to a speedy
marriage. I need hardly tell you how the thoughts of
becoming a bride fluttered my virgin heart, only to
think of being naked in bed with a fine fellow like
Arthur, who I only too truly guessed would be for-
midably armed with a Cupid's spear commensurate
with the very ominous bunch in his trousers, which
always had a peculiar fascination to me. So rather
more than a week ago we were made man and wife.

Letters from Laura and Eveline, 1903

L ike all the best love affairs it had been as accidental as it
had been unexpected.

For well over a year now, Louis Hurt had been Stella's ardent and devoted swain, and she was only too well aware that
her Mamma thoroughly approved of him. Indeed, Mrs Mary
Ann Boulton was doing everything in her power to promote
the match. Louis was constantly at the house, invited to luncheons and dinners, and frequently asked to spend weekends
with the family. On one occasion he had stayed for an entire
fortnight.

Stella liked Louis and sometimes she even fancied herself

a little in love. He was predictable, gentlemanly, hard-working and, most importantly, utterly devoted to her. But these virtues were also his vices. Louis wanted her, but he wanted her on his own terms. His spaniel-like attentions could be irksome and he was possessive to the point of jealousy when it came to other beaux, which meant that Stella was very sensibly rather less than frank with him about her nocturnal escapades in the West End.

Truth be told, dear Louis was really rather dull and disapproving. He was not at all in favour of fun or frivolity, and he was very decidedly against dragging up. It was only on very rare occasions, on high days and holy days, that he could be persuaded to consent to accompany her to the theatre or to a ball or a party in her full drag glory.

And though he certainly had considerable charm of manner and equally considerable charm of person, his conversation could be dreary and repetitive. When he was not droning on about his work with the Post Office, he would talk about Alderwasley, about his ten brothers and his four sisters, until her poor head ached with trying to keep up and sort the one from the other. And he spoke rather too much about 'Mother', who sounded very formidable and dragon-like and not at all the sort of person that Stella felt she would like as her Mamma-in-law.

Louis was never in the right place at the right time. Whenever she did want him he would be away – in Wales or Wiltshire or Worcestershire or some other wild place – and when she did not want him, there he was, with his fine grey eyes which seemed to be imploring and beseeching her, and yet at the same time judging her, reproaching her, constraining her. So much so that Stella found herself looking forward to his long absences, and dreading his returns.

For Mrs Mary Ann Boulton these were the happiest of happy days, and 1867 the happiest of happy years. Ever since Ernest, at her behest – nay, upon her insistence – had given up work in the January, he had blossomed forth. He seemed happier than he had ever been, and the dark, gloomy days of the London and County Bank were quickly forgotten. His health still gave her cause for concern. She still fretted and worried that he was consumptive (there was a decided propensity to consumption on Mr Boulton's side), and he was often pale and exhausted.

But Ernest had such a gift for friendship, and she so much enjoyed meeting his friends and helping them in their little theatrical enterprises. There was Mr Frederick Park, Mr Martin Cumming, Mr Charles Pavitt, Mr Cecil Thomas, Mr Albert Wight and half a dozen others whose names she could not possibly be expected to remember. They were constantly at the house. Indeed, Frederick, or Fred, or even 'Fanny' as the others had called him in jest, was so much with them that he seemed almost like a brother to Ernest.

Boys would be boys, and there was much joshing and many colt-like high spirits. And why ever not? She had been highly amused when Ernest first told her about his new name. 'He laughed and told me that he did go by the nickname of "Stella".' Stella. In Latin, star. Most pretty and most appropriate, and when the boys were gathered together in her home, sometimes she could not help herself from joining in the fun and addressing him as 'Stella' too, to hoots and whoops of delight.

They were all mad for the theatre, and constantly singing and playing and dressing up and putting on little private theatricals. She had never seen anything as comical as plump Mr Cumming playing a dowager duchess, and Fanny and Stella, as she now started to think of them, made extremely convincing ladies. Fanny, it was true, made a handsome – rather than a beautiful – woman, and looked older than his years, unlike her Stella, who utterly astonished and silenced all and sundry with his beauty, his conspicuous beauty, as a young woman.

Mrs Mary Ann Boulton was much in demand as prompter, stage manager and wardrobe mistress. 'On one or two occasions I gave a dress,' she said later. In truth, it was more like a dozen dresses when she added them all up in her mind, but who was counting? It was a little embarrassing for the boys to procure dresses for private theatricals, and yet so easy for her to help with buying bits and pieces, pinning and sewing, making and altering. Besides, she enjoyed being a part of it all. But she needed all her skills of diplomacy to smooth and soothe those little differences of opinion which seemed to flare up with alarming frequency. It was not for nothing, she had begun to realise, that acting was also called the histrionic art.

Then in the autumn of 1867 came an invitation to dinner at the home of Mr and Mrs Richards. The invitation was not especially unusual or unexpected. Mr Richards was a stockbroker, a friend of Mr Boulton's and connected to him by way of business. But when Mrs Richards had whispered so confidentially to Mrs Boulton that a personage, none other than Lord Arthur Clinton, the Honourable Member for Newark, and son (but not heir) to His Grace, the late Duke of Newcastle, was attending she had got herself into one of her states and dressed herself with the utmost ceremony for the occasion, almost as if she were going to be presented at court.

For some reason – which Stella could not now recall –

neither her Papa nor Gerard were able to go with them to the Richards's. It was to be just Mamma and herself. Of course, she was only too well aware that she would be expected to sing for her supper. But she was quite happy to do so.

Stella was, she freely admitted, more than a little intrigued at the prospect of meeting Lord Arthur. As far as she was aware, she had never met a real Lord before, and it would be interesting to do so. She had no idea of what to expect. He might be ninety years old and deaf as a post. Or, like so many of the men she met, he might want to talk about huntin', shootin' and fishin' all night, and she would have to sit there and politely try to stifle her yawns.

Lord Arthur Pelham-Clinton could not be described as handsome in any conventional sense. He was of the middle height, slightly built and inclined to stoop. He wore a small, neat moustache and long side-whiskers. The top of his head was already as bald as an egg, a fact he cleverly disguised by combing over the hair from one side of his head to the other and plastering it down with plenty of Rowland's Macassar Oil, a remarkable product guaranteed, it was said, to 'nourish and preserve the hair, and make it grow thickly on all bald patches'.

Lord Arthur seemed older and wiser than his years. There were dark shadows under his eyes, and his lips were full and red, making a strange and not unpleasing contrast with the pallor of his complexion. There was something about him that caught Stella's attention from the moment they were introduced, a certain gleam in his eyes, a certain vigour in his handshake, a certain smile, a certain intense gaze, a certain *je ne sais quoi*, as Fanny would have it with her cheap French phrases.

Stella blushed and smiled, and smiled and blushed, and

was suitably modest when she felt that modesty was called for, and suitably bold when she needed to be bold. Sometimes she would look up and catch him gazing at her appreciatively and would find herself colouring under the penetrating scrutiny of his dark eyes.

Lord Arthur made a special effort to put her at her ease. He begged her to call him Arthur, asking her for her opinion and asking her questions about herself before hastening everybody into the drawing room to hear, he said with a smile that melted her heart, young Mr Boulton sing. And so Stella had sung the hauntingly sad 'Fading Away', and sung it with such sweetness and with so much intensity that she felt the first prickings of a tear or two in her large and very beautiful blue-violet eyes.

> Rose of the garden,
> Blushing and gay,
> E'en as we pluck thee,
> Fading away!
>
> Beams of the morning,
> Promise of day,
> While we are gazing,
> Fading away!

As she took her bow, which was really more of a curtsey, she looked over to Lord Arthur and thought she saw the glint and glimmer of an answering tear in his eyes. And then she was certain.

Her friendship with Lord Arthur had, to use her Mamma's phrase, very quickly 'ripened into intimacy'. Arthur, as she must now learn to call him, had asked her Mamma that very night if he might call upon them in Dulwich, and naturally Mamma was in transports of delight at the prospect, though Dulwich was, of course, just another of Mamma's pretty fictions, as their house was firmly within the rather less genteel borders of Peckham Rye.

The household was thrown into a feverish frenzy of expectation and preparation. Though Papa very manfully decreed that Lord Arthur must take them as he found them, Mamma worked herself up into a state of the greatest excitement and the greatest agitation. Within a day or two of their first meeting, she had told anyone and everyone in Peckham Rye about Lord Arthur, and was happily discoursing about the late and dear Duke as if they had been on terms of the most intimate acquaintance.

When, upon Arthur's first visit, it became clear that Stella was his particular object, all thoughts of Louis Hurt flew the rickety coop of her Mamma's mind. With a variety of sage nods and winks, knowing looks and sighs, and with many significant shakings of her artificial curls, she gave Stella to understand that she, and therefore her Papa (though Stella had never known him to give an opinion upon any of her beaux), thoroughly approved of her new suitor. Where once 'dear Louis' had held sway, now 'Lord Arthur' reigned supreme. Though pressed repeatedly to call him Arthur, Mrs Mary Ann Boulton invariably used his title, laying particular and empathic stress upon the word '*Lord*'.

There were luncheons, dinners, evening parties and musical parties. Arthur's public passions were theatrical. He could play and sing and act, and though his talents in these arenas could in no way compare with Stella's, they were complementary. He would play her accompaniments, sing duets with her, and act the part of the handsome hero to her dazzling heroine in the two-handed drawing-room entertainments that Stella loved to perform.

Lord Arthur was constantly at Peckham Rye. He was shown off, like a prize ox, casually displayed for the delectation and edification of Mrs Mary Ann Boulton's friends and neighbours, who had, she felt, never fully appreciated her or her family's true gentility. Quite apart from what he could and would do for Ernest, Lord Arthur, with his social and political connections, would, she thought, be of immense help to Mr Boulton and his business, and no doubt he would be able to put something in Gerard's way when the time came. At last, she thought to herself, things are finally coming right.

But the path of true love did not always run smoothly. Within weeks of their first meeting, there were those two unfortunate and disagreeable episodes to contend with.

Ernest and Mr Cumming were arrested in the Haymarket. It was all a mistake, a lark. In an excess of youthful zeal, and perhaps even a little in their cups, they had donned their stage costumes and gone out to carouse among the gay ladies. They had meant no harm, and it was of course completely preposterous of those ladies of the night to assume that either Ernest or Mr Cumming was – and here Mrs Mary Ann Boulton shuddered – 'interfering with their calling'. And then, by a terrible fluke, the same thing had happened again, this time with Ernest's friend, Mr Campbell, a gentleman with whom she was not acquainted (and frankly with whom she had no wish to be acquainted).

Mr Campbell was apparently 'a man perfectly well-known to the police', though of course Ernest could not possibly have been aware of that fact. How the police and the newspapers dared to insinuate what they did was beyond her. They had

had the temerity to suggest that Ernest and Mr Campbell were 'apparently plying for men, so much so that a disturbance ensued'. Thankfully Mr Boulton had arranged matters, and Ernest had been released with a small fine and a stern talking-to. They had decided as a family that it had been much ado about nothing, a comedy of errors – a conclusion which, fortunately and very much to her relief, Lord Arthur Clinton seemed to share.

Mrs Mary Ann Boulton's ears had pricked up with alarm when, during the early days of the courtship (for surely no other construction could be placed upon it?), Lord Arthur casually made a reference to 'my fiancée'. And she had bristled defensively a week or so later when she read in *The Times* that 'a marriage is arranged to take place between Lord Arthur Clinton, M.P., and Miss Matthews'.

Love or money? It sounded like the title of one of the plays that Ernest and his young friends were so fond of performing. Mrs Mary Ann Boulton knew that in the world of the theatre love would always triumph in the end, but away from the limelight, in the dark and difficult present, she feared that gross Mammon often won the day. She trembled at the thought. All she could do was hope and pray, and double and redouble her efforts to snare Lord Arthur for Ernest. Fortunately, her fears proved groundless when Lord Arthur announced that he had relinquished his engagement to Miss Matthews, or as some of the less savoury newspapers hinted, Miss Matthews had shown him the door.

And then there was the question of Lord Arthur's bankruptcy. Mrs Mary Ann Boulton's poor fuddled head could not understand the ins and outs of it all, but it appeared from the crumbs that Lord Arthur let drop, and from what was reported in the newspapers, which she could not keep herself from reading avidly, that he had been ill advised – not to say wilfully misled – over money matters by unscrupulous people and had got himself into difficulties. It was so easily done, so very easily done, and she had every sympathy, though debts of £34,134 did seem extraordinarily excessive and beyond her ability to comprehend.

There were some unsavoury details: Lord Arthur, it seemed, had unfortunately availed himself of the services of a pawnbroker, a Mr Attenborough, and pledged a number of items with him, the tickets for which, she had read with incredulity, had been stolen by a servant. It was very much to Lord Arthur's credit, she reflected, that in the absence of proof, Lord Arthur had not informed the police of the theft nor, indeed, dismissed the man in question.

It appeared that Lord Arthur had a generous nature – Mrs Mary Ann Boulton might even go so far as to say an *over*-generous nature. The sum of £1,694 owed to Messrs Ortner, Houle and Co. for items of jewellery given as presents was very considerably more than what she herself spent annually on keeping house. She was surprised to discover that Lord Arthur had given his intended bride 'in all, five diamond rings'. She could not help comparing – a little uneasily, it had to be said – the cost of one of these diamond rings, apparently £75, with the huge sum of £210 for 'a chest containing plate and cutlery' given as a gift to one Lieutenant Jones, a fellow officer of Lord Arthur, which bespoke a deal of manly friendship and affection existing between them.

It was unfortunate, it had to be said, that Lord Arthur's generosity, his over-generosity, cast a slight shadow over Ernest's coming-of-age party in the December of 1867. Mrs Mary Ann

Boulton had been planning it for months, if not years. A supper party for family and friends in their house in Dulwich to celebrate her darling boy's majority. There was to be champagne, a full supper, presents and surprises, and entertainments, both musical and dramatic. Naturally, she wrote to Lord Arthur first as guest of honour, and she received a charming reply:

> My dear Mrs Boulton,
>   Pray accept my most sincere thanks for your most kind invitation which I accept with the greatest pleasure, especially as it is to celebrate the coming of age of your son, Ernest, for whom I entertain the most sincere regard. Believe me to remain
>   Sincerely yours,
>   Arthur Pelham-Clinton

'*Your son, Ernest, for whom I entertain the most sincere regard.*' Mrs Mary Ann Boulton savoured those words over and over again.

Then, at the very last minute, Ernest had informed her that Arthur had 'said he would be very pleased to send any little thing down to supper if Ernest would like him to do so'. When she finally got to the bottom of things, she was horrified. It seemed that Lord Arthur had ordered and intended to pay for an entire supper from Buck's the Caterers. Apart from throwing her into complete disarray (and how typical of menfolk to be so oblivious of her existing arrangements), Mr Boulton had put his foot down and decreed that they could not accept such a gift, especially when Lord Arthur had been declared a bankrupt barely a fortnight earlier.

Mrs Mary Ann Boulton asked Ernest to most politely decline Lord Arthur's offer. 'My answer to my son when he told me of having received the letter was: "Then write and tell Lord Arthur that it would not do for you to name such a thing to your Mother or she would be offended." Those were my words,' Mrs Mary Ann Boulton declared. 'Everything was provided.'

But matters had not ended there.

'When I was dressing for the evening on my son's birthday, two persons arrived from Buck's and said they had been desired by Lord Clinton to provide a supper and my words were these: "I feel sure that Lord Arthur means this kindly but it is a mistake."'

Lord Arthur wrote her a very pretty letter of apology: 'I fear I offended and caused annoyance to you on Friday last – if so pray let me offer my sincerest apologies &c &c.' And so the matter was forgotten, and the perfectly smooth surface of their relations polished back to full lustre. When she reflected upon the incident, there was, she concluded, more to delight than to dismay. It had all sprung from Lord Arthur's 'most sincere regard' for Ernest, from an ebullition, from an excess, of those manly feelings of affection towards her darling boy.

And really, what on earth could be wrong with that?

13

Lord Arthur's Wife

MARRY! If you are for pleasure, marry; if you prize
rosy health, marry; and even if money be your object, marry. A good wife is Heaven's last, best gift to
man, his angel and minister of graces innumerable,
his gem of many virtues, his casket of jewels. Her
voice, the sweetest music; her smiles, his brightest
day; her kiss, the guardian of his safety, the balsam
of his life; her industry, his surest wealth; her eco-
nomy, his safest steward; her lips, his faithful
councillors; her bosom, the softest pillow of his
cares; and her prayers, the ablest advocates of
Heaven's blessings on his head.

The Ladies' Treasury, March 1867

Fanny could not give two hoots for the law, for Chelmsford,
or for the firm of Gepp and Sons. But her allowance from
Papa depended on her sticking her articles out. Fortunately Mr
Gepp Senior was not a harsh taskmaster. Indeed, it sometimes
struck her rather forcibly that Mr Gepp Senior was as eager to
see the back of her as she was to see the back of him. Fanny's
absences from the firm multiplied. Her recent and severe bout
of scarlet fever had meant blessed months away from Gepp and
Sons, and even then she was still as weak as a kitten and would
often feel unwell and unable to face her duties. Weekends were
stretched and stretched until they almost joined up. Then

there were holidays to be taken, and of course rehearsals. Endless rehearsals. Mr Gepp rarely questioned her absences, and her pleas to be excused – so she could rehearse or perform or have a costume fitted for such worthy causes as the Benefit for the Infirmary – were greeted with a combination of bewilderment, resignation and, truth be told, sighs of relief.

Fanny ended up spending rather more time in London than she did in Chelmsford. She was in London almost every weekend, and when Stella fell in love with Lord Arthur Pelham-Clinton and they moved into Mrs Peck's establishment in Southampton Street, Fanny was a regular and welcome visitor. She slept in the little dressing room which opened off Stella and Arthur's bedroom. It was not an entirely satisfactory solution from either of their points of view. It was perfectly understandable that a young married couple in the first flush of passion needed privacy, and Fanny had no perverse wish to listen to Stella squealing like a stuck pig every time she brought a steamer home or Arthur chose to exercise his conjugal rights. It was all *most* unladylike.

Equally, the same problems arose on those rather less frequent occasions when Fanny wished to entertain a gentleman overnight, or just for an hour or two. Indeed, there were times when Mrs Peck's first-floor front bore a passable resemblance to a cheap knocking shop, and come the morning Fanny was never sure who she would find there in various and interesting states of *déshabille* and disarray, and it would require all her reserves of skill and cunning to smuggle out these waifs and strays without either Sharp-eyed Maria or Slow Eliza from Norfolk spotting them.

There were other difficulties to contend with. As the older, unmarried and – she was not ashamed to admit it – plainer sister, living with her quite exceptionally beautiful younger sister and her sister's aristocratic husband in the cramped surroundings of Mrs Peck's first-floor front, Fanny sometimes felt that she was playing gooseberry to Stella and Arthur, that she was in the way, that she was under their feet. But when she voiced these nagging concerns, Stella would fly into a fit of hysterics and declare that she could not, she would not, do without her dearest Fanny; that they could never, would never, be parted.

There was much muttering and much speculation in the servants' hall of 36 Southampton Street about the new tenants on the drawing-room floor. By common consent, it was felt the *he* was all right. At least he was polite and nearly always said please and thank you and the like. And even if he didn't have two farthings to rub together, it was still something to have a *real* Lord, the son of a Duke, in the house after so many to-ings and fro-ings of plain and ordinary Misters.

But young Mr Boulton was another kettle of fish altogether. He might be called Mr Boulton, but everyone was convinced that he was, in truth, a she.

Secretly, Eliza Clark rather liked Mr or Miss Boulton. He was only a year or two older than herself and, if he was in the mood, he would chat to her in a friendly, interested sort of a way and ask her questions about her life in Norfolk before she came to London; about her previous service; and about her sweethearts. Eliza could always tell straight away what sort of mood he was in. Some mornings he would smile and bustle about and sometimes even give her a hand with the dusting or the bed-making. On other days he would sit silently, scowling, lost in his own angry thoughts, furiously smoking thin cigarettes or cigars.

'I thought Boulton was a female all the time he was there,' Eliza said later. It was the small things that convinced her, like the fact that he (or she) 'used powder to her face' and sang very prettily with 'a womanish voice'.

One thing she did puzzle over was the dresses that Mr Boulton and Mr Park wore when they went out in all their finery in the evening. They were not the sort of dresses that respectable ladies wore. Quite the opposite. 'I have been to the Theatre and have seen Ladies dressed as Boulton and Park were,' was the only way she could blushingly phrase it in court; she could not bring herself to speak the word 'whore' in front of gentlemen. 'When they went out dressed as Ladies, Boulton wore white muslin, and Park, black silk, made low, and like ladies wear.'

'I used to accuse him of being a female,' Eliza said. As the weeks went by, she had become quite bold, and as she bottomed out the rooms every morning, she used to think of a dozen different ways of getting him to admit that he was in truth a she. It was their little bit of fun. But she could never get a straight answer. 'He used to pass it off as a joke.'

Maria Duffin, by contrast, was a sharp-eyed, sharp-tongued, inquisitive, clever sort of a girl, a cockney girl who had seen far more of the world than was strictly good for her, and quite the opposite of Slow Eliza. 'I never could satisfy myself whether Boulton was a man or a woman,' Maria said. And it was true. Sometimes she was convinced that he was a woman in disguise. At other times she was not so sure, and she sometimes suspected that he was a man, a man who dressed up as a woman.

'Boulton generally dressed as a Lady,' Maria said. In the mornings he would wear a loose flowing gown or wrapper, the kind of gown, she was reliably informed, that gay ladies wore to their 'work' inside houses of ill-repute. 'When he went out with Lord Arthur in an evening he always dressed in women's clothes. I have seen him only once or twice dressed in gentlemen's clothes.'

And then there was Mr Park, Boulton's particular friend, who used to come at the weekends, regular as clockwork, and stay two or three nights. Here was more perplexity, more bewilderment, more confusion. What exactly was Mr Park? Was he a man or a woman? Maria was not sure. Sometimes he would be dressed as a man and sometimes as a woman.

Certainly, the sleeping arrangements had struck Maria as decidedly odd. 'When Boulton was there he slept in the same room, and in the same bed with Lord Arthur Clinton,' she said, frowning at the memory. 'There was a small dressing room leading out of Lord Arthur's bedroom. There was a bed in that room, and Park slept in that bed. The entrance to the dressing room was only through Lord Arthur's bedroom. There was no other door to the dressing room. When Park was away, Boulton did not occupy that bed, but continued to sleep with Lord Arthur Clinton.'

Maria Duffin knew this because it was her job to take the hot water into the bedroom every morning. Of course she would give a cursory knock and, with barely a second's pause, enter the bedchamber. It was a game. She wanted to catch them out, she wanted to catch them at it, to find out once and for all whether Boulton was a man or a woman or some sort of in-between. And there they would be, huddled together, half-asleep and half-entwined, and quickly covering themselves over with the bedclothes.

It was she who first saw the card with 'Lady Arthur Clinton' engraved upon it. It was true that at the time she was poking and prying about the room while Lord Arthur and Boulton were absent – she could not remember exactly when – but most likely when they were away in Scarborough in the October. When she pointed it out to Eliza, she of course had taken it as proof positive of what the household had suspected all along: that Boulton was a lady dressed up as a man.

But still Maria's doubts persisted. There was something not quite right, something that did not fit. But she could not, for the life of her, put her finger on what it was. One morning, as she was making the beds, Maria decided to come right out and ask him.

'I beg your pardon,' she said, 'but I really think you are a man.'

Boulton had looked at her a little oddly and then laughed gaily.

'I am *Lady* Clinton', Stella had said grandly, '– Lord Arthur's *wife*,' laying particular stress on the word 'wife'. Then she waggled the fingers of her left hand in front of Maria's face and invited her to look at her wedding ring and keeper. Maria had looked, and she knew that that should have settled matters. But she was still left feeling uneasy and confused. Despite Lady Clinton's dramatic revelation, she was still all at sea, still uncertain, and had a feeling deep down that Lady Clinton was not a Lady at all. Turning it over and over in her mind, she felt very uncomfortable. She would take her mother's advice and leave this house. Perhaps Mr Lindley in Catherine Street would take her back.

F anny and Stella had sworn that they would never let Arthur come between them, but of course he did. It had all begun innocently enough and with the best of intentions.

Fanny was used to listening to both sides of the story. It seemed to help both Stella and Arthur to have a third party, a confidential friend, a sister, a sister-in-law, someone to whom they could pour out their troubles, who would do her best to try to smooth out their differences. And what troubles and what differences! There were a thousand and one irritations, a thousand and one little altercations peppering every day. To be quite candid, Stella was highly strung. At her worst, she was a hissing, spitting Virago, and there were raised voices, slammed doors and flouncings-out at least half a dozen times a day.

If she was not spitting venom, Stella would sit with a darkening face in a darkened room, gazing into nothingness, contemplating the unfathomable abyss of her own mind. She was not getting on with Arthur. She wondered if they had ever got on. And more importantly, she questioned whether they ever would get on and whether it had been doomed before it had even begun.

She was very much afraid that Arthur had misled her, if not deceived her. His courtship had been assiduous. He had flattered her and attended her and bombarded her with expensive trifles and *bijouterie*. He had made out that he was a man of means, prepared to take her to wife and keep her in a style befitting Stella, Lady Clinton.

But she had been sold a pup – or rather, a puppy. Arthur was a declared bankrupt. He was a wastrel, a feckless profligate drowning in an ocean of debt so vast and so deep that it was improbable, if not impossible, that he would ever escape. And still his debts mounted. Still he spent money like water. Still he borrowed. They were sinking lower and lower, and the bitter irony of it all was that it was she who had to venture forth nightly and sell her arse to passing trade to put food on the table and pay the rent. She should have listened to and profited from those endless and tedious lessons about the importance of money that dear, dull Louis Hurt had tried to drum into her.

O f course, if Stella had bothered to ask Fanny for her opinion before rushing headlong into matrimony, Fanny could and would have told her that marriage was not a state to be entered into unadvisedly, lightly or wantonly, as she believed the Form of the Sodomisation of Matrimony ran, but reverently, discreetly, advisedly and soberly. (On this last point, Fanny could testify that Stella was certainly not sober before her marriage to Arthur, and had rarely been sober since. Not that she was judging her. If Fanny had a sovereign for every time she herself had fallen down dead drunk, she would be a rich woman.) But Stella had been so determined to have Arthur's ring on her finger that she was deaf, dumb and blind to all advice and sisterly counsel.

Stella was wilful, vain, moody, petulant and quarrelsome. At the same time she was loyal, brave, exciting and beautiful. Stella's beauty was her greatest gift and her greatest curse. She was a perfect beauty, and that meant she could get more or less whatever she wanted simply by snapping her fingers or fluttering her eyelashes.

In Fanny's considered opinion, Stella's account of Arthur's courtship was partial and jaundiced. It was certainly true that Arthur had laid siege to her, but only because she had *wanted* him to lay siege to her. From the moment she first met Arthur, Stella had set her cap at him. Her ambition knew no bounds. She wanted to be Stella, Lady Clinton. And more. If Fate so decreed that his two older brothers were to die suddenly and without issue, Arthur would be Duke of Newcastle and she his beautiful Duchess, and then the whole world would have to bow and scrape and curtsey to her. She had visions of living at Clumber, or in the grand town house in Pall Mall, and driving in the park in an open carriage emblazoned with her personal cipher.

But, upon reflection, Arthur was a far from ideal husband for Stella. Stella was too volatile, too explosive. She needed a strong man, a man who would stand for no nonsense, a man with a firm hand who would give her a good slap (as Fanny herself had had to do upon occasion) when she got out of control. Stella was utterly oblivious to Arthur's finer qualities: to his kindness and his thoughtfulness, to his loyalty and his devotion. It was true that Arthur had not been quite honest with Stella; true that he was mired in the most terrible debt; true that he lacked direction and drive; but Stella's withering contempt, her constant carpings and criticisms had reduced him and diminished him. She had humiliated and emasculated him. And what – Fanny asked herself with a rhetorical flourish – had it profited her?

Arthur, it was clear, needed the love and support of a good woman. He needed a wife who would encourage him, a wife who could organise him, a wife who could direct him. A wife who was a helpmeet to her husband; a quiet, good, kind wife, but a wife nonetheless who could stand beside her husband as an equal; a wife who could mingle effortlessly with his family and friends, at ease in the drawing rooms of London and at home in the country. A knuckling-down sort of wife, unafraid of hard work and hard times. A wife, in short, like the kind of wife that Fanny thought *she* would make. There. She had dared to think it. She had dared to whisper it. And once thought, once whispered, she could not unthink it, she could not unwhisper it.

Fanny, Lady Clinton. It had, she thought, a certain ring about it. Really, quite a definite ring about it.

14

The Toast of the Town

Oh! the dresses, neat, eccentric,
Individualised and queer;
Oh! the dresses various coloured,
As the flowers that deck the year;
Oh! the dresses, breezy, airy,
Most expansive, startling, grand;
Oh! the dresses, quite peculiar,
As the fossils on the strand.

'Cantab', 'The Spa at Scarborough:
A Reminiscence', 1864

The *Scarborough Gazette and Weekly List of Visitors* (founder, publisher and proprietor: Mr Solomon Wilkinson Theakston) was the most venerable and the most select of the dozen or so newspapers that served the genteel resort and spa of Scarborough.

Those with a curiosity to discover what was going on in the wider world – in, for instance, the North Riding of Yorkshire; in England, Wales, Ireland and Scotland; in Continental Europe; or in far-flung countries sweltering under scorching suns – did *not* turn to the *Scarborough Gazette and Weekly List of Visitors*. Nor did those who wished to read of war and revolution, of famine and pestilence, of great adventures and daring deeds, give themselves the bother of consulting the *Scarborough Gazette and Weekly List of Visitors*. And those Mr

Gradgrinds from the world of manufacturing, trade and commerce who needed hard facts and adamantine figures as mental grist for their dark Satanic mills were emphatically not subscribers to the *Scarborough Gazette and Weekly List of Visitors*.

The *Gazette* (the abbreviation used by all but its most particular readers) held no truck with such worldly events. News was an unwelcome and unpleasant intrusion into its elegant and serene pages. It had been published, week in and week out, since 1845, which was the very year that the railway came to Scarborough and the very year that the town's first built-for-purpose hotel – the Crown Spa Hotel – opened for business.

Vulgar rivals and cheap imitators had periodically attempted to usurp the position of the *Gazette* as the town's social lodestar, as its finely calibrated chronometer of gentility. The *Scarborough Advertiser and List of Visitors* had lasted a mere four months, while the grandly named *James Greasley's Scarborough Times and Weekly List of Visitors* survived just a matter of weeks. It was true that the *Scarborough Herald and Weekly List of Visitors* had mounted a more sustained siege, lasting, much to everyone's surprise, for two years and two months, before withering on the vine. The *Scarborough Gazette and Weekly List of Visitors* sailed on, unperturbed and imperturbable, through rough seas, storm and tempest, as Scarborough's ship of social state.

The entire purpose of the *Gazette*, its beginning, middle and end, was polite society and the social round. Week in, week out, the *Gazette* would appear at exactly the same time on a Thursday morning with two or three, and sometimes more, pages devoted to listing those visitors to Scarborough considered to fall within the pale of polite society. For ease of social gradation visitors were grouped together according to which hotel, apartment or other establishment they were residing in during their stay, and these selfsame hotels, apartments and other establishments would be listed in strictly *de*scending order of gentility.

Scarborough's long season stretched from March to almost the end of November, and every day of every week the train would shudder slowly to a halt alongside the railway station's famously long platform, and from its first-class carriages would be disgorged and deposited, like the shining pebbles washed up on the Strand, a fresh batch of distinguished visitors to make new patternings in Scarborough's endlessly shifting social sands.

And what pebbles, what patterns, what sands! When Royalty, in the ample figure of the Prince of Wales, graced the town with a visit in 1869, the news caused much fluttering in the breasts of the ladies of Scarborough. Some were propelled into a positive frenzy of excitement and gave themselves up to endlessly promenading the fashionable shopping streets, or genteelly loitering in the gardens and parades in their best bonnets, in the forlorn hope of dropping a curtsey to His Royal Highness.

The Peerage was well represented, with a fair sprinkling of Dukes and Duchesses and Dowagers, Lord This's and Lady That's, as well as a baker's dozen of baronets or their relicts. There were any number of Honourables, and an even larger number of assorted, untitled relations: annuitarians of all shapes and sizes; cousins of multiple and dizzying removes; swathes of elderly maiden aunts and blustering port-nosed uncles; and plenty of plain – in the fullest sense of the word – Misses. Almost without exception these assorted relations were as poor as church mice – poorer even, if such a thing were possible – but they kept up appearances wonderfully well and never ceased bragging about and basking in the reflected glory of their wealthier kin.

Then there were those from the middle ranks of society: an abundance of elderly and wealthy widows; plenty of plump ladies of a certain age richly dressed in Macclesfield silks garnished with gold and diamonds; ruddy-faced gentleman farmers and their ruddy-faced lady wives, who always looked a little uncomfortable in their Sunday best; surgeons, lawyers and portly parsons and lean preachers with their wives and children, as well as the odd Collector or lesser-ranking official of the East India Company spending his six months' home leave by the sea. Without any particular distinguished connexion but with plenty of money, they had managed to establish a precarious toehold in Scarborough society by dint of lavish hospitality and a willingness, bordering on the slavish, to flatter and praise and pander to their social betters.

Scarborough prided itself on not being narrow, on not being hidebound. The wealthy, as well as the well-born, all had their contribution to make and it would be foolish to make too many hard and fast rules. All were meticulously recorded in the hallowed pages of the *Scarborough Gazette and Weekly List of Visitors* as if it were the Book of Life itself.

Apart from those invalids – real and imagined – who came in search of a cure and assiduously drank the vinegary, brown chalybeate waters famed for their aperient properties – 'it strengthens and exhilarates the bowel,' according to *Theakston's Guide to Scarborough* (author and publisher: Mr Solomon Wilkinson Theakston) – and discovered by the enterprising Mrs Thomasin Farrer in the reign of good King Charles, matrimony was the main purpose and preoccupation of Scarborough's visiting gentlefolk. Like a vast flock of migratory birds that each year flew to the farthest shores to seek out a mate, so the distinguished and the not-so-distinguished, the rich and the poor, the plain and the beautiful, the old and the young, the hopeful and the hopeless, those with a past and those with a future, flocked to Scarborough for the annual mating season where rich and brilliant plumage, elaborate courtship rituals, dancing and singing, struttings, couplings, feints and sleights made it a sight to behold.

There was a mild flutter of anticipation among the readers of the *Gazette* of Thursday, 15th October 1868 when that august organ, struggling gallantly with the spelling of Stella's given name, announced that 'Lord Arthur Pelham-Clinton, M.P. and Mr Earnest Boulton, Esquire' would be appearing next Tuesday and Wednesday at the Spa Saloon, Scarborough in a dramatic double bill, *A Morning Call* and *Love and Rain*.

The subsequent sudden and dramatic postponement of the entertainment at the Spa Saloon took everybody by surprise. Mr George Reeve Smith, the manager, took the unusual step of publishing the text of the terse telegram he had received from Lord Arthur:

> Oct. 20, 1868. – Clinton, London, to Smith, Spar.
> Ernest Boulton very unwell. Cannot leave London to-day. Will start by nine train to-night. Pray postpone entertainment until Wednesday.

It was felt by everyone to be a most gentlemanly telegram, and there was widespread speculation as to what the sudden indisposition of Mr Ernest Boulton might be. It was to be hoped that it was neither serious nor contagious (especially not the latter, in case Lord Arthur contracted the contagion, and then who knew what might happen). But the anxious matrons of Scarborough were reassured by the fact that Mr Boulton would clearly be well enough to travel later the same day, though everyone knew that travelling through the night was ruinous to health. Indeed, there was such a wave of sympathetic interest in the wellbeing of these two young men that when they arrived in Scarborough bleary-eyed and half-asleep early on the Wednesday morning, both performances were completely sold out.

In its edition of Thursday, 22nd October 1868, the *Gazette* recorded, erroneously, the names of the two distinguished visitors who had arrived the day before: 'Pelham-Clinton, Lord Arthur M.P.' and 'Belton, Ernest Esq.' They were staying at the Royal Hotel, where the startlingly named 'Mr D. Anus' was also listed as residing. Though considerably less expensive than the newly built Grand Hotel with its 365 bedrooms (one for every day of the year), the Royal was nevertheless highly regarded by *Crosby's Guide* as 'the oldest and most aristocratic' of the Scarborough hotels.

The more enthusiastic readers of the *Gazette* were curious, more than a little curious, to see Lord Arthur Pelham-Clinton in the flesh. Apart from being the third son of a very distinguished Duke, he had been, it was said, quite a hero during the dreadful Indian Uprising, though no one could remember the exact details of his gallantry. More to the point, he was the Member for Newark (and quite a rising Member, it was said, with the patronage of Mr Gladstone assured by virtue of being his godson).

It was a trifle unusual, Scarborough conceded, for a rising Member to tread the boards so enthusiastically; such theatrical propensities seemed more than a little odd, especially as the interests of most gentlemen from similar stock began and ended with blood sports. But whether there was any impropriety in it was quite another matter. Scarborough noted that Lord Arthur had appeared on the professional stage alongside the Marquis Townshend's troupe of 'Noble Amateurs', and so as far as society was concerned that was the end of it. Any endeavour, theatrical or otherwise, which numbered in its ranks at least one Marquis must be a highly respectable, if not positively praiseworthy, pastime.

There was one aspect of Lord Arthur's life in which Scarborough took a particular and kindly interest. He was known to be unmarried at the present time, and in the eyes of Scarborough society an unmarried Lord was an unmarried Lord and therefore an extremely desirable commodity for their many unmarried daughters. Though there had been rumours of engagements, indeed of several engagements, none of them had fruited into matrimony. It could well be that Lord Arthur was currently engaged. Scarborough would cross that bridge when – and if – it came to it. But a man was innocent until proven guilty. Scarborough would therefore treat Lord Arthur as *not* engaged to be married – and go on treating him as such until proof positive was offered to the contrary.

According to the well-thumbed copy of *Dod's Peerage, Baronetage and Knightage of Great Britain and Ireland* in Mr Theakston's Library (founder and proprietor: Mr Solomon Wilkinson Theakston), Lord Arthur Pelham-Clinton was twenty-eight years of age – the perfect age, in the opinion of many, for a man to marry; an age when the impetuosity of youth gives way to manly maturity, when wild oats have been sown (and sometimes unfortunately reaped), and when most men are soberly considering taking a well-brought-up wife with a comfortable fortune.

Then, of course, Lord Arthur was a bankrupt and his name had been in the newspapers. Though the shame and stigma of bankruptcy might well damage the chances of other, lesser, men in the matrimonial market, the wealthy matrons of Scarborough with spinster daughters on their hands saw it as a positive advantage. It was a truth universally acknowledged that a single man *not* in possession of a good fortune must be in want of a rich wife. And the same could surely be said for Lord Arthur's theatrical consort, Mr Boulton or Mr Belton (the *Gazette*, puzzlingly, had it both ways), who was very likely a most superior sort of young man, although rigorous interrogations of the pages of *Dod's Peerage* had not, as yet, borne fruit.

S tella played the roles of Fanny Chillingtone and Lady Jane Desmond to the hilt, with plenty of stage whispers and alouds and asides, managing half a dozen lightning-quick costume changes which delighted the audience and brought forth storms of applause. She was beautiful and she was fascinating, and the audience could not keep their eyes off her. She effortlessly ran through the gamut of emotions, being, by turns, thrillingly bitter and bitingly sarcastic, aristocratically haughty, foot-stampingly impatient and curl-tossingly petulant. She was mischievous, worldly, calculating, but could switch in a flash to vulnerable, fearful and tearful. She simpered, she flirted, she smiled and she was coy. She was compelling and she was dazzling. She sparkled and she shone like the diamonds she wore on stage, reflecting and refracting all the wonderful, the multifarious, the flashing and the fleeting moods of Woman Incarnate. The audience loved her.

Unsurprisingly, the *Gazette* was positively fawning in its praise of the actors. The Spa was 'honoured' and its frequenters 'delighted' by the 'two charming little drawing-room pieces'. The *Gazette* was especially in awe of 'the very easy "at home" character of the acting' which quite obviously reflected 'the *au fait* acquired by the social position of the actors'.

Lord Arthur and his companion were invited to attend the sumptuous studios of Mr Oliver Sarony in order that a series of photographic likenesses might be taken. In the commodious dressing rooms of Sarony's studios ('an establishment with every convenience for carrying out Photography to perfection', his advertisements in the *Gazette* proclaimed), they were to dress themselves as Sir Edward Ardent and Mrs Chillingtone. Mr Sarony took no fewer than thirty-four different negatives for a sequence entitled 'Man and Wife'. In a long and exhausting session, Stella was also prevailed upon to pose in other attitudes and costumes, including as a nun at prayer, which made a most striking and soulful image.

The photographs sold like hot cakes, and Mr Oliver Sarony struggled to keep up.

'Was there a popular demand for these photographs?' Stella's barrister asked him in court nearly three years later.

'Yes,' the photographer replied. 'There was a great demand.'

'They sold freely to the Gentlemen and visitors in Scarborough?'

'Very fast, as fast as we could print them.'

The most popular photographs were those of Stella alone, and were purchased, in the main, by admiring and incredulous gentlemen. Lord Arthur may have been the most sought-after bachelor by the matrons of Scarborough, but it was Stella who caused the greatest excitement among the gentlemen of the place. Encouraged by the warmth of her reception, which seemed to verge on adulation, Stella determined to venture out in full drag in the town, where her presence created a most extraordinary commotion – especially among the gentlemen. Hats were doffed. Bows were made. Introductions were effected. Arms were proffered and eager invitations to luncheon, to tea and to dinner fell like confetti at her feet. Scarborough had never seen anything quite like it. She was the toast of the town, and seemingly all eyes were upon her.

They were not always friendly eyes. Despite her conquering the hearts of most of the gentlemen in Scarborough, there were a few who obstinately refused to succumb to Stella's many and various charms, a few who manifested hostility towards her, towards the very idea of her, who brindled and bridled at the very mention of her name. One such was Mr Wybert Reeve, 'lessee and manager' of the long-established Theatre Royal in Scarborough, a sworn and bitter rival of the Spa Saloon and the Spa Theatre, which had in recent years leeched his audiences away.

When Lord Arthur and Stella decided to attend a performance at the Theatre Royal, Mr Wybert Reeve felt compelled to call the police.

> Lord Arthur had the impertinence to introduce Ernest Boulton *in female attire*, and sit with him in a prominent place among the Ladies and Gentlemen assembled in the dress circle in my theatre.
>
> On hearing of it I at once desired the police, if possible, to take them into custody. They, however, contrived to leave the theatre with the crowd.
>
> The next morning I wrote to Lord Arthur Clinton, expressing in strong terms my annoyance, and explaining the order I had given to the police if he dared to repeat the offence.

Notwithstanding this, and my refusal to accept an apology, he afterwards applied to me to allow them both to appear in a piece entitled *A Morning Call* on the stage of this theatre, which I at once decidedly refused.

It was a narrow escape for Lord Arthur and Stella. Mr Wybert Reeve's visceral anger and animosity towards them was a stark reminder, a warning, that not all gentlemen could be beguiled, dazzled and seduced by Stella's beauty and by Stella's charms. Burlesque on stage was one thing: acceptable to some, offensive to others. But it was quite another thing when men dressed as women walked the streets; when they dared to take their places – their *prominent* places – among the serried ranks of ladies and gentlemen in the Dress Circle; when they smirked and simpered and giggled and flirted with gentlemen as if they were real women. It was all wrong. It was more than wrong. It was unnatural and it was criminal, and (in the opinion of Mr Wybert Reeve and many other gentlemen with whom he had discussed the matter with much huffing and puffing) if there was not a law against such goings-on, there ought to be. Lord Arthur and his catamite may have evaded capture for now. But such creatures should take heed, they said. They will get their comeuppance. It was only a matter of time.

'Yr Affectionate Fanny'

Don't be too particular
When you come to woo;
Lay aside your spectacles
Worthy bachelors, do!
When wives are young and dutiful
Honeymoon's pleasures abound;
But who would wish for a beautiful
Honeymoon all the year round?
Then don't be too particular!

John Orlando Parry, 1843

Everyone was agreed. Stella was impossible. Quite impossible. Completely, absolutely and utterly impossible.

Not just annoying. Not just irritating. But infuriating, exasperating, maddening. She was entirely selfish and entirely self-absorbed. She was easily bored and took no pains to conceal her boredom. She was frequently rude and often offensive, especially when she was in her cups, a condition which was the rule rather than the exception.

Stella never listened and she never learned. She was impatient and intolerant. She was dismissive of the feelings of others, belittling and humiliating them as and when the mood took her.

Stella demanded everything as her right and as her due. She took, took and took again. But she gave nothing in return.

There were rarely any pleases, and even fewer thank-yous, no gratitude, no recognition of a service rendered, of a gift given or a compliment bestowed. Nothing, not even a smile.

And she was quick to take umbrage over the slightest slight, real or imagined. She could sulk for days or weeks. She was even quicker to anger. Her tempers and her tantrums were things frightening to behold: sudden and violent sea tempests that wrought a terrible havoc and then blew themselves out as swiftly and as bewilderingly as they had blown up. Afterwards, Stella would in some mysterious fashion be calmed and cleansed, drained and purified of the poison within her, while Arthur and all those around her were left clinging to the flotsam and jetsam of their wrecked lives and emotions.

Stella was a prolific writer of letters, though notes might be a better word to describe the shower of missives that assailed Arthur by every post. She was not much given to writing love letters (though of course she delighted in receiving them). Her letters tended to be short and to the point, ranging in tone from the firm and instructive to the impatient and irritable, with only very occasional oases of affection and regard in between.

Arthur could usually tell what sort of mood Stella was in from the way she signed her letters. 'Stell' was a rare and good augury. It was her comfortable name, her familiar name. It meant that she was at one with the world, at her ease, in her wrapper, with her stays loosened, her stockings rolled down and her curling papers in.

'Stella' was almost as good. Stella was a great and formal beauty. Stella was the cold light of the moon and the stars in the sky, and her love burned with the hard, clear flame of eternity. Stella was poetic and soulful, the dark and mysterious muse of Spenser or of Swift. Stella's love was pure and untainted. An alabaster love, smooth and icily beautiful.

'Ernest' or 'Ernest Boulton', 'E' or 'E.B.' were admirably brisk and determinedly businesslike. They were common-sensical, down-to-earth, feet-on-the-ground names and they spoke of wanting to get things organised, of wanting to get things done. Ernest and Ernest Boulton, E and E.B., were often exasperated and irritated, angry and annoyed, and some-times driven to distraction or to drink, or both, by Arthur's enduring and ever-expanding catalogue of failings and inadequacies.

'Stella Clinton', on the other hand, was decidedly inaus-picious. Stella Clinton was a stormy-petrel sort of a name, a name presaging destruction and disaster; a threatening, lower-ing, darkening sky of a name. Stella Clinton was a shot across the bows, or the rumour and rumble of approaching cannon. Stella Clinton was regal and haughty, imperious and imperial, a Roman matron, a Boadicea, a Bess of Hardwick, a Virgin Queen. Stella Clinton was glorious, and Stella Clinton was magnificent. But woe betide those who dared to cross her, for there was no escape from her vengeance, no escape from her cold fury.

On rare occasions there was no signature at all, just an angry full stop jabbed and stabbed onto the page. When in receipt of one of these anonymous missives, Arthur knew that a terrible storm was about to break above his head and that if he had any sense he would run for cover.

Stella bombarded Arthur with letters and notes. At the time of leaving Mrs Peck's establishment in Southampton Street – and it was a moot point as to whether they left of their own ac-cord or whether they were evicted by that good lady – things between himself and Stella went from bad to worse, and in the course of a week, or even less, he received not so much a flurry as an avalanche of letters by almost every post.

Arthur staggered under the weight of these letters instructing him to do this, ordering him to do that. Peremptory and insolent notes, reproaching him and rebuking him, telling him he was good for nothing and interrogating him about actual and alleged infractions. And these said instructions, injunctions and orders, once executed, were immediately and abruptly countermanded, usually without explanation or apology. No wonder Arthur sometimes did not know whether he was coming or going.

'My dear Arthur,' Stella's missives invariably began:

'I am just off to Chelmsford with Fanny where I shall stay till Monday. We are going to a party there tomorrow night . . .' 'We were very drunk last night, consequently I forgot to write to you . . .' 'I am very tired and seedy.'

'How *can* you be so absurd?' . . . 'I must of course trust to you about the things you promised . . .' 'Now no promises please, as this is *no* joke.'

'A game pie or two might be nice as a little present to me . . .' 'If you have any coin I could do with a little . . .' 'Send me some money, Wretch . . .' 'I wanted the money so it's rather a bore.'

'I shall leave here by the 10.40 train. Meet me . . .' 'Why *cannot* you tell me the truth for once and say you did not come to the station at all? . . . ' 'It is now five o'clock and no letter for me, of course, not that I expected them, but your everlasting promises are *sickening* . . .' 'When you write let it be a very proper letter.'

'I have waited in for you just two hours and a half. I need not tell you I am extremely put out about it . . .' 'I do not like to be treated with such rudeness and if you had any feelings of a gentleman you would know that to be impunctual shows great ill breeding.'

'I am quite tired of waiting and shall not return tonight, nor at all if I am to be treated in this way. I will call tomorrow at one o'clock and shall expect you to be in . . .' 'We cannot go on in this way . . .' 'I am most annoyed.'

'I am consoling myself for your absence by getting screwed . . .' 'And now, dear, I must shut up.'

'We cannot go on in this way,' Stella had written. Arthur entirely agreed. He was exhausted. He yearned for some respite and some repose from the terrible strain of living with Stella. Never had he stood in greater need of a confidential friend, and it was with some relief that he turned to Fanny for guidance and support. Fanny, the older, wiser, calmer sister. Fanny, who knew Stella inside-out and upside-down. Fanny the diplomat, smoother of passages and privy counsellor to the secrets of Stella's heart.

After one particularly epic and exhausting confrontation, which ended as usual with Stella flouncing out, he wrote despairingly to Fanny, who replied by return. 'My Dearest Arthur,' she began on her familiar blue notepaper, emblazoned with the monogram 'F.W.P' in gilt lettering (so very clever and so very economical a device, used with equal facility by Frederick William Park *and* by Fanny Winifred Park).

'My Dearest Arthur,' she wrote, 'You must really excuse me from interfering in matrimonial squabbles (for I am sure the present is no more than that) and tho' I am as you say Stella's *confidante* in most things, that which you wish to know she keeps locked in her own breast.

'My own opinion on the subject varies fifty times a day when

I see you together,' Fanny continued.

> She may sometimes treat you brusquely, but on the other
> hand see how she stands up for your dignity and
> position, so that really I cannot form an opinion on the
> subject.
>
> As to all the things she said to you the other night, she
> may have been tight and she did not know what she was
> saying, so that by the time you get my answer you will
> both be laughing over the whole affair – as Stella and I
> did when we quarrelled and fought down here. Don't
> you remember when I slapped her face?

Arthur of course remembered that day very clearly. As he un-
derstood it, it was not the first time that Fanny had slapped
Stella's face (or indeed, the first time that Stella had slapped
Fanny's).

'Do not think me unkind, Dear, as really I have told you all
I know and have not an opinion worth having to offer you,'
Fanny concluded. 'Goodbye Dear, Ever yrs, Fan.'

Arthur's correspondence with Fanny was not all gloom and
agonisings over Stella. He wrote her a charming letter offering
his congratulations on the occasion of her twenty-first birthday
and promising a suitably handsome gift – funds permitting. It
prompted a gushing reply:

'My dearest Arthur,' Fanny wrote:

> How *very* kind of you to think of me on my birthday. *I*
> require *no* remembrance of my Sister's husband as the
> many *kindnesses* he has bestowed upon me will make me
> remember him for many a year and the Birthday present

he is so kind as to promise me will only be one addition
to the heap of little favours I already treasure up.

'I cannot echo your wish that I should live to be a hundred,'
Fanny continued archly, in reply to Arthur's earnestly expressed hopes, 'though I should like to live to a green old age –
green! did I say? *Oh Ciel!*, the amount of paint that will be required to hide that very unbecoming tint!

'My "campish" undertakings are not at present meeting with
the success which they deserve,' she confided, 'whatever I do
seems to get me into hot water somewhere but *n'importe*,
what's the odds so long as you're happy? Once more with
many many thanks, believe me, Your affectionate Sister-in-law,
Fanny Winifred Park.'

'What's the odds so long as you're happy?' It was a joyous
sentiment, and so typical of Fanny. It was an attitude of mind in
contrast, in marked contrast, Arthur could not but help thinking, to the sullen moods and gloomy introspections of Stella.
Fanny lived for the moment. She was careless of tomorrow. If
she got into hot water, as she called it, she would laugh gaily
and simply shrug it off. It was, Arthur reflected, a very appealing quality, a very attractive quality.

'Is the handle of my umbrella mended yet?' Fanny jovially
enquired. 'If so, I wish you would kindly send it to me, as the
weather has turned so showery that I can't go out without a
dread of my back hair coming out of curl. Let me hear from you
at any time,' she concluded. 'I am always glad to do so, Ever yr
affectionate Fanny.'

'Ever yr affectionate Fanny.' These words stayed with him.
To be sure, they were innocent and innocuous enough, but
for reasons he could not immediately fathom, the words took

root in his mind and he was surprised to feel a curious light-
ness in his heart when he thought of them, as if Fanny's
joyous spirit had in some mysterious fashion entered into his
soul.

The Dragon of Davies Street

Ann Empson, a lady of determined appearance,
who eyed the prisoners with no friendly aspect.

Reynolds's Newspaper, 5th June 1870

M iss Ann Empson was a lady of singular, not to say start-ling, appearance. She was tall and spare and grey, and she scowled a great deal. And when she was not scowling, her face wore a fell and determined expression, as if life were a battle that must be fought to the bitterest of bitter ends.

Miss Ann Empson was conspicuously unmarried, and it was clear from the very severe and resolute tone with which she declared her state of spinsterhood in court that she had nev-er contemplated matrimony and never would, which came as something of a relief to London's eligible bachelors as Miss Empson was not an easy person. Not at all an easy person.

Miss Ann Empson maintained a small establishment at num-ber 46 Davies Street, in the fashionable environs of Bond Street, where she condescended to let lodgings – chambers, as she grandly termed them – to suitable single gentlemen with an irreproachable character. But such suitable single gentlemen rarely stayed for long after they discovered, in very short order, that Miss Ann Empson was a fire-breathing Dragon, clearly descended from a long and distinguished line of fire-breathing Dragons.

There were long lists of rules and regulations, strictly enforced and invigilated by the indefatigable Miss Empson herself, who policed and patrolled her kingdom with admirable – if fearsome – zeal. Infringements and infractions rarely, if ever, escaped detection, and were invariably punished by a vigorous tongue-lashing or by summary expulsion from her kingdom, and very often by both.

Miss Ann Empson constantly seethed and was always out of temper. If it was not this, it was that. If it was not one thing, it was another. If it was not some*thing*, then it was some*one* giving her cause for complaint. She fumed and smouldered and burned with perpetual indignation and rage at the world, so much so that there were those who swore they detected a faint bituminous odour about her, though it was more likely that these sulphurous exhalations were a consequence of the numerous nips of brandy she felt it necessary to imbibe throughout the day to help settle her stomach.

M iss Ann Empson was still seething, still fuming, even after all this time. It was disgusting. There was no other word for it. She felt physically sick every time she thought about it. Under her roof. In her bed. (Not *her* bed, exactly, but near enough.)

It had all begun so well. Lord Arthur Pelham-Clinton seemed to fit the bill perfectly. Blood, after all, was Blood, and having little or none of that commodity coursing in her own veins, Miss Empson was all the more eager to have a resident gentleman of irreproachable Bloodstock. Lord Arthur was a Lord, the son of the late Duke of Newcastle, no less, and an Honourable Member to boot.

What with it being so close to Christmas, Miss Empson had been resigned to not getting a let for the drawing-room floor until after the festive season had passed. And then Lord Arthur had turned up out of the blue and charmed and delighted her so much that she was putty – yes, *putty* – in his hands. Indeed, so charming and so delightful had he been that she had waived her usual month's deposit, and even advanced him the not inconsiderable sum of ten golden sovereigns on a note of hand. In retrospect, she thought that she must have taken temporary leave of her senses. Either that, or Lord Arthur had unusual powers of Mesmerism which he had exercised in order to make her agree to things that went so very much against the grain.

Matters had not stopped there. Incredibly, given her strict and sacred injunctions against overnight visitors in any shape or form, Miss Empson found herself weakly agreeing to allow Lord Arthur's country cousin, a Mr Ernest Boulton, to stay in Davies Street on those occasions when he was up in town, and she was even persuaded to buy – yes, *buy* – a single bed for that express purpose. As she said, she was putty in his hands. *Putty*.

Things started to go wrong almost immediately. Lord Arthur moved in, and within a day she had smelt a rat. Or rather, two rats, in the form of the two young men – though that was rather a loose description – who arrived very shortly after him. One of them was Mr Boulton, the country cousin, the other a Mr Park – but she could not remember which was which, which was not at all surprising as they seemed to be two peas from more or less the same pod. All she could say with any certainty was that one was dark and one was fair, and that one was pretty and the other plain.

The manner of Miss Ann Empson's giving evidence at Bow Street Magistrates' Court was refreshingly bracing.

'Are you married?' Mr Straight, for the defence, gently enquired of her after she was sworn.

'Certainly not!' she replied with a snort of contempt. 'I am a *single* woman,' she said, glaring at the assembled multitude, daring any or all to contradict her.

It was clear from her abrasive tone that Miss Empson was angry and aggrieved and spoiling for a fight.

Mr Straight tried another tack. 'Have you been drinking this morning?' he asked.

It was a reasonable enough question. The unhealthy pallor that so many fashionable young ladies struggled to achieve by dint of draughts of strong vinegar and copious quantities of ingested chalk was emphatically not exhibited by Miss Ann Empson. She spurned such fashionable conceits and instead defiantly sported a ruddy and flushed complexion entirely congruent with numerous nips of brandy. There was something, too, about the way she slurred certain words, about the gleam and the glaze of her eyes, and about the fixity of her fell expression, which suggested she had not, for the time being at least, taken the Pledge.

'Have you been drinking this morning?' Mr Straight asked again.

'I could not speak so well as I do if I had,' Miss Empson replied combatively. There was loud laughter. For some reason, the spectators crammed into Bow Street appeared to find Miss Empson funny, and she had barely to open her mouth before guffaws of laughter broke out. Miss Empson was simultaneously offended and pleased by the laughter and played up to it wonderfully.

'You had better answer the question,' Mr Flowers the magistrate sternly interjected.

'Have you been to a public house to-day?' demanded Mr Straight.

'On my oath I have not,' answered Miss Empson, swaying slightly. 'I have not had any drink at home. A policeman brought me here in a cab, but I don't know who it was.'

There was much more in the same vein, but slowly, with much difficulty, Mr Straight got down to the meat and drink of Miss Ann Empson's evidence. Lord Arthur Clinton had lodged with her for a fortnight before she was obliged to evict him. Shortly after he had taken possession of his rooms, his young cousin from the country had turned up and enjoyed 'a mutton chop and bitter beer at Lord Arthur's expense' and had stayed that night. So far, so good.

Miss Empson rarely hesitated when it came to exercising her ancient rights and privileges as a landlady and regularly entered her tenants' apartments for a good snoop around while they were out. So on the morning after his country cousin had spent the night, Miss Empson found herself in Lord Arthur's bed-room feeling puzzled and perplexed.

'I was surprised,' she said, 'to see that the new bed I had bought had not been slept in.' Had Lord Arthur's cousin changed his mind and returned to the country? It was possible. But a thorough examination of the bedding suggested that the country cousin had 'slept with Lord Arthur in the same bed', which raised some unpleasant, some very unpleasant, specula-tions in her mind.

A night or two later, while on one of her regular patrols, Miss Empson had seen a woman coming out of Lord Arthur's rooms, which was strictly forbidden under the draconian laws of the establishment.

'I saw Lord Arthur go on tiptoe to let her out,' she said.

'I saw him through the kitchen stairs letting a lady out, as I considered.

'I complained to Lord Arthur that he had brought a woman to my house. He said it was a man. Lord Arthur assured me it was a man. He represented him as his cousin.' But Miss Empson was quite certain of what she had seen. There was no two ways about it. It was a woman.

'I complained of it as an abuse of my latch-key,' Miss Empson declared indignantly, much to the amusement of the public gallery. But, shocking and disgusting as the presence of this woman in her house was, at least it put paid to those earlier and very unpleasant speculations.

A day or so later, she had caught the two young men, Mr Boulton and Mr Park, in the very act of moving in, which again was strictly forbidden. This sort of cheap trick might pass unnoticed in certain common lodging houses, but it would not do in Davies Street. It would not do at all. There they were, bold as brass, in Lord Arthur's rooms with their boxes just brought up and about to be unpacked. Miss Empson confronted them.

'I said to them, "You have brought your boxes up, and I will make you take them down." I did so. One of them turned round and said, "I wish never to see your house again," and I replied "I'll take good care you don't."

'He said, "Why not?" and I replied, "Because I let the rooms to Lord Arthur Pelham Clinton."'

'I'm not having this,' she told them in no uncertain terms. 'I *will* not have it. I *shall* not have it.'

Miss Empson was ruddy with the glow of this remembered triumph and glared out defiantly at the courtroom, armed and ready to repel all boarders, doubters and naysayers.

Not long after this, Miss Empson mounted an expedition

deep into the heart of Lord Arthur's territory. No stone was to be left unturned, no drawer unopened, no letter unread. She went through everything with a fine-tooth comb. She pried and probed and poked about her, and she was rewarded, if that was the right word, by the discovery of an entire wardrobe of 'lady's wearing apparel: bracelets, necklets, chignons and the like, silk dresses, shawls and everything that ladies wear, kid boots and more'. There were pots of paint and rouge and powder, and an assortment of other feminine necessities, the particulars of which she felt it indecorous to enter into.

Miss Empson put two and two together. It dawned upon her that when Lord Arthur said that the woman he had surreptitiously let out was a man, he was almost certainly telling the truth. Miss Empson was shocked and revolted. Under her roof, in her bed. If that was their pretty game then they were out, out on their ears, that very night. Of one thing she was sure. She would need a nip or two of brandy – and probably several nips – before her stomach could be settled that night.

In Bow Street Magistrates' Court, Miss Empson was confused. Boulton and Park were there in the dock and she recognised them both as the two young men she had turned out. One was dark and one was fair. One was plain and one was pretty (though not so pretty now, she noticed with satisfaction). But which was Boulton and which was Park? Lord Arthur had told her that his country cousin was called Boulton, but surely this could not be so. In court, Boulton had been identified as the dark, pretty one, but she was as sure as sixpence that the young man who had spent the night in Lord Arthur's bed, the young man whom she had seen dressed as a woman, was the plain, fair one. She pointed to him in the dock.

'The prisoner nearest to me – Park – who I call Boulton, is

the one who slept with Lord Arthur,' she said. 'That is the one. It was the one with the golden hair.'

Fanny shifted uncomfortably on the hard wooden bench of the dock as she was fingered by the redoubtable Miss Empson. She did not like to be reminded so graphically of her all-too-brief and doomed liaison with her sister's husband. Needless to say, Arthur had fallen at the first fence. Under interrogation by Stella he had crumpled and confessed all, and even tried to save his own sorry and scrawny neck by implying that it was Fanny who had made all the running.

Stella had been incandescent with rage. She did not know which was worse: Arthur's infidelity or Fanny's betrayal. But if she blamed anyone, she blamed Fanny. Arthur was weak, in-decisive and painfully susceptible to flattery. Stella could well imagine how Fanny had flattered and simpered, and simpered and flattered until poor foolish Arthur did not know whether he was coming or going, at which point Fanny would have pounced like a cat on its unsuspecting prey.

There had been tears and tantrums, scenes and slappings. Arthur was devastated and appalled. Fanny could only hang her head in shame and beg her sister's forgiveness. But Stella was adamant. She renounced her husband, disowned her sister and did what all sensible married women should do in such cir-cumstances: she went home to her Mamma.

17

'Come Love'

Love is a pretty pedlar
Whose pack is fraught with sorrows,
With doubts and fears,
With sighs and tears,
Some joys – but those he borrows.

Robert Jones,
'The Muses Gardin for Delights', 1610

Why Stella had even bothered to keep this short note was a mystery. It had been hurriedly scrawled in pencil on a torn and crumpled half-sheet of paper. Stella was not much given to keeping billets-doux. She was so accustomed to receiving letters from ardent swains and besotted beaux that she had become careless of such epistolary declarations. And in comparison to so many of the epic letters of love and adoration and despair that she received from young and not-so-young gentlemen, this short note barely ranked as a Valentine.

It was addressed in a decidedly shaky script to 'Mr Ernest Boulton at Mrs Dickson's, 118 Princes Street, Edinburgh' and contained the briefest of brief messages:

Darling Erné,
    Do come up tonight. Everybody is too drunk to mind. Donald is here and wants to see you. Come love.

Always for ever thine.

JSF

Bring Mr P.

'JSF' were the initials of Mr John Safford Fiske, the United States Consul in Edinburgh, who had recently fallen head over heels in love with Stella Boulton. 'Donald' was Donald Sinclair, a friend and fellow sodomite of John Safford Fiske. And the mysterious 'Mr P.' of the postscript was Harry Park, Fanny Park's older brother, who was spending a few days in Edinburgh with Stella. Eight years earlier, Harry had fled a charge of 'having indecently exposed himself and trying to incite a Police-Constable to commit an indecent offence'. Now, as 'Mr Charles Ferguson', Harry was living quietly in the out-of-the-way and unpronounceable small town of Lesmahagow in Lanarkshire, or Abbey Green, as its more anglicised and prosperous residents preferred to call it.

T he year 1869 had not been kind to Miss Stella Boulton. In fact, it was decidedly cruel, beginning with her startling discovery of a brazen and heartless infidelity on the part of her *caro sposo*, Lord Arthur Clinton, with none other than her beloved sister, Mrs Fanny Winifred Graham (*née* Park).

It had, according to Arthur, only happened the once, in fearsome Miss Ann Empson's drawing-room floor in Davies Street. But once was enough. Of course, she blamed Fanny. Arthur was easily led and it was not the first time that he had had his head turned by the tricks and wiles of a designing and unscrupulous woman.

It was a bitter blow. She tore up the cards engraved with that luminous title 'Lady Arthur Clinton' and reverted to her maiden name. She was now just plain Miss Stella Boulton (though her many gallant admirers would protest vociferously at the epithet 'plain' when applied to the lovely Miss Stella).

It was perhaps as well that she had returned home to Peckham Rye. Within weeks she was ill. Very ill. Gravely ill. It had all begun a year or so earlier with a nasty suppurating boil on her anus (or her 'arse-quim' as Fanny was fond of calling it). She had been under the care of Dr Hughes, who treated the sore with the vigorous application of poultices, ointments, antiseptics, douches, injections, disinfectants and dressings, as well as supplying her with a formidable battery of different medicines. Nothing seemed to work.

She had suffered from it almost constantly while she was living with Arthur, and, really, was it any wonder that she was so often out of sorts, short-tempered and snappish? But Stella had winced and grimaced with the pain and carried on as if nothing was the matter. Someone, after all, had to pay the rent and put food on the table, and as Arthur was so mired in debt and seemingly so incapable of earning money, it was left to her to manage matters as best she could. So Stella still had to go out on the pad, tattered and torn, and instead of moaning with pleasure, real or simulated, she moaned with pain. It was all the same to the punters. Stella sighed. The things she did for love.

Dr Hughes had been called to the house and his manner had been very grave and subdued. He said that the boil had turned into an abscess and now the abscess had turned into a *fistula in ano*. Stella was not exactly sure what a *fistula in ano* was. All that she knew was that it was agonisingly painful, and that the longer it went on, the worse it became. Dr Hughes said if Stella did not submit to the knife, he would not answer for the consequences. Indeed, matters had reached such a pass that even with an operation, there was no guarantee of success. Any delay would be fatal.

T he operation was a success. Within a fortnight Stella was feeling better, and the pain was very much diminished. In time, Dr Hughes assured her, it would disappear altogether.

One consequence of this near brush with death was that Fanny was forgiven and the sisters were reconciled. Upon being informed of the gravity of Stella's illness, Fanny rushed to her sister's bed of sickness and begged for forgiveness. It was graciously granted. Stella was not one to hold a grudge. Besides, she missed Fanny more than she cared to admit. Husbands and lovers might come and go, but when all was said and done, the love of a sister was rarer and more precious than rubies and pearls.

As the spring turned to summer, and the summer turned to autumn, Stella was very much improved in health. But she felt increasingly restless in Peckham Rye. Having been mistress of her own establishment, such as it was, in Southampton Street, it was hard for her to bow to the superior claims of her Mamma to be mistress in her own house. So when, in late September, Louis Hurt invited her to go and spend a few months with him in Edinburgh for a change of air, Stella accepted with alacrity. However dark and damp and dour Edinburgh in the winter might be, at least she would be free, like a bird set free from a gilded cage.

During her convalescence, there had been moments of reflection and introspection when she questioned whether she had done the right thing in giving Louis up. There was much to recommend him. He was tall and handsome. He was from a good family. Like Arthur he had been educated at Eton, but unlike Arthur, he had made his own way in the world. He was hard-working, sensible and solvent. His prospects were good, and most importantly of all, he was utterly devoted to her.

Louis had courted her assiduously and her Mamma, always determined – over-determined, perhaps – to see her marry well, had entertained the highest hopes for the match. Louis was always a welcome visitor at Peckham Rye, often spending as much as a fortnight with them before rushing off to remote and rustic places to inspect post offices.

But Stella had always had her doubts. In truth, Louis was more than a little dull. He was strict and strait-laced. He did not approve of her career. He did not approve of drag. He did not approve of her campish ways. He did not approve of her going out on the pad. He did not approve of unpaid bills, un-made beds, dirt, disorder or disarray.

Louis was reluctant to call her Stella. He called her Ernest, or Ernie, but never Stella. And though he never exactly put it into words, Stella sensed that he disapproved of her friendship with Fanny. All he wanted her to do was to behave herself, to conform, to grow her moustache, to be more manly and mas-culine, to be less mincing and to try to be Ernest Boulton, the beloved boy of Louis Hurt. Now, at a time when she felt weak and helpless, Louis's strong arms, his unfaltering love and his certainty seemed very appealing.

S tella's worst fears about Edinburgh were not fully realised. It was certainly dark and damp and dour, but it was also austerely beautiful, and the cold winds from the North Sea were refreshing and invigorating after the fugs and smogs of London. Louis had been there for a year or more and had com-fortable chambers in Princes Street, in the very heart of the city.

Mrs Dickson, the landlady, seemed to be a good soul, and mercifully there was none of that poking and prying about of uppity servant girls that had so plagued Stella at Mrs Peck's in Southampton Street.

There was bound to be a fly in the ointment, though, and this time the people who lived above were being tedious, as people who live above generally are, and had complained about the noise of the piano, most especially about her 'playing weekday tunes on the Sabbath'. Mrs Dickson had tactfully requested Stella to 'leave it off on a Sunday'.

There was much to discover, much to learn and much to enjoy. Stella professed herself charmed by everything she found, even though in her heart of hearts she still sometimes hankered after London, after Coventry Street and the Haymarket, after the Alhambra and the Burlington Arcade, after the theatres and the streets and the shops, after that great erotic tide that bore down upon her and engulfed her, sweeping her up and taking her where it willed.

Stella had only to set foot in the streets of Edinburgh to draw gasps and stares. Many, but by no means all, of these gasps and stares were hostile. The rest were of the bewildered, the curious, the frankly interested and the downright flirtatious variety. Stella revelled in the attention. 'Nothing like him had ever been seen in Edinburgh before,' Mr John Doig, a colleague of Louis's, declared. 'He was spoken about a great deal, and a great number of people expressed doubts about his sex.'

There was no shortage of gentlemen callers. In fact, there was a surfeit. Stella's debut in Edinburgh caused quite a stir in certain circles and in no time at all she was besieged on all fronts by beaux. There was that roguish rough diamond, Mr John Jameson Jim, who, after a severe bout of brain fever (brought on, he confessed, 'by drinking and girls'), had seen the light and abruptly transferred his gruff and manly attentions to Stella, falling for her hook, line and sinker. 'Have you the same love as ever for me?' he would write in the plaintive and pleading tone of a lovesick youth.

Or there was plain and honest Jack from the small town of Musselburgh, just outside Edinburgh, who, not to put too fine a point on it, was desperate to pass a night with Stella, and not solely for the charm of her conversation. Plain and honest Jack favoured a bold and direct approach when it came to matters of the heart. '*Will* you stay tonight?' he demanded in pencil. 'You are a *great* cow if you don't.'

Or the very charming and helpful young man behind the counter at Messrs Kensington and Jenner who had been so understanding and so accommodating in the matter of a new gown in silk moiré for Stella which she ordered on the last day of March. He had given her such a knowing look, a loaded look so redolent of meaning, that Stella blushed and hardly knew where to put herself.

And finally there was Mr John Safford Fiske, who was as fine a specimen of American manhood as she had yet met. He was tall, but not too tall; muscular, athletic and lithe; manly and masculine, with sensual lips and large soulful eyes which melted her heart – as well as various other organs – when their loving gaze turned upon her.

Fortune had always smiled upon Mr John Safford Fiske. He had led a charmed and happy existence and was, in consequence, charming and happy. From the moment of his birth to parents of modest means in the small and unexceptional town of Ashtabula on the shore of Lake Erie, a benevolent Fate had steered John Safford Fiske safely through the treacherous waters of life. All those who knew him (or knew of him) were convinced that he was destined for great things.

His talents were prodigious. At Yale he had demonstrated a facility for languages, both living and dead, and for history, ancient and modern. He had a passion for literature, especially for poetry, and was conspicuously widely and well read. But he was no dry and dreary scholar, slowly desiccating in his tower of ivory. Here was a manly man, a man of strong ruddy flesh and bright ruby blood, fleet of foot, sound in wind and limb, a man well-endowed with strength and courage as well as virtue and learning.

When, after a distinguished career at Yale, John Safford Fiske accepted the position of Deputy Clerk for the New York State Senate in Albany, there were those who prophesied a bright future in the world of politics or the world of diplomacy, or both. He exuded trust and integrity, and he effortlessly married an innate authority with an easy charm. People looked to him and up to him. They relied on him to frame arguments, suggest solutions, resolve disputes and generally make the world a better place.

John Safford Fiske himself entirely concurred with all these estimations and expectations of greatness to come. He had always held that Fortune and Fate helped those who helped themselves, which was why, in the summer of 1867, he had not hesitated to take the bold step of writing directly to Mr William H. Seward, United States Secretary of State, to ask, quite charmingly, for the position of United States Consul in Edinburgh. He was supported in his application by Judge Joseph Mullin of Watertown, New York, who praised his protégé as 'a young man of unblemished character, perfect integrity and unquestionable ability'.

Appointing Mr Fiske as United States Consul, Judge Mullin wrote, 'will do no discredit to the department or the country' and will 'aid a young man who is destined to do honour to both'. Mr Fiske 'intends devoting himself to literature', Judge Mullin continued, and 'seeks a place abroad with the aim of extending his knowledge of man'.

The application was successful and so, in the autumn of 1867, the twenty-nine-year-old Mr John Safford Fiske arrived in the New Athens ready and eager to take up his consular duties. They were not especially arduous. Much of his work was ceremonial. Going here and going there. Attending this and attending that. Receptions, banquets, balls and dinners. Listening, smiling, being charming. He was admirably suited to such duties. With his strength, wisdom, youth and vigour allied to an absolute certainty of his own destiny, Mr John Safford Fiske was the perfect embodiment of his young nation's values and aspirations, of its sense of its own importance and of its coming greatness.

John Safford Fiske had a plan. He wanted to marry, and to marry well. He would need a wife, a wife with a fortune to place at his disposal so that he could fulfil his literary and his political ambitions. His present means were more than adequate to meet his needs, but even in the great democracy of the United States, it was money that talked, and talked the loudest; money that opened doors; money that made the world turn; money that bought influence and brought power. He needed money, and the fastest and easiest way to acquire money, and lots of it, was to marry, and to marry well.

In fact, Mr John Safford Fiske was preparing to surrender himself to matrimony. Fortune and Fate had again smiled upon him and provided him with a young, beautiful and charmingly dressed heiress. She was American, born and bred into one of the best and oldest families on the East Coast, so he could be quite sure of her pedigree.

She was coming to Edinburgh in the spring. She was coming to see him. She was expecting him to propose to her and he was determined to do so. They would marry that summer and then, after a year or two in Edinburgh, he would be appointed ambassador, perhaps to London or to Paris, where he would live in splendour and serve with distinction before returning to Washington and the Senate.

John Safford Fiske's attitude to marriage was modelled on that of the Ancient Greeks. Marriage was a duty and a necessity. The world must turn, children must be born and the sacred cycle of nature perpetuated. Men needed wives for dynastic purposes and for domestic harmony. But he would reserve his love and his lust for boys and for young men, as he had done, carefully, discreetly and quietly, throughout most of his adult life. Women for duty, but boys for pleasure.

Of course there would be curbs on his freedoms. As a married man, he would have responsibilities towards his bride, but as soon as the children came, he hoped that he might be left alone to pursue young men. 'After we were married I could do pretty much as I pleased,' he mused. 'People don't mind what one does on £30,000 a year, and the Lady wouldn't much mind as she hasn't brains enough to trouble herself about much beyond her dresses, her carriage etc.'

From the moment of his arrival in Edinburgh he had sought out 'adventures', as he called them, and had established a delightful network of charming and handsome young men, including the brothers Donald and Robbie Sinclair. It was Robbie to whom he felt closest, Robbie with 'his smiling face', his 'clear gray eyes' and the 'vivid roses' in his cheeks – or so it was until the fateful moment when Stella Boulton swept into Edinburgh like the devouring North Wind and turned his world upon its head.

There were women and there were men and then there was Stella. John Safford Fiske had never before met anyone like her and he knew for a certainty that he would never do so again. She was fascinating. She was compelling. She seemed to him to be half-man and half-woman, but more, infinitely more, than the sum of her two parts. Stella was, he wrote, 'Laïs and Antinous in one'. An amalgam, a coalescence, of Laïs the Corinthian, the most famous, the most beautiful and the most expensive courtesan of the Ancient World, the muse of Demosthenes, and Antinous, the most beautiful and most beloved boy of the Emperor Hadrian. It was, he wrote, 'a ravishing thought'.

Who could fail to fall in love with two such beings, united in one perfect body? Fiske knew he was powerless to resist. It was more than love, more than lust. It was a kind of madness. A rapture. He could not sleep and he could not eat. Thoughts of Stella, in drag or out of drag, as a man, as a woman or as a hermaphrodite, filled his waking and sleeping hours. His chambers became a secret shrine to Stella, where he would worship her votive images in the privacy of his bedroom and hold her four carelessly written little notes about inconsequentialities in a bundle to his heart and feel a terrible joy and exultation.

He wanted her. More than he wanted anything else. More than he wanted a wife and a fortune. More than he wanted power and glory. More, perhaps, than life itself. He knew only too well that the more he wanted her, the more he risked all. But he was prepared to give up everything for her.

'Come love,' John Safford Fiske hastily wrote in pencil to Stella. 'Always for ever thine.' Despite its brevity, despite its drunken scrawl, this torn and crumpled half-sheet of paper was nonetheless as ardent and authentic a declaration of enduring love as Stella had yet received, which was perhaps why she treasured this brief note so much and kept it clasped to her breast.

18

Un Souvenir d'Amour

All Cracks are found so full of Ails
A *New Society* prevails
Call'd Sodomites; Men worse than Goats,
Who dress themselves in Petticoats.

John Dunton, *The He-Strumpets:*
A Satyr on the Sodomite-Club,
1707

Miss Fanny Winifred Park, also known as Mrs Fanny Graham, as Miss Vivian Gray (and by a variety of names
unfit for polite ears), was beginning to feel decidedly worried.
The sore on her bottom which had first appeared in January
had not gone away. If anything, it was getting worse and becoming more painful. At first she had assumed, quite naturally
and quite reasonably, that it was a mere wound of love; a
passing soreness and discomfort; a consequence of being
rather too energetically sodomised. In any event, she had decided to rest up for a few days and be deliciously *hors de
combat*. She would allow things to settle, to right themselves,
before venturing forth again with renewed vigour and renewed
appetite. Not that her appetite in that department could ever be
described as feeble. *Quite* the reverse. But the soreness had not
gone away, and now she was feeling extremely uncomfortable
and very low.

It was a nuisance that both Stella and Harry – the two people who might best advise her – were in Scotland: Stella selfishly still ensconced in Edinburgh with her former paramour, Louis Hurt, and Harry officially still in disgrace and in hiding, though Stella had confidentially informed her that Harry was being *very* indiscreet. Short of travelling all the way to *l'Ecosse*, she had no one to give her counsel. One or two friends, though, had bravely hazarded a look at her bottom, and amid some extremely vulgar and very unwelcome general observations, the particulars of which she need not enter into, said they thought that her poor cunny looked *very* sore.

What was she to do? If it was – horror of horrors – the pox, she could hardly go to the family doctor, explain that she had been sodomised to the point of insensibility and was now suffering from *un souvenir d'amour*. She was not sure she could trust him to keep quiet, and if it got out it would kill her poor Papa. Even if she went to another doctor, there might well be tiresome questions, and there was no guarantee that the police would not be dragged in.

Chancre of the anus or a pox in the arse was rather more common – at least in women – than most doctors either knew or cared to admit. It was a distasteful aspect of an already disagreeable branch of diagnosis. National honour no less than national decency was at stake. William Allingham, a doctor specialising in diseases of the rectum, was, like many others, convinced that anal sex (and in consequence, anal syphilis) was altogether a Continental, and specifically a French, phenomenon. 'In France this cannot be uncommon,' he asserted. 'I trust it is not common in America. I cannot say that in this country it is altogether unknown, but I hope and think it is infrequent.'

William Acton, the most celebrated venereologist of the age, agreed. Appearances were deceptive. The 'immense prevalence' of anal warts in female prostitutes in the metropolis of London might lead some to conclude that there was an equally immense prevalence of anal sex. 'Foreigners noticing these appearances in our foul wards go away fully convinced that unnatural crimes are very common in London,' he wrote. But 'a greater error than this cannot occur'. According to Acton, anal warts in female prostitutes were simply vaginal warts that had migrated.

This theory of migration was equally useful to Acton and his colleagues in explaining away those cases of anal syphilis which did present themselves. Syphilis in the vagina migrated to the anus either by discharges from syphilitic chancres in the vagina 'running down' to the anus, or through menstrual fluids following the same route. Sometimes anal syphilis might be the consequence of accidental or stray contact between the penis and the female anus, of the sort that might reasonably be expected to occasionally occur in the throes of passion. But the most obvious explanation, that anal syphilis was a consequence of anal sex, was an unwanted and unwelcome truth, a truth better buried than bruited abroad.

In a break with tradition, George Drysdale, a doctor and pioneering sexologist, was considerably more frank than most of his English colleagues when he stated that anal syphilis was 'frequently to be seen in the female venereal hospitals'. Anal sex was, he said, commonplace among female prostitutes. 'There are very few of the older prostitutes', he said, 'who do not lend themselves to these practices, as well as many of the younger ones; however, they always maintain an obstinate silence when questioned on this point.'

There was a long-held suspicion that some men turned to

sodomy as a way of avoiding venereal disease. As early as 1707, in *The He-Strumpets: A Satyr on the Sodomite-Club*, the playwright John Dunton attributed the growing popularity of sodomy to an epidemic of the clap among female prostitutes. The poem 'Don Leon', a paean in praise of sodomy supposedly written by Lord Byron, suggested that sodomy with boys was a specific against being 'infected with rank disease'. And the anonymous author of *Extraordinary Revelations*, the penny pamphlet about Fanny and Stella, described sodomy as an 'abomination by which lust defies disease'.

Although reports of rectal syphilis and gonorrhoea in men were uncommon, they were not unheard of. In 1851, the French syphilologist Philippe Ricord recounted the cautionary tale of 'G—', a young man of twenty-five, 'of a good constitution, and enjoying excellent health', who consulted him about 'a recent cutaneous eruption' of ulcers around his anus 'for which he pretended he could assign no cause'. Ricord was convinced that these ulcers were syphilitic chancres. He cross-questioned the young man who finally confessed that:

> after a dinner party, when too liberal a quantity of generous wine had made him lose his reason and forget his manliness, he had slept with a friend, to whose beastly appetite he had sacrificed himself. He remembered having suffered greatly during the connection, and having passed blood on the following and subsequent days.

George Drysdale was once again out of step with his colleagues when, in 1861, he asserted that 'sodomy is common enough, especially in the prisons, where the most uneducated and degraded of the community, being shut up together, and left in idleness, take this mode of passing the listless hours':

> Instances now and then occur of gonorrhoea and chancre of the anus, which the patients, when pressed hard, either confess, or tacitly admit to having been contracted by these unnatural practices, though at first they always deny that the disease has such an origin, and ascribe it to an unclean water-closet &c.

Henry James Johnson, a former surgeon at the London Lock Hospital, which specialised in treating venereal diseases in female prostitutes and among the poor, had come across a very severe case of chancre of the anus in a man which strongly suggested that it was a consequence of anal sex. 'I saw one case which I did not doubt must have been a case of that description,' he testified at Fanny and Stella's trial. The state of this man's anus could, he said, admit of no other explanation but that he had been 'repeatedly' sodomised. 'At the time we were perfectly convinced of it.'

D esperate circumstances called for desperate measures. Miss Fanny Winifred Park was by now all but certain that she had contracted the pox. She still hoped for the best, at the same time fearing the worst. It was just conceivable that it might yet turn out to be some kind of local irritation, an ulcerating pile, perhaps, or something akin to Stella's fistula. But Fanny had an awful feeling that it was syphilis. The pain from the sore was excruciating; she could not sit and she could not sleep. That she needed to see a doctor, and sharpish, was not in dispute. But which doctor?

She had heard from friends that sometimes the doctors in the hospitals and the dispensaries asked fewer questions when confronted by young men with problems in their bottoms. Getting the required letter of recommendation from a subscriber to the hospital's charitable fund was the easy part. That was not difficult to obtain if you mixed in the right society and made up a story about some respectable young man of your acquaintance who had fallen upon hard times and could not afford to see a doctor.

Armed with her ticket-of-admission letter, Fanny would transform herself into that respectable young man. She would dress herself up in appropriate clothing, not her own well-cut suits from her Papa's tailor, but the sort of clothes that would have come from a fripperer's shop; second-, or third- or fourth-hand; frayed and worn and cheap, and probably none too clean. It was like dragging up, Fanny thought to herself, only in reverse.

Renowned as she was for playing 'principally dowagers' on the amateur and semi-professional stage, Fanny was convinced that she could give this particular role her all. After all, she had had plenty of experience of young men from the lower strata of society. Like her older brother Harry, she had a decided and definite penchant for the working men of London; a fascination, a reverence for their animal instincts, for their strangely hesitant and yet passionate approach to the business of fucking which so exactly coincided with her own needs. She knew them inside-out. She knew what clothes they wore, down to their undergarments; she knew how they spoke, how they acted, how they smelt. She would give the performance of her life.

She would become that shy young man, a mercer's clerk,

perhaps, who had unaccountably got this sore on his bottom.
If the doctor asked point-blank how she – or rather, he – had
acquired it he/she would blush and hang his/her head in shame
and say that he/she had been drunk and could remember nothing at all. If there was any funny business, if there was the least
sign of the police being called, she could leg it. All the hospital
would have was a false name and a description of a shabbily
dressed young man who might have been a clerk.

Fanny turned up at Charing Cross Hospital one afternoon
in mid-February dressed in an old cutaway coat and 'wearing a
pair of shabby plaid trousers'. As part of her disguise she had
not shaved for two or three days. The hospital was very busy,
and clearly she would have to wait for a long time. She paced
up and down, down and up the long stone corridor waiting to
be called. She could not sit still on the hard wooden benches
that lined both sides of the corridor, partly because of the pain
of the sore on her bottom, and partly because of nerves. She
was always nervous before a performance.

'He was walking backwards and forwards in the passages,'
the hospital hall porter, George Layton, recalled, 'which is contrary to the rules of the hospital and I asked him to take a seat.'
Fanny was on the point of issuing the sharpest of sharp retorts,
but recollecting where she was and why she was there, bit her
lip and duly took a seat on a wooden bench.

S omething very strange had happened this year. Not one,
not two, but *three* young men – three in almost as many
weeks – had presented themselves in Dr Richard Barwell's consulting room at Charing Cross Hospital with afflictions of the
rectum. Was it a coincidence, or was there something more singular going on – something more sinister? He had dealt with

the first case summarily. The young man – a rather common specimen and gaudily dressed – had turned up one afternoon in early February complaining of a sore on his bottom. Dr Barwell's suspicions were aroused by the young man's rather affected, effeminate way of speaking. Naturally he had enquired of this young man how long he had had this sore and how it might have come about. Was it some sort of injury? The young man hesitated. In a manner of speaking, yes, he said, it was a sort of injury. He smiled a confiding sort of smile. And then he admitted everything.

'He confessed to the act of sodomy,' Dr Barwell recounted indignantly in court. 'He confessed how he had got this sore, so cynically – almost *boastfully*, or *jauntily*, I should rather have said – that I would have nothing to do with him. I drove him away.'

Dr Barwell rarely lost his temper, but on this occasion with this young man, he had lost his temper badly, very badly indeed. He had, quite literally, driven this young sodomite away, pushing the frightened youth out of his consulting room and propelling him down the corridor while people looked curiously on. He had thought about it many times since and always with revulsion. It was not so much the affliction that he objected to. He had seen dozens of cases of syphilis of the anus before, invariably in women, and he had shrugged his shoulders and treated them. Such things went on, and he would not sit in judgement. Even the fact that this was a case of syphilis of the anus in a young man, revolting as that was, rare as that was – for he had never seen another case – even that fact was not the cause of his loss of control. Nor was it simply the absence of any remorse, any sense of shame, on the part of the young man, shocking as that was. No, what had made him lose his reason, what had driven him over the edge, was this young man's evident *pleasure* – pleasure which seemed to be commingled with *pride* – pride in the act of sodomy; a pleasure that he had the temerity to boast about; a pleasure that he assumed, that he presumed, others would understand and somehow share. That was what had made Dr Barwell see such violent red.

In just a matter of days, another man had fetched up in his consulting room. Dr Barwell had asked what the matter was, and after some hesitation the man said he thought he was suffering from 'a gonorrhoeal discharge, as he himself called it, from the anus'. Dr Barwell was taken aback. The man was nondescript; neither young nor old, not obviously effeminate, and he clearly had some education. Most of Dr Barwell's patients would never even have heard of the word 'gonorrhoea', let alone use the word in front of him. The man was civil and had the grace to look somewhat ashamed of himself. Dr Barwell decided that he would treat him.

Dr Barwell could not now believe that yet a third man had turned up with a venereal affliction of the rectum. The young man sitting nervously in front of him was dressed in 'rather common clothing' which was a little too tight upon his slim frame. He had a sore bottom, he explained, or rather, a sore upon his bottom that would not heal or go away. Dr Barwell looked at him sharply. The young man seemed reluctant to meet his eyes and hung his head as if he were ashamed of himself. How had this sore originated, he asked, and for how long had he had it? The young man hesitated. About three or four weeks, he thought. And he had no idea how he came by it. Dr Barwell could tell he was lying but said nothing.

S o far, so good, thought Fanny to herself. The rather stern-looking doctor had given her one or two very penetrating glances before asking her to bend over and drop her trousers. That, at least, was something she was well practised in. She wanted to giggle but repressed herself sternly. At least he was examining her and would, presumably, treat her. It was all going according to plan. She winced with pain as the doctor parted her buttocks.

'I examined him and found a syphilitic sore upon the anus, a primary sore,' Dr Barwell recalled. 'It was an open sore, called a chancre, and the anus gaped sufficiently to show the mucous membrane, and the sore upon it. The sore was at the back part of the anus, on the edge of the margin of the mucous membrane.'

There was no doubt in Dr Barwell's mind that this young man's chancre 'would have been communicated by a person who had the disease, and not by slight or mere contact'. While he could not be absolutely certain that this young man had been sodomised (though the gaping anus strongly suggested that he had), at the very least there had been direct and prolonged sexual contact between a syphilitic penis and this young man's anus.

The sore was not the worst he had ever seen, but nor was it slight either. 'With energetic treatment such a sore would be healed in two months or ten weeks, sometimes much sooner,' Dr Barwell said. He gave Fanny a battery of medicines: iodide of mercury, bichloride of mercury, iodide of potash and a weak solution of carbolic acid as a mild disinfectant.

Twice a week, every week, as winter turned into spring, Fanny put on the same old cutaway coat and the same shabby plaid trousers and attended Dr Barwell's surgery at Charing

Cross Hospital in character as a poor but respectable clerk.
Dr Barwell remained stern and aloof, and Fanny knew better
than to engage him in conversation. Sometimes he would examine her bottom and sometimes merely take her own account.
Mercifully, the sore was healing, and Fanny learnt to recognise
the little grunt of approval Dr Barwell made when things were
progressing well.

In April 1870, after almost two months of treatment,
Fanny's visits to the hospital abruptly ceased. Dr Barwell was
mildly surprised, as this person had been assiduous in keeping
his appointments. But it was common for attendance to fall off
once the sore had healed. This young man was almost cured,
though not quite, and Dr Barwell would have liked to have
continued seeing him for a few more weeks yet.

But before he knew it there were two policemen standing
on the doorstep of his house on a Saturday morning in the
middle of May. A young man had been arrested upon suspicion
of sodomy, they said, and they 'insisted upon his accompanying them to see if he could identify his patient'. Dr Barwell
refused. He was a doctor, not a policeman, and he would have
no part in these proceedings if he could help it. He had strong
professional obligations of confidentiality, even to avowed or
suspected sodomites, and he was, he said, 'most unwilling to
be mixed up in such an unpleasant business'. But the policemen would not take no for an answer. If Dr Barwell refused,
they would apply to Mr Flowers for a summons, forcing him to
make the identification. And if he refused to answer that summons, he would be in contempt of court and they would arrest
him. He had no choice in the matter.

'And so,' as the *Lancet* reported, 'Dr Barwell was thus most
unwillingly made a witness for the Crown.'

19

The Battle of the Bottoms

'Mamma dear,' said the youth, 'what is the meaning of the word bugger?'

'Bugger, my child? Why do you ask?'

'Because I heard my tutor call the coachman a damn bugger.'

'Well, my child,' replied the Marchioness, 'a bugger is a person who does his fellow an injury behind his back.' Cough.

The consulting room at Newgate Gaol had rarely been so crowded. Crammed inside along with Fanny and Stella, there were no fewer than six doctors, four prison warders, three detectives, two medical orderlies, Mr Abrams the solicitor and a gentleman from the Treasury who was there to represent the public interest. There was barely room to swing a cat.

That afternoon in early June was especially fine and warm, which was all very well outside in God's fresh air, but in the dank and airless confines of Newgate, with its unmistakable and pervasive smell of prison rot – a rank combination of unwashed bodies, disease, sewage, despair and hopelessness – the stench and the heat were overwhelming. Several of the gentlemen in attendance felt decidedly faint, and only the strong odour of carbolic in the consulting room prevented them from actually keeling over.

Fanny and Stella had been transferred to Newgate at the end of May. As the web of conspiracy seemed to grow ever larger, and the case against them assumed greater and greater seriousness, the House of Detention in Coldbath Fields was deemed inadequate to contain such dangerous prisoners.

In Newgate they could be held 'in close prison', or solitary confinement, so that the contagion of sodomy and effeminacy which they both carried within their bodies would not taint the other prisoners. 'We are of the opinion that there is much danger of contamination among younger prisoners,' a Report by the Departmental Committee on Prisons had concluded when considering this very subject. 'They are of an age when curiosity stimulates the inherited or acquired depravity which is so often found in young criminals.'

The extraordinary scene in the consulting room at Newgate Gaol was the consequence of an impasse between the Crown, who wanted unambiguous and unarguable forensic proof that Fanny and Stella had been repeatedly sodomised, and the defence, who wanted to prove the exact opposite.

As things stood, the defence appeared to be at a slight advantage, having already despatched Dr Hughes, Dr Harvey and the splendidly named Dr Le Gros Clark to examine Ernest Boulton and Frederick Park in the House of Detention a fortnight earlier. Their conclusions, reached after a very thorough examination, were the very opposite of those reached by Dr Paul, the police surgeon who had examined Boulton and Park the morning after their arrest, and by Dr Barwell, who said he had treated Park for syphilis of the anus. According to Dr Hughes, Dr Harvey and Dr Le Gros Clark, there was nothing abnormal about these two young men's penises, and nothing in, on or around their anuses or rectums which betrayed any evidence of unnatural crime – just a small scar, a cicatrix, on the outside of Stella's anus where she had been operated upon for *fistula in ano* early in 1869.

Now half a dozen 'eminent medical gentlemen' – from both sides, and from no side, of the argument – would examine these young men for forensic signs of sodomy. And to ensure that everything was above board and out in the open, the examinations would be conducted while they were all assembled together in the consulting room of Newgate Gaol. According to the newspapers the examinations were to take place 'by the direction of the Government', a decision taken at the highest levels, and it was said that the Attorney-General himself had taken personal charge of the case.

'Eminent medical gentlemen' was how they were described in the newspapers, though there was medical eminence and there was medical eminence. The undoubted star of their troupe was Dr Alfred Swaine Taylor of Guy's Hospital. He was remarkable for the fact that he was a Professor twice over, simultaneously holding two chairs at Guy's: in chemistry and in medical jurisprudence. He was the most celebrated medical jurist of his day, having almost single-handedly pioneered the science of forensic medicine.

Dr Taylor's first book, *A Manual of Medical Jurisprudence*, was published in 1836, when he was just thirty years old, and had already run to eight editions. He had appeared as an expert witness in over four hundred trials, and he was feared and loved in equal measure by the guilty and the innocent.

With his shock of dark hair, now streaked with silver, Dr Taylor looked much younger than his sixty-four years. He was insatiably curious about everything, a polymath, with interests ranging from the physics of geology to the chemistry of photography. He was an expert in poisons and in the classification of gunshot wounds, and an early pioneer in the use of chloroform. By a strange coincidence, it was Dr Taylor who had administered chloroform to Ernest Boulton during the operation for *fistula in ano* performed by Dr Hughes at the Boulton family home in Peckham Rye in February 1869.

By an even stranger coincidence, it was Dr Taylor who, thirty-six years earlier, had performed the post-mortem dissection on the young actress Eliza Edwards, and made a startling, not to say disturbing, discovery: Eliza Edwards was in fact a man – of sorts.

By a third bizarre coincidence it was as a student at Dr Taylor's celebrated series of lectures, in the early 1850s, that Dr James Thomas Paul had first heard about sodomy and sodomites, and about young men who dressed as young women. He had been inspired, if that was the right word, to discover more, and it became quite a passion with him. The wheel had turned full circle, but Dr Paul would not be there to meet his old mentor. The defence were adamant. They would not brook his presence.

Hot on the heels of Dr Taylor in the stakes of medical eminence came Dr Frederick Le Gros Clark, Fellow of the Royal College of Surgeons, Examiner of the University of London, Chair of Surgery at St Thomas's Hospital, Examiner of Surgeons to the Royal College of Physicians and so on and so forth. Dr Le Gros Clark was already well acquainted with the private parts of the two young men in women's clothes, having examined them just a fortnight earlier in company with Dr

Hughes and Dr Harvey. None of them could find any sign of sodomy, insertive or receptive, so Dr Le Gros Clark could be counted as a witness for the defence.

The third medical gentleman who could justly lay claim to eminence was Dr Henry James Johnson, a distinguished surgeon who for the best part of forty years had specialised in *les souvenirs d'amour*, the diseases of love. Now nearly seventy, Dr Johnson was still remarkably upright and remarkably active. He had a large private practice in Suffolk Place, off Trafalgar Square, and those gentlemen unfortunate enough to contract a dose would hasten in a closed carriage to his consulting rooms where they could be assured of the best and most up-to-date treatment for their condition.

For two years, from 1832 to 1833, he was the House Surgeon at the old London Lock Hospital, which had been set up in 1746 to provide free treatment for syphilis and other such afflictions to the poor, and it was here that he had developed his formidable knowledge and expertise in all diseases venereal.

In 1851, after recovering from a long illness from which he fully expected to die, he published *Gonorrhoea and Its Consequences*, which was among the first books to argue that gonorrhoea was an infectious disease in its own right: not a local irritation; not a weakened form of syphilis; and emphatically not an unfortunate consequence for the male of the species of those constricting 'vaginal spasms' experienced by women (especially prostitutes) when overly aroused during sexual intercourse.

With Dr Johnson, the real medical eminence of their group ended. Dr William Hughes, who was also one of the party, was of course a highly respected and respectable doctor in general practice in Fenchurch Street, but he could lay no conceivable claim to expertise on the subject of sodomy or post-sodomitic symptoms. Dr Hughes was there for one reason only: having operated on Boulton's fistula a year earlier, he was privy to the pertinent medical history of one of the young men in question.

Equally, Dr Barwell was under no illusions about the reasons for his own presence in the consulting room at Newgate Gaol on this sticky afternoon in June. He was there because, like Dr Hughes, he had compelling and pertinent medical knowledge of one of the defendants: the young man he now knew to be called Frederick Park. Having treated this young man for an unambiguous and unarguable chancre of the anus, he supposed himself to be a witness for the prosecution.

Dr John Rowland Gibson, the Surgeon of Newgate Gaol, was the sixth and final member of this medical troupe. It would have been an impossible professional discourtesy for him not to be present in his own consulting room while the two prisoner-patients under his care and control were examined by colleagues. By any standard of medical etiquette, he had to be present and he had to participate in the proceedings.

To give him his due, Dr Gibson's many years of experience of attending to the medical needs of the very worst of God's creatures must have given him insights into the dark depravities and feralities of the criminal body and the criminal mind, insights not usually granted to doctors. Among Dr Gibson's many duties was to testify as to the sanity – or otherwise – of murderers and rapists and other hardened criminals, and to certify that those executed within the prison walls were properly dead when taken down from the gibbet. With such a rare and unusually solemn practice, Dr Gibson might be expected to detect those outward bodily signs and deformations – visible only to the trained eye – which betrayed the inner diseased pathology of the criminal and the degenerate.

Likewise, with his long experience of criminals, Dr Gibson might well be able to intuit certain incorporeal qualities about his patients, such as patterns of lying, auras of deceit, miasmas of criminality, airs of guilt – or even innocence. In any and in all events, Dr Gibson would bring something different and strange to these very different and very strange proceedings.

Notwithstanding the eminence of the six medical gentlemen present, only three of them had any actual experience of the signs and symptoms of sodomy: Professor Taylor with Eliza Edwards, almost forty years previously; Dr Johnson, who claimed to have seen one certain case of receptive sodomy among the outpatients of the Lock Hospital – again, almost forty years earlier; and Dr Barwell himself, who, after a lifetime of professional innocence in such matters, had this very year seen three young men with afflictions of the rectum in as many weeks. With the best part of 150 years' combined knowledge and experience, these six doctors had examined the back passages of just five confirmed sodomites.

British doctors laboured under a disadvantage when it came to trying to determine whether or not Ernest Boulton and Frederick Park had been sodomised. If it was the case indeed, as one and all were only too ready to proclaim, that sodomy was a rare and alien fungoid in the sexual flora of the British Isles, then it stood to reason that British doctors would neither have, nor need to have, forensic knowledge or experience of the tell-tale signs of sodomy.

It was widely felt that any disagreement between the six eminent medical gentlemen on whether or not these two young men had been sodomised would be detrimental to the reputation of the medical profession. The *Lancet* confessed to 'a feeling of apprehension lest a new scandal may be caused by directly conflicting medical testimony' in 'this very grave case' and felt sufficiently exercised to devote an entire editorial to the delicate subject of knowledge (or rather, the lack of knowledge) of sodomy among English doctors.

So how could a fair verdict be reached, a verdict based on sound scientific principles and on observable forensic evidence? The *Lancet* felt 'most strongly' that the Government 'should place the medical evidence for the prosecution in the hands of a select committee of medical men'. Given the dearth of home-grown experience in 'this very repulsive subject', the *Lancet* urged the Government to recruit the two leading French specialists in sodomy, Monsieur Ricord and Monsieur Tardieu, to work in coalition 'with two English medical men of the highest eminence'.

In the consulting room at Newgate, Fanny and Stella lay upon identical couches, their nakedness covered by coarse brownish sheets with the words 'Newgate Prison' emblazoned in letters three inches high. Both of them were sorry sights now: pale, unshaven and undernourished. Their plucked and tweezered eyebrows were beginning to grow out of shape, and their eyes were dull. Neither of them appeared to evince any surprise at the presence of so many people in the consulting room. Mr Abrams had no doubt warned them what they must expect, and they waited patiently for what they knew must happen.

Apart from the mandatory bath in filthy water upon admission to Newgate Gaol, facilities for washing were almost non-existent. 'The two things most neglected in Her Majesty's prisons are cleanliness and godliness,' recorded one inmate of Newgate. Apart from a damp rag and the occasional basin of brackish water grudgingly allowed before a court appearance, prisoners were unable to keep themselves clean. Fanny and Stella had done their best, but their private parts and their backsides were in an unwashed and decidedly unpleasant state.

Quite apart from the closeness of the room, the malodorous state of Fanny and Stella and the overwhelming stench of prison rot (to which only Dr Gibson seemed oblivious), the atmosphere in the room was tense. As the *Lancet* had prophesied, the medical gentlemen present were in profound and uncomfortable disagreement. The hospitable preliminaries of Dr Gibson had fallen flat, and even Dr Le Gros Clark's fabled 'dignified courtesy of manner' failed to ease the tension.

Each medical gentleman took his turn to examine the two young men. Their genitalia would be looked at first: penis, testicles and scrotum lifted, pulled, squeezed and peered at; foreskin rolled back; and the meatus, the lips of the urethra, pinched and prised apart to see if there was any discharge. Then they would be asked to turn over and lie flat while their buttocks were carefully parted and scrutinised, before they were instructed to stand up and bend over the couch while their anuses were minutely examined.

Dr Johnson had bought with him a large and powerful lens for the purpose of magnification, and also a speculum, the hugely unpopular and painful device shaped like the beak of a duck used to force open the vaginas of prostitutes suspected of being diseased. Which in a way was entirely right and proper, if it was true that these young men had so unmanned themselves, so unsexed themselves, that they had allowed men to use them as common prostitutes.

29th April 1870: An excited crowd looks on as Ernest Boulton and Frederick Park in full drag leave Bow Street Magistrates' Court the morning after their arrest at the Strand Theatre

'And such a stock of togs was there.' The police raid Fanny and Stella's secret dressing-rooms in Wakefield Street and confiscate their entire drag wardrobe

Stella Boulton, 'the most wonderful impersonator of female character ever before the public' with 'the most perfect soprano voice', photographed in Scarborough in October, 1868

'Rose of the Garden, blushing and gay' – the captivating Stella Boulton dressed as a man

Dressed in silk and suitably padded, bewigged and with a very generous application of paint, Fanny made a handsome woman

Fanny (left) – 'a gabbling, good-natured, prattling, gossiping, charming young man', photographed with an unknown gentleman in Chelmsford in 1868

Fanny, with her 'sterner features', had a natural bent for playing domineering duchesses and dowagers of a certain age

A love triangle: Fanny (standing) and Stella (front) with Lord Arthur Pelham -Clinton

Stella and Fanny dressed in character in the sort of drawing-room entertainment they toured to small country houses and market-town assembly rooms

Stella and Charles Pavitt on tour in Essex in 1869

The shocking case of 'The Female Personators' was front-page news all over the country

The Comical Countess and Carlotta Gibbings

Stella, now blonde, in New York circa 1875, in a portrait by the celebrity photographer Napoleon Sarony

Stella as a shepherdess of the golden age, circa 1880

Sisters. Side by side and shoulder to shoulder. Sisters for better or for worse: Stella rests her head on her beloved Fanny's breast

E ven if they had not actually read the controversial works of the sodomite-hunter Professor Ambroise Tardieu, or the marginally less rabid, marginally more rational discourse of his recently deceased German colleague Dr Johann Ludwig Casper, most of the medical gentlemen present had a broad idea of what they were looking for.

There were, Professor Tardieu had decreed, three 'characteristic signs of passive pederasty'. First, *infundibulum*, or a funnel-shaped depression of the anal cleft caused by the intense pressure applied by the penis of the insertive sodomite to the anus of the receptive partner in order to gain ingress.

Second, erasure of the *rugae*, the characteristic puckerings and ridges around the anus. The mechanics of sodomy eroded and erased these *rugae*, literally wore them away, partially or completely, and when such erasure was present, sodomy must be presumed to have been the cause. When, as a young man, Professor Taylor had examined the anus of 'Miss Eliza' Edwards post-mortem, the *rugae* had been entirely obliterated. Such was the alchemy of sodomy that the anus resembled female labia.

Third and most tellingly, excessive or extreme dilation of the anus was invariably apparent to the naked eye. Again, at the post mortem of Eliza Edwards in 1833, it had been 'noticed by all present' that his/her 'anal aperture' was greatly enlarged, 'much wider and larger than natural'.

But in cases where anal dilation was not immediately apparent to the naked eye, it was necessary to test the dilatability of the anus, to discover how quickly it would dilate when stimulated by the repeated insertion of the physician's lubricated finger, imitating, in so far as it was possible, the repeated insertion of the sodomite's erect *membrum virile*. The quicker the dilation, the greater the likelihood that sodomy had been practised.

'Beware,' Tardieu warned doctors. Some sodomites were skilled in evading the detection of anal dilation. 'They clench their buttocks, but it will suffice to quickly change position, or put them on their knees in a kneeling position, or simply prolong the examination until they tire of contracting their muscles, to triumph over this gross fraud.'

There could have been little danger of Fanny and Stella clenching their buttocks so as to deceive the doctors. Six doctors, six fingers, and multiple insertions by each doctor meant that by the end of the examinations, which lasted well over two hours, the dilatability or otherwise of their anal sphincters became almost meaningless.

The examinations were conducted in almost complete silence. There was no discussion, no commentary, no exchanges of opinion, save one when Dr Barwell pointed out to Dr Johnson a scar on the prisoner Park's anus which, he said in a triumphant tone, was the scar left behind by the syphilitic chancre he had treated some months earlier.

But Dr Johnson politely begged to differ. 'No,' he said. 'That is only a small varix,' a varicose vein. 'It was quite small. It was not so big as a marrow fat pea – hardly so large as an ordinary garden pea,' he said later.

Dr Johnson used his magnifying glass and examined the supposed scar more closely. 'What you see is nothing but the light reflected from the glistening side of the varix. There is no scar whatever,' he told Dr Barwell. 'I then handed him the glass to look for himself and he declined it, implying that he could see as well, I suppose, without a magnifying glass as with one. At any rate he declined it.'

By the time the examinations were completed, the heads of all those nineteen persons present were spinning with the heat and the stench and the strangeness of the task they had been engaged in.

Of the six doctors present, five were agreed that there were no signs of sodomy present upon the bodies of the prisoners, no scars or cicatrices consequent upon a syphilitic chancre, no evidence to suggest unnatural practices – apart from a certain feyness, a certain delicacy, a certain femininity (more marked in Boulton than in Park, but nonetheless present in both). Dr Barwell alone dissented.

All six were however agreed that the *rugae* had been partially obliterated around Park's anus, with five of them reading little or nothing into this state of partial destruction, and Dr Barwell again dissenting. Equally, all six agreed about the presence of a crop of condylomatous warts around both young men's anuses, but disagreed as to the origins and meaning of these warts, with Dr Barwell, as usual, dissenting most violently.

Unpleasant, humiliating and painful as the prolonged examinations had been, this was good news for Fanny and Stella. A majority of the six eminent medical gentlemen had found in their favour. 'It may be relied upon as a positive fact,' *Reynolds's Newspaper* reported breathlessly, 'that the result of this examination undoubtedly tended to throw some doubt upon the medical evidence adduced before the police magistrate.' It now seemed doubtful, at least to *Reynolds's Newspaper* and to some others, that the prosecutions of these two young men could or should proceed. For a brief, shining moment it almost seemed possible – perhaps even likely – that Fanny and Stella might be released without charge.

He, She or It

There is not the slightest doubt that England is
hastening towards the border which divides the
sexes; already persons have over-stepped and stand
alone, hated and despised.

The Englishwoman's Domestic Magazine, 1871

D r Henry James Johnson, one of the six eminent medical
gentlemen who examined Fanny and Stella in Newgate
Gaol, had been most forcibly struck by the startling, the really
quite startling, *womanliness* of their bodies, especially about
their bottoms. They were men, and yet they were not men.
They were women, and yet not women. They were something
indeterminate, somewhere in-between. The whiteness and
smoothness and translucency of their skin, with their slender
waists, the gentle curve of their hips and their shapely buttocks,
all bespoke womanliness. Above and beyond the womanliness
of their bodies, there was an indefinable aura of femininity
about them, he could not put it more precisely than that, which
was all the more powerful because it was so mysterious, so hard
to pin down.

Of course Dr Johnson was only too well aware that these
young men had regularly dressed themselves as women, wearing corsets to give themselves wasp-waists and tight-laced bodices to squeeze and push their breasts upwards and outwards.

They had tweezered their eyebrows and plucked their beards and used every artifice: wigs, paint, pads and God only knew what else to create a convincing illusion of womanliness. There could be no doubt that such practices, long adhered to, long indulged in, might very well lend a permanent air of womanliness to any young man. Constant tight-lacing, quite apart from constricting and deforming the disposition of the internal organs to an alarming and dangerous degree, did have the effect of permanently altering the bodies of young women, giving them impossibly small waists and shapely hips and buttocks. But even making allowances for the effect of such practices, Dr Johnson still found these young men troublingly womanly.

'The smallness of the anus, the tightness of the sphincter, and the smallness of the rectum' were all, Dr Johnson said, what he might expect to find in a healthy young woman. These characteristics were, he added, most marked in Frederick Park's posterior, 'if possible more so even than in Boulton'.

Was it possible that the womanliness of Fanny and Stella was actual, rather than assumed? Could there be a biological explanation for the troubling emanations of femininity that both these creatures exuded? Were they, perhaps, a species of hermaphrodite? An amalgam of male and female? Not masculine and not feminine, but a combination of the two genders commingled to produce a strange hybrid?

From the moment of Fanny and Stella's arrest, attitudes were divided, like the Red Sea. There were those who regarded them as wicked and wilful sodomites, all the more wicked and all the more wilful because they deceived, they tricked men into thinking that they were women. And then there were those who took the view that Fanny and Stella were indeed hermaphrodites, bodily or mentally, or most probably a mixture of both: degraded certainly, but also unfortunate and to be pitied, because their actions – however reprehensible and however offensive – were the consequence of instincts ordained by a freakish and perverse Nature.

As the details of the case against them began to unfold, *Reynolds's Newspaper* had gone from calling them 'the Young Gentlemen in Woman's Clothes' to describing them as part of 'the Hermaphrodite Clique' and 'the Hermaphrodite Gang'. Other newspapers implied their innate duality by calling them 'men-women' or 'he-she ladies' or variations on this theme. Even before their arrest, many found it impossible to believe that Fanny and Stella – particularly and most especially Stella – were men. Wherever they went, whoever they met, in drag, or out of drag, as Fanny and Stella, or as Frederick and Ernest, there were always those who had their doubts as to their exact gender. Were they men? Or were they women? Or were they a rare and remarkable matched pair of hermaphrodites?

In January of the previous year, Fanny and Stella, in company with Charles Pavitt, had formed a small touring theatrical company called 'Her Majesty's Servants'. They made their debut on 27th January 1869 at the tiny but grandly named Theatre Royal in the small Essex town of Stock. 'By special request', the actors performed 'Mr. H. J. Byron's comedy of *One Hundred Thousand Pounds*, the characters of Alice and Mrs. Barlow being played respectively by Boulton and Park, who are designated in the programme, Miss Ernestine Edwards and Miss Mabel Foster'.

'During the piece Miss Edwards sang "Fading Away" with a care and taste that brought down the house,' the *Essex Herald* reported, clearly not able to fully grasp the fact that Miss Ernestine Edwards was, in truth, Mr Ernest Boulton. Other newspaper correspondents could only marvel at the perfect illusion of femininity that Stella/Ernestine created: 'Listening to his extraordinary voice, and criticising, however narrowly, his wonderfully feminine appearance and manner, it is really difficult for a moment to believe that he is not a really charming girl.' Indeed, Miss Ernestine Edwards was so perfect and so charming that the anonymous correspondent went on to hint orotundly that Miss Edwards had to be a species of hermaphrodite. 'Certainly,' he declared, 'if some of Nature's journeymen had not been at work, "Mister" Boulton, we hesitate almost to write this prefix, would have incontestably been a woman.'

Later that same year, Stella and Charles Pavitt toured Essex and Hertfordshire with *A Drawing-Room Entertainment*, devised and written by themselves and designed to be performed in country-house drawing rooms, assembly rooms and village halls. 'We agreed to share the profits and divide the expenses,' Charles Pavitt recalled. 'The entertainment usually comprised a short opera, a humorous dialogue, and a laughable sketch. In all these the ladies' characters were represented by Ernest Boulton.' Sadly, there was no role for poor Fanny.

Wherever they went, Stella shone, and even though the playbills unambiguously declared that all the female parts were performed by Mr Ernest Boulton, all who saw her could hardly believe that she was not in reality a beautiful and charming girl. 'We may add that Mr. Boulton very cleverly personates female characters,' wrote one reviewer, 'and that it is difficult for a spectator to realise the fact that he is a "make-up" for the occasion. His song, "Fading Away" is exceedingly feminine.'

Off stage, as well as on stage, Stella had more than her fair share of admirers who seemed unable to comprehend that the beautiful young woman they saw singing and swooning on stage was in reality a young man. Bouquets were invariably the order of the day.

'On one evening,' Charles Pavitt recalled, 'Boulton had as many as *fourteen* bouquets thrown to him.' And there were any number of invitations to supper from gentlemen, and from ladies. All of them wanted Stella to attend 'in his female costume', and 'several sporting gentlemen wanted him to go in his lady's costume into the hunting-field, but he would not go.'

Even when Stella was dressed as a man, even when she introduced herself as Ernest, even when she shook hands as manfully as she could and spoke as gruffly as she could manage, many men simply refused to accept that she was a man. The delicacy of her body, the softness of her voice, the brilliancy of her eyes, the smoothness of her skin, the lustre of her hair, the sweetness of her scent, the smallness of her hands and the daintiness of her feet were all, and in every way, female, feminine, womanly.

Quite apart from those gentlemen admirers who simply could not or would not believe that Stella was a man, even when it was written in black and white, even when Stella protested that she was indeed a man, even when she dressed in men's clothing, there were also those with no conceivable amatory interest in her who were equally convinced that she was a woman.

A few weeks before her arrest, dear, dull Louis Hurt wrote to Stella from a remote inn in Scotland, where they had spent a night or two in the course of Louis's interminable inspections of post offices. Stella had worn male clothing, but had signally failed to convince anyone that she was a man. 'My darling Ernie,' Louis began:

> The landlord of the inn from which I write tells me that
> all the men whom we saw here the other day were
> positive you are a woman. He assured them you were
> not, although he seems not to have been certain himself.
> He said you moved about and stood like one but that
> your thighs, which he examined when you were going
> upstairs, were not so plump as a woman's.

No doubt it reminded them both of an unfortunate incident eighteen months earlier when Louis had dragged a reluctant Stella off on a tour of post offices in Wales and the West Country – for the good of her health, he said. The 'rustics in Devizes and Newport' had taken it upon themselves to write to the Postmaster-General himself accusing his roving inspector of travelling upon official business with a woman disguised as a man in tow. If it had not been so serious, it would have been funny, especially when the said rustics intimated their belief that Mr Hurt's companion was a woman of low repute, little realising how close they had come to hitting that particular nail on the head. It had taken the urgent intervention of Lord Arthur Clinton, MP, to clear matters up.

Mr Flowers, the magistrate at Bow Street, also appeared to be convinced that Fanny and Stella were in fact women, or some variation on a womanly theme, despite the weight of evidence and despite their own assertions and protestations: 'I really thought they were women, and I expressed that opinion at the time,' Mr Flowers said in court some three weeks after Fanny and Stella's first appearance there. 'I was in hopes that the defence would be that they were women.'

Of course, there were some men whom Stella was quite happy *not* to tell: steamers or punters, the men *she* picked up (because she was nothing if not choosy) in the Haymarket and round and about, the men who paid her money, and good money too, thinking she was a beautiful young whore, so different from the usual run of ruined and raddled harridans. It was easier for them not to know, and it was not hard to keep them in the dark. Most were so drunk they didn't know whether they were coming or going, let alone by the front or the back door, and even if they were sober, they hardly cared.

Some of them, of course, knew she was a man because they had had her before, or they had guessed, or they had groped her and found something they were not expecting. Or she had told them on an impulse or out of caprice to see what, if anything, would happen. Usually they carried on regardless; most were past the point of no return. A few even seemed curious and asked if she was one of those rare and wonderful creatures that was man and woman in one, the very idea seeming to arouse them sexually.

In his riotous and unreliable *Recollections*, Jack Saul, the celebrated Mary-Ann, recounts Stella confiding in him that she once seduced a handsome gentleman by the name of Mr Bruce in the Star and Garter Hotel in Richmond by purporting to be a hermaphrodite.

> 'I pretended to resist his attempts to get at my cunny,'
> Stella said, 'and at last blushingly told him that I was one
> of those unfortunate beings (which perhaps he had heard
> of) who had a malformation, something like the male
> instrument – in fact, it was capable of stiffening, and

always did so under excitement, exactly as a man's would do.'

'But, darling,' Stella said, addressing herself to Mr Bruce, 'It is quite harmless, and can do no mischief like the real male affair. Now you, I know, will be too disgusted to want to kiss me, although I am dying for you to afford me that pleasure.'

Mr Bruce assured Stella that he had often heard of hermaphrodites and was curious to know more.

But despite Stella's many triumphs in the endless battle of love, there were occasional defeats. Another admirer who believed, at first at least, Stella to be a woman was Mr Francis Kegan Cox – or Captain Cox as he preferred to be called. Captain Cox was every inch the swell. He was a partner in the auctioneering line, having had what might tactfully be termed a chequered past. After nine years in the army he had sold his commission and spent the several years knocking around Australia and New Zealand looking for opportunities, of which none presented themselves.

Back in London, he landed on his feet and secured an enviable position as Secretary to the Civil Service Club.

'I resigned that office voluntarily,' Captain Cox admitted in court. 'There was a complaint made against me.'

'Like mistakes in arithmetic?' Mr Straight, for the defence, enquired sarcastically.

Captain Cox cleared his throat and swallowed hard. 'Sums were entered into the books without names, carelessly,' he countered.

From the debacle of the Civil Service Club, Captain Cox

found his way to the City where he and an unnamed gentleman set themselves up as auctioneers. In September 1868, Stella was sitting at luncheon in the Guildhall Tavern, Leadenhall Street, in company with Lord Arthur Clinton and Mr W. H. Roberts, Lord Arthur's solicitor, loan arranger and general fixer, when the Captain walked in.

It transpired that Captain Cox and Mr Roberts were previously acquainted. Introductions to Lord Arthur and Stella were effected, and Captain Cox was invited to join the luncheon party. He needed no pressing. He was strangely and powerfully drawn to the young man who had been introduced to him as Mr Ernest Boulton, but Captain Cox was dashed and damned and blowed if he believed that for an instant. Even though 'he' was dressed from top to toe in male attire, it was clear to him that Boulton was a girl, a very pretty girl, and a very flirtatious girl at that. There could be no doubt about it. She was coming on exceedingly strong to him.

'It was from the manner Boulton's hair was done, and from the smallness of his hands and feet, as well as his general manners, that I formed an opinion he was a woman,' the Captain said later in Bow Street.

Stella was equally smitten. The Captain was a fine, swaggering figure of a man and, at thirty-five years old, in the prime of his life. He was the cock of the walk. Tall, strong, upright and confident in matters of the heart (and other organs), he did not scruple to indicate in every possible way that he was very taken with Stella.

Stella, in turn, was flattered, flirtatious and on flamboyant form.

'Oh you City birds have good fun in your offices', Stella said in a tone of mock complaint, 'and you have champagne!'

The Captain rose gallantly to the bait.

'You had better come over and see,' he replied meaningfully, and that very afternoon a radiant Stella and a less than effervescent Lord Arthur Clinton turned up at 1 Gresham's Buildings, being the Captain's flashy rented offices.

'My partner arrived whilst we were there and we had champagne,' Captain Cox continued. Lord Arthur's nose was clearly out of joint. After all, he and Stella were living together as man and wife, and he had not long since ordered – but not yet paid for – engraved cards bearing the legend 'Lady Arthur Clinton'. Of course, Arthur knew that Stella frequently went out on the pad to sell herself to men for much-needed cash to keep them afloat. Though he was not exactly happy about this arrangement, he could see the advantages. What he did not care for, not one jot, was being made to play the cuckold in public. And after one particularly loaded exchange between Stella and this man Cox, he left the room and slammed the door, and went for a walk to cool his heels and cool his head while the flirtation continued apace.

'I treated Boulton as a fascinating woman,' Cox said later.

'Have you had a large experience in fascinating women?' asked the sarcastic Mr Straight. Captain Cox objected to this question, very strongly. But Mr Straight was not to be deflected. 'Have you had a large experience in fascinating women?' he repeated.

'I have known a great many women in my time,' was the guarded reply.

'Were you in the habit of making advances of this sort on your first acquaintance?'

'It would always depend whether there was an advance made,' the Captain answered.

'Do you state that there was an advance made by him?'

'I do. Boulton went on in a flirting manner with me, and I kissed him, she or it, at the time believing he was a woman.'

There. He had said it. He had kissed Ernest Boulton.

Captain Cox's confession brought forth gasps and giggles from the public gallery.

'But you don't mean to say Boulton kissed you?'

'Well, he did something very like it,' Captain Cox replied.

'You anyhow kissed him?'

'I certainly did.' (Laughter.) 'Shortly after that Boulton complained of being chilly. My partner whipped the cloth off the table, put him in an armchair, and wrapped up his feet in the cloth.'

A few days later, Lord Arthur and Stella attended one of the Captain's auction sales at the Roebuck Tavern in Turnham Green. Lord Arthur's spirits seemed entirely restored and a jolly time was had by all. There was a piano in the public bar and Stella sat down and sang divinely, later taking the opportunity to slyly slip the handsome Captain a photograph of herself in men's clothes.

As in all the best romances, the dashing Captain Cox had sealed his love with a kiss and it was left to the imagination of the gentle reader, or, in this case, the minds of the coarse-grained, foul-mouthed chorus that comprised the public gallery of Bow Street Magistrates' Court, to determine if the love affair between Captain Cox and Stella was ever consummated. And if the raucous laughter, squints, leers and half-mumbled lewd comments emanating from that quarter were anything to go by, the public gallery had already reached its unanimous verdict.

There was an unhappy coda to the romance. Somehow or other Captain Cox got wind of Stella's true gender.

'I afterwards heard something about Boulton's sex,' Captain Cox told the court, carefully avoiding naming who it was who had tipped him off, though the odds were on the dubious Mr Roberts who was simultaneously trying to prevent Lord Arthur from being cuckolded and the Captain from being cruelly duped. When he found out, Captain Cox was incandescent with rage.

'After this I went to Evans's. I saw Boulton there. Park and Lord Arthur Clinton were with him. I went up to the table where Boulton, Park and Lord Arthur were sitting, and used abusive language. "You — infernal scoundrels," I said. "You ought to be kicked out of the place." I said more to the same purport, and kept walking up and down by the table. I afterwards promised not to create a disturbance, and left.'

M r Pollard, the most senior solicitor at the Treasury, had been very sympathetic and understanding. With scrupulous politeness he had called him Captain at every possible opportunity, tut-tutted over his treatment at the hands of the Civil Service Club and listened to stories of his army life and his Antipodean adventures with every appearance of animated interest.

It was with the greatest delicacy and the greatest difficulty that Mr Pollard brought the conversation round to the vexed topic of his giving evidence. Captain Cox shuddered and shivered. He was understandably reluctant to appear as a witness and admit to kissing – if that was all it was – a woman dressed as a man who turned out to be a man after all. He was a former officer and still some sort of gentleman.

Mr Pollard urged and persuaded. In cases like this, he said, cases of interest and importance to the Crown, cases which reflected on the national character and the national honour, there would of course be expenses. *Generous* expenses. Mr Pollard underlined the word 'generous'. A man like Captain Cox could hardly be expected to neglect or abandon his important business to help secure the conviction of two pernicious sodomites without some adequate disbursement from the Crown for his time and his trouble. And so it had been agreed. A dusty Treasury ledger records the receipt of 'a letter from Captain Cox applying for his expenses as a witness'.

Sadly, Captain Cox did not live to collect his disbursement from the Treasury, though his widow and his children were no doubt very grateful. The gallant Captain died two weeks to the day after he gave his evidence in Bow Street, of smallpox, the death certificate stated, and also quite possibly of shame.

A Bitches' Ball

I have heard of 'a bitches' ball'. It might mean two
things. It might be a ball for prostitutes, and it
might be a ball for men prostitutes. I have taken
part in a ball for male prostitutes at my father's
house about two years ago.

> Malcolm Johnston, also known
> as The Maid of Athens, 1884

Miss Carlotta Westropp Gibbings requests the pleasure
of your company at a Ball at Haxell's Hotel, West Strand
on Friday, 7th April at 9 o'clock.

There was the greatest excitement about Carlotta's ball. It
went without saying that it was to be the most perfect
and the most dazzling ball ever given. A brilliant ball to launch
a brilliant season, the most brilliant season they had ever
known – and by the end of it none of the young men who liked
to dress as young ladies expected anything less than to be engaged to be married to a peer of the realm or a prince from
foreign parts.

It would most emphatically not be one of those poky, secret-
ive, sad little balls they sometimes attended, in a room above a
public house or in a low tavern in some out-of-the-way place
no one had ever heard of, with a solitary pianist picking out ancient waltzes on a rickety piano and the air thick with cheap

tobacco smoke, beer and sweat. And there was to be no riff-raff, only the *crème de la crème* of gentlemen and the choicest ladies from their circle. Certainly no trollops off the streets (though, strictly speaking, this meant that many, if not most, of their friends would face disqualification).

No, Carlotta's ball was going to be held in a proper ball-room, on the second floor of Haxell's Hotel, which, if not the biggest ballroom in London, was one of the most elegantly ap-pointed. There was to be a small orchestra. There was to be champagne and a proper supper served at the stroke of mid-night. And there were to be at least two dressing rooms for the ladies and a smoking room for the gentlemen. And between the dances, there were to be musical interludes and singing. Everything, absolutely everything, was to be, as Fanny said at least a dozen times a day, *comme il faut*.

Best of all, Stella had been prevailed upon to return from her exile in Edinburgh and grace the proceedings with some songs. She was to come a few days early and stay in Haxell's Hotel as Carlotta's guest. It would be the first time Fanny had seen her sister for six months and there was a great deal of catching up to do.

Fanny was in a whirl of excitement and expectation. She was in her element, advising her dearest Carlotta on every as-pect of the ball. They had planned it together, down to the last detail, and it was to be all perfection. By rights, of course, it should have been Carlotta's Mamma who organised this ball to launch her daughter upon an unsuspecting world, but her Mamma was in Clifton, Carlotta had explained, and was dour and sour and rather too fond of going to Mr Charlesworth's church. So Fanny had stepped in and become Carlotta's trus-ted and truest friend; her wisest counsel; an older sister and a maiden aunt rolled into one. *Tante Fanny*. She rather liked the sound of that.

Carlotta was Fanny's newest and, with the exception of Stella, her most intimate friend. They had met quite recently, just before Christmas, at a *bal masqué* at Highbury Barn, one of the few places where young men dressed as young ladies were welcome and where they had formed quite a little society of friends.

Fanny and Carlotta had hit it off immediately and had become more or less inseparable. Almost like sisters. They had much in common. Like Fanny, Carlotta had been dragging up since she was fourteen or fifteen years old. 'I have known the slang term "drag" about five months,' Carlotta later proclaimed in court to gasps and giggles. 'I have gone about dressed as a woman but I *never* went out so dressed with the intention of walking in the street.'

Which was, perhaps, just as well, Fanny mused to herself charitably, for her sweet-natured Carlotta was no oil painting. In fact, she was decidedly plain, labouring under the multiple disadvantages of an overly long neck, broad and most unwomanly shoulders and a complete absence – a perfect desert – of chin which, to be frank, made her look a little simple.

Fanny could sympathise. She, too, had once laboured – and indeed laboured still – under some disadvantages of the person, and yet she had turned these disadvantages to triumphs, winning many victories in the endless battle of love. Personality counted for much, but there was a great deal she could teach her dear Carlotta about the dark arts of dressing well, of painting herself, of arranging her coiffure, and generally making a little go a very long way. Every pot has its lid, thought Fanny, and properly dressed and properly lit – the dimmer the better, dare she say it! – even Carlotta might appear to advantage and prove irresistible to the gentlemen at her ball.

D rag balls were a regular feature of life in London, though few aspired to – or indeed, achieved – the brilliance and opulence of Miss Carlotta Westropp Gibbings's ball. There was a clear distinction to be made between public and private drag balls. Many advertised themselves publicly as masquerade balls, as fancy dress balls, or, like the entertainments at Highbury Barn, as *bals masqués* and were open to all comers.

In April 1864, the diarist Arthur Munby 'chanced to see an advertisement of a masked ball at some pleasure gardens in Camberwell: admission *one shilling*'. Munby was intrigued. 'Who would be attracted by such a ball?' he asked himself and decided to find out. He was hoping, perhaps, to strike a rich new vein of the working-class women he loved to encounter and to write about obsessively in his diaries. 'Only about fifty or sixty people were present,' Mundy recorded, 'most of them in fancy dress of a tawdry kind.' The ball was held in a large wooden shed.

> Several of the girls were drest in men's clothing, as sailors and so on: one, as a volunteer in uniform, I took for a man until someone called her Jenny.
>
> Moreover, not a few of the youths were elaborately disguised as *women* of various kinds; some so well, that only their voices showed they were not girls – and pretty girls.

'This is a thing new to me,' Munby wrote censoriously, 'and is simply disgusting.'

Private drag balls were a very different kettle of fish. They were strictly by invitation, and entry was usually by password only. They were often small, hole-in-the-wall affairs, with not more than a dozen or so dancers, and held in an odd assortment of venues: in rooms above taverns; in out-of-the-way halls and assembly rooms; in cellars, stables and barns; and sometimes in private houses.

Drag balls were held regularly at the Druids' Hall in Turnagain Place in the City of London. Even though the hall was unlicensed for drinking and dancing, the police seemed happy to turn a blind eye until the summer of 1854 when two men were arrested in full drag. John Challis, aged sixty, was 'dressed in the pastoral garb of a shepherdess of the golden age', while his companion George Campbell was 'completely equipped in the female attire of the present day', a court heard. 'There were about a hundred persons present,' Inspector Teague told the magistrate, Sir Robert Carden, 'and from eight to ten men were dressed as females.' Challis and Campbell had, he said, 'rendered themselves very conspicuous by their disgusting and filthy conduct'. Challis in particular was 'behaving with two men as if he were a common prostitute'.

A few years after Fanny and Stella's arrest, no fewer than forty-seven men were arrested when police burst in on a private drag ball at the Temperance Hall in Hulme, a desperately poor district of Manchester. The organisers had gone to considerable lengths to keep out prying eyes, fastening lengths of black crepe over the windows and employing a blind accordionist as the only musician. But Detective Sergeant Jerome Caminada had been tipped off, and he and his officers had climbed onto the roof of an adjacent building in order to spy on the proceedings. What they saw amazed them. Half the men were in drag and the other half in a variety of exotic costumes. The men in drag were performing, Caminada testified, 'a sort of dance to very quick time, which my experience has taught me is called the "Can-Can"'.

Admission to the ball was by password only but Detective Sergeant Caminada had somehow found it out. Knocking on the door of the Temperance Hall, he uttered the word 'Sister' in a mincing voice and the door opened to reveal a man dressed as a nun. Then there was panic as policemen and local volunteers rushed in to round up the revellers.

T hings had got off to a less than perfect start, Carlotta thought irritably. She had always intended that her ball should be small and select, with no more than a dozen couple at most. The whole thing was to be an austerely beautiful and romantic affair, untainted by the sort of brutish behaviour which characterised so many low drag balls.

She had to confess that she was very far from pleased to discover that Fanny had been dispensing invitations broadcast to the ragtag and bobtail of her acquaintance and then had the nerve to tell *her* that this one and that one simply had to attend, or that she had already promised so-and-so that they could come. The upshot was that there were now forty-eight guests, quite double the original number. She was sure that she did not know half of them, and equally sure that she would not *wish* to know them.

Mr Edward Haxell, the jovial proprietor of Haxell's Hotel, was in his element. Young Mr Gibbings's ball was going swimmingly and all the young men and the young men dressed as ladies seemed to be enjoying themselves enormously. 'They changed partners for the dances,' he recalled later, 'and there was nothing wrong in any way during the whole night.

'There was no impropriety of attitude that I saw in the room, not a *vestige*,' he insisted. 'I heard the observation made about how well the young men were acting.' It was true that some of the young men – the young men dressed as young men, that is – had danced with each other, which was a little odd when you first saw it, but after a while it seemed perfectly natural, indeed, rather charming, and Mr Haxell wondered idly to himself why this did not happen more often in situations where there was a dearth of ladies.

He had counted thirteen young men dressed as ladies, though there might of course have been more. It was sometimes hard to tell the real thing from the fake. Miss Gibbings, Miss Boulton and Mrs Graham of course he knew well. And he had been previously introduced to Miss Cumming and Miss Thomas. Miss Peel he knew by reputation only as Mr Percival Peel, rumoured to be nephew to the late Sir Robert Peel, the former Prime Minister.

Miss Stella Boulton – or Lady Stella Clinton, as he had heard her referred to more than once – made an utterly convincing young lady. When she had first arrived at Haxell's a few days before the ball, Miss Gibbings introduced her as 'the best amateur actress off the boards', and Mr Haxell could well believe it. She seemed to light up even the dullest room from the moment she entered. She was, in the truest sense, enchanting. No wonder everyone seemed to fall instantly under her spell. He was even a little in love with her himself.

'I heard Boulton sing his popular song "Fainting Away", I think three times, with great *éclat*,' he said later in court. (Or was it 'Fading Away'? He could not be sure.) 'I spoke to the Master of the Band about Boulton's singing, and when he sang a second time, he went straight up to him and said, "It is the most perfect man's soprano voice that I *ever* heard!" '

Of course, when the police started nosing around and asking questions, everyone was falling over themselves to say how Carlotta's ball had all gone off so perfectly, with so much propriety, with so much sweetness and light. Everyone, that is, apart from Jack Saul, whose bawdy recollections of that night were closer to the bone, in every sense.

On the surface, he said, everything about the ball seemed to be above board. Both the gentlemen and the ladies conducted themselves, for the first hour or two at least, with the greatest propriety. But as the evening wore on, and more and more champagne was consumed, the ball started to turn into a bacchanal, and the ballroom became a brothel.

'There seems to be,' Jack Saul mused with some relish, 'such a peculiar fascination to gentlemen in the idea of having a beautiful creature, such as an ordinary observer would take for a beautiful lady, to dance and flirt with, knowing all the while that his inamorata is a youthful man in disguise.'

The gentlemen could hardly contain themselves at the sight of so many young-men-dressed-as-ladies and even those who were long past the first flush of youth, those with sterner features, like Fanny Park, or those with stouter builds were positively chased around the ballroom. Jack Saul noticed Mr Haxell nodding and smiling and encouraging his guests to enjoy themselves, seemingly unaware of what was going on under his very nose. 'No doubt the proprietor was quite innocent of any idea of what our fun really was,' Saul wrote, 'but there were two or three dressing rooms into which the company could retire at pleasure.'

These dressing rooms which Carlotta had insisted upon

were supposed to be intimate retreats for the young men dressed as ladies to refresh themselves and to repair their toilette. But in reality they resembled nothing so much as dimly lit bordellos where drunken guests fumbled and frolicked with each other.

Tiring of drinking and dancing, Jack Saul recalled, 'I sat for a while on a sofa by myself, watching the dancers and taking notice of all the little freedoms they so constantly exchanged with one another.'

Both Fanny and Stella caught his eye. Fanny was 'dancing with a gentleman from the City, a very handsome Greek merchant', while Stella was enjoying the attentions of Lord Arthur Clinton who, Jack Saul observed, 'was very spooney upon her'.

> During the evening I noticed them slip away together, and made my mind up to try and get a peep at their little game. So I followed them as quietly as possible, and saw them pass down a corridor to another apartment, not one of the dressing rooms which I knew had been provided for the use of the party, but one which I suppose his Lordship had secured for his own personal use.
>
> I was close enough behind them to hear the key turned in the lock. Foiled thus for a moment, I turned the handle of the next door, which admitted me to an unoccupied room, and to my great delight a beam of bright light streamed from the keyhole of the door of communication between that and the one in which my birds had taken refuge.

Jack Saul knelt down and put his eye to the keyhole. He could see and hear everything. 'Lord Arthur and Boulton were standing before a large mirror,' he recalled. Stella was busy unbuttoning Lord Arthur's trousers. 'Soon she let out a beautiful specimen of the *arbor vitae*, at least nine inches long and very thick. It was in glorious condition, with a great, glowing red head.'

Stella 'at once knelt down and kissed this jewel of love and would, I believe, have sucked him to a spend, but Lord Arthur was too impatient.' Picking Stella up, Lord Arthur flung her down backwards on the bed to reveal 'a beautiful pair of legs enveloped within lovely knicker-bocker drawers. They were prettily trimmed with the finest lace, and I could also see pink silk stockings and the most fascinating little shoes with silver buckles.'

Matters proceeded apace. Lord Arthur quickly put his hands into Stella's drawers and 'soon brought to light as manly a weapon as any lady could desire to see, and very different from the crinkum-crankum one usually expects when one throws up a lady's petticoats and proceeds to take liberties with her'.

'What's this beautiful plaything, darling?' Lord Arthur asked in an erotic frenzy 'as he fondled and caressed Boulton's prick, passing his hand up and down the ivory-white shaft and kissing the dark, ruby-coloured head every time it was uncovered'.

'Are you a hermaphrodite, my love?' he demanded. 'Oh I must kiss it: it's such a treasure!'

Jack Saul was riveted. 'How excited I became at the sight you may be sure,' he recorded. 'I was determined not to frig myself, as I was sure of finding a nice partner when I returned to the ball-room. Still, I would rather have had Boulton than anyone else. His make-up was so sweetly pretty that I longed to have him, and him have me.'

Jack Saul could see how Stella's body seemed to shake and spasm as Lord Arthur's finger 'postillioned her bottomhole'.

Seeing how agitated he had made her, he took that splendid prick fairly into his mouth and sucked away with all the ardour of a male gamahucher; his eyes almost emitted sparks as the crisis seemed to come, and he must have swallowed every drop of that creamy emission he had worked so hard to obtain.

After a minute or two Lord Arthur wiped his mouth, and turned Stella around so that her bottom was in the air.

Opening the drawers from behind, he kissed each cheek of the lovely white bum, and tickled the little hole with his tongue. But he was too impatient to waste much time in kissing, so at once he presented his prick to Boulton's fundament, as he held the two cheeks of his pretty arse open with his hands.

Although such a fine cock, it did not seem to have a very difficult task to get in, and he was so excited that he very nearly came at once. But keeping his place, he soon commenced a proper bottom fuck, which both of them gave signs of enjoying intensely, for I could fairly hear his belly flop against Boulton's buttocks at every home push, whilst each of them called the other by the most endearing terms such as:

'What a darling you are! Tell me, love, that you love me! Tell me it's a nice fuck!'

And then the other would exclaim:

'Tush; push; fuck me; ram your darling prick in as fast

as it will go. Oh! Oh! Quicker, quicker: Do come now, dearest Arthur; my love, my pet! Oh! Oh!! Oh!!!'

The Wheels of Justice

We hope and believe that not one winding of this
filthy business will be left unexplored, nor one of
those concerned in it be left unexposed or unpunished. Now that we have got our hand on the
cockatrice's den it is of the utmost moment that we
should not take it away until we have cleared out its
last recesses and subjected every one of its inmates
to the just penalty of his guilt.

Pall Mall Gazette, 8th June 1870

For Louis Hurt in Edinburgh, the dramatic arrest of Fanny
and Stella had come as a bolt from the blue. He was struggling to make sense of what had happened. Events seemed to
be moving so swiftly and, apart from the extensive and sal-
acious reports in the newspapers, which were already a day or
more old by the time he saw them, he had no way of knowing
what was happening. Of course, he had written and telegraphed to Mr and Mrs Boulton, but they appeared to be
almost as much in the dark as himself.

Louis was angry and confused. He had warned Ernie over
and over again about the undesirability – let alone the dangers
– of dressing up as a woman. 'I am rather sorry to hear of your
going around in Drag so much,' he had told him sternly just
days before. 'You know my sentiments.'

Stella was only too well aware of Louis's sentiments on

the subject of 'Drag', which he always spoke of and wrote of with a large capital D, as if to emphasise his disgust and his disdain. His pompous pronouncements, his admonitions and his injunctions on Drag were endlessly repeated.

Though Louis was a trifle dull (in truth, rather more than a trifle), he more than made up for it with his spaniel-like loyalty and devotion to his Ernie. Within a week of Fanny and Stella's arrest he had asked for, and been granted, a leave of absence from the Post Office, but was also in receipt of a terse request from the Postmaster General himself to provide a full written explanation of his relations with the young men in women's clothes. 'I suppose I shall be called up to resign,' he gloomily confided to John Safford Fiske.

Louis's plan was to go to London and do what he could. If it was at all possible, he would visit Ernie in prison. He would certainly go and see Mr and Mrs Boulton at Shirland Road in Maida Vale and offer what help he was able. And he would rally Ernie's friends and acquaintances and see what could be done. Lastly, he would find out what the implications were for himself.

Louis feared the worst. The newspapers were full of rumours and speculations about cliques and claques of young men who dressed as women, of peers and politicians, of scandal and disgrace, of imminent arrests and round-ups. The police were no fools. It would not take them long to realise that Ernie had spent the past six months living with him in Edinburgh. Ernie was always so careless. Letters would be found. Compromising letters. Letters to 'My darling Ernie' from 'Your loving Louis', and whatever else he had committed to paper in his dark and lonely moments. He would be arrested and quite possibly – quite probably – charged with sodomy. Mrs Dickson would be questioned. He turned pale at the prospect.

For the moment, however, he was free: free to find out what exactly the police knew, and perhaps more importantly what they did not know – yet; and free, for the moment, to flee if matters should take a turn for the worse. 'Do you advise my going to New York?' he enquired of John Safford Fiske.

It was almost certain that Fiske would be implicated too, along with Harry Park and Donald Sinclair and John Jameson Jim and all the others in their little society of friends. All except poor Robbie Sinclair, who was now beyond the reach of the police, dead of consumption at just twenty-three.

Once he was in London, Louis began to feel reassured. He had spoken to Abrams, the solicitor, who said the situation was grave, certainly, but not perhaps as grave as he had first imagined. His opinion, his hope, was that the Metropolitan Police and the Treasury had overreached themselves. They had levelled grave and grandiloquent charges of sodomy and conspiracy to commit sodomy. But such grave and grandiloquent charges required clear and unambiguous evidence. And so far, the Metropolitan Police and the Treasury had signally failed to produce any evidence worthy of the name. There was – as yet – no evidence of sodomy; and no evidence of invitations to sodomy; no evidence of any attempts to induce, incite, entice or inveigle any other men into committing sodomy.

Even the evidence of the chief prosecution witness, a young man named Hugh Mundell, had gone to their credit. 'Miss Stella' and 'Mrs Fanny', as he persisted in calling them, had made efforts, strenuous efforts, to inform that gullible young man that they were, in fact, men dressed up as women, even penning a note to that effect. It had made not a ha'p'orth of difference. Mr Hugh Mundell still refused to accept that they were men. Really, if this callow young man was the best that the

Metropolitan Police and the Treasury could muster, then the defence was, according to the optimistic Mr Abrams, almost home and dry.

The medical evidence of sodomy, which had at first seemed so compelling and so convincing, also failed to hold water. It was certainly true that Dr Paul, the police doctor, had detected alarming signs of sodomy written upon the bodies of Fanny and Stella. And Dr Barwell, from the Charing Cross Hospital, had sworn on oath that he had treated Frederick Park for a syphilitic chancre upon his anus which could only have been the consequence of sodomy.

Powerful as this evidence was, it had been weakened – mortally weakened – by the mass examinations of the parts of Ernie and Fred which had taken place at Newgate Gaol. Five out of the six eminent medical men present could find no signs of sodomy, not a shadow, not even a trace – insertive or receptive – upon either of them.

Louis was feeling altogether more sanguine. 'I am heartily glad that I came here,' he told Fiske in the middle of May. 'Case looks well at present. Abrams says there is no warrant issued against me. I have just seen a crowd standing round Ernest and Park's photos in a shop.'

By Herculean endeavours, Louis managed to squeeze and push himself into the public gallery in Bow Street. 'I was in Court and rather regretted going when I saw how pale and worn poor little Ernie looked,' he wrote to Fiske. 'It made me so unhappy. I managed to say a word or two to him. Tomorrow I hope to have a short interview with him.'

'My dear John,' Louis wrote to Fiske after his short and unhappy interview in Newgate with his poor little Ernie, pale and wan and half-frightened to death, but still putting a brave face on it all, 'Ernest begs you will destroy any letters from him you may have. I hope you will if you have not already done so.'

Fiske had already burned all Stella's letters in his possession. But unfortunately his love letters to Stella were already in the hands of the police. The last and most passionate of these had been posted just twelve days before the arrest of Fanny and Stella. It was addressed to *'un ange qu'on nomme Erné'*, an angel named Erné, and no one who read it could have the slightest doubt of his feelings towards Stella:

> My darling Ernie,
>
> I have eleven photographs of you (and expecting more tomorrow) which I look at over and over again – I have four little notes which I have sealed up in a packet. I have a heart full of love and longing – and my photographs, my four little notes and my memory are all that I have of you – when are you going to give me more? When are you going to write a dozen lines of four words each to say that all the world is over head and ears in love with you and that you are so tired of adoration and compliments that you turn to your humdrum friend as a relief. Will it be tomorrow? Or will it be next week? Believe me, darling, a word of remembrance from you can never come amiss, only the sooner it comes the better.
>
> Yours always
> *jusqu'à la mort*
> John S Fiske

It did not take long for the newspapers to obtain the text of this damning letter, though when the contents were published most people felt it was foolish rather than filthy. 'I have just seen a

copy of the letter,' Louis wrote to Fiske. 'There is nothing indecent in it (of course) but it is in the most high flown language.
After this letter, I can't understand why your rooms haven't
been searched; perhaps because you have been Consul. Post
going — Yours, L.'

It was certainly true – and not a little surprising – that neither
Louis Hurt nor Fiske had yet been interviewed by the police
in connection with the case, especially given the furore surrounding it. Fiske's diplomatic status as United States Consul
in Edinburgh may well have given the police pause for thought
and protected him, at least in the short run, from Inspector
Thompson's unwelcome attentions.

But Mr Abrams was firmly of the opinion that prevention
was better than cure. Both Mr Hurt and Mr Fiske would be
well advised to make themselves available for interview by the
Metropolitan Police. Such a move would clearly demonstrate
candour and help dissipate the cloud of suspicion hovering
above them. Inspector Thompson's enquiries were far from
concluded. Putting themselves forward for voluntary interview
was a hundred times, nay a thousand times, preferable to waiting for Thompson to arrest them.

Louis was firmly persuaded by the urgings of Mr Abrams,
but Fiske hesitated. He still hoped against hope that it might
all go away. After all, the very worst the police had against him
was that foolish letter he had written to Erné and, as Louis said,
there was nothing actually indecent in it. It was hardly compelling evidence of sodomy. It was unfortunate that his letter had
damaged Erné's case. But he could not help that. He had himself to think about now.

It was quite possible, perhaps even probable, that the police
would leave well alone. Scotland was a different jurisdiction

from England, and there would be all sorts of legal complexities to surmount.

F inally, however, on 3rd June, Fiske decided to come to London to see if matters could not be resolved. He would not countenance an interview with Inspector Thompson. But he would call on Mr Poland, the barrister leading the prosecution against Erné and Fred Park. He would tell Mr Poland that his letter was utter nonsense. It would be a frank and a manly chat. He would tell Mr Poland that he was about to be married and that these unfortunate and unfounded allegations risked his future happiness. And Mr Poland would listen sympathetically and nod his head wisely and all would yet be well.

One of Fiske's most urgent tasks the day after he arrived was also far from congenial. It was downright distasteful. The indefatigable Mr Abrams had opined that both he and Louis Hurt should take the precaution of being examined for signs of sodomy by an eminent medical man. Though Mr Abrams remained optimistic, if the worst came to the worst, it might prove very useful, very useful indeed, to have irrefutable medical evidence that neither he nor Louis had ever indulged in sodomy. Dr Alfred Harvey was the man he had in mind. He had already minutely examined Boulton and Park and detected no signs of sodomy.

Fiske's next task was equally uncongenial. He had to call at the Legation of the United States for a painful interview with Mr John Lothrop Motley, United States Minister in London. 'Mr Fiske called at the Legation on the 4th instant,' Motley wrote in a confidential memorandum to the Secretary of State in Washington:

in order to communicate the fact that his name was
implicated in the disgraceful affair of the men in women's
clothes, and to request some introduction in writing
from the Legation to the Counsel charged with their
prosecution. He thought he could make explanations to
that personage which might relieve him from the
suspicions resting upon him.

In the course of the interview, Fiske revealed the extent of his
friendship with Erné.

He admitted that he had made the acquaintance of the
prisoner Boulton at Edinburgh, that he had introduced
himself to him, that he had requested him to put on his
female attire, that he had received him familiarly at his
own house (not in women's clothes, however) by
invitation eight times, and that he had written letters to
him, three of which were in the hands of the prosecution.

Fiske turned up at Mr Poland's chambers the following day to
request an interview, only to be sent word through his clerk
that Mr Poland regretted that such an interview between a prosecuting barrister and a potential witness – and perhaps even a
potential defendant – was impossible and unthinkable.

Fiske was left reeling. It was a serious and unexpected re-
versal. Had the twin goddesses of Fortune and Fate ceased to
smile upon him? He shivered and – as he returned to Edinburgh – for the first time in his life he was frightened of what
the future might hold.

T he wheels of justice might grind slowly but they ground inexorably. Inspector Thompson's telegram was handed to Detective Officer Roderick Gollan of the Edinburgh City Police on the morning of 9th June, kindly requesting him to call upon Mr John Safford Fiske at his chambers at 136 George Street and search the premises for any evidence, written or photographic, that might connect him to Ernest Boulton.

Fiske was still at home when Detective Officer Gollan called at George Street mid-morning. He did not appear to be at all surprised by the policeman's visit. In fact, he seemed to be expecting it. Gollan began to methodically work his way through the cupboards and drawers in the sitting room and the bedroom, slowly and thoroughly reading every letter he came across. In the pen drawer of his desk he found three letters and two telegrams signed 'Louis', and concealed in a hatbox in the bedroom were a dozen or so photographs of young men (rather effeminate young men, it seemed to Detective Officer Gollan) and some newspaper cuttings about the case of the Young Men in Women's Clothes.

'I asked Mr Fiske if there was anything else,' Gollan testified in court later. 'After a little hesitation he said if I would leave the room he would produce the remainder that he had that could refer to the case.'

'What did you say to that?'

'I said I would not leave.'

'What took place then?'

'He said, "I will admit to you my weakness", and he went and produced from behind the grate of the chimney piece a box containing an album containing a number of *cartes de visite*.'

'Had you seen it when you were searching?'

'No.'

'What further took place?'

'He said, "I have got a number of letters from Mr Boulton, but I have destroyed them."'

'Did he say anything further?'

'He said, "I have written some foolish notes to Boulton but meant no harm by them."'

Detective Officer Gollan left George Street having spent almost two hours searching. He sent a telegram to Inspector Thompson listing what he had found and awaited further instructions. They were not long in coming. At around 4 p.m. the same day, John Safford Fiske heard a loud knock at the front door. Detective Officer Gollan had come to arrest him and to take him into custody.

Mr John Lothrop Motley despatched a confidential memorandum to the Secretary of State in Washington:

In cipher:

Mr Fiske – Facts as to his imprisonment in London and application for bail.

I have now to state that John S. Fiske, United States Consul in Edinburgh, was on the 9th instant arrested at that place and brought to London the next day. He is now held in Newgate on a Bench Warrant awaiting his trial.

He was required to find bail in four sureties of £500 each. He has employed able counsel as I am informed for his defence, and I have requested the United States Vice-Consul General at London privately to watch the case.

Mr Fiske of course hopes to establish his entire innocence of any misdemeanour, but he does not, as I understand, deny familiar acquaintance with Boulton, one of the men in women's clothes indicted for felony, for conspiracy and for misdemeanour, nor the authorship of certain letters to him now in the hands of the prosecution.

I am informed that he wishes to send in his resignation, but if his letter to that effect can only be written on Newgate paper, I have caused it to be intimated to him that it should not be written.

For John Safford Fiske, Fortune and Fate had turned into the Furies and wreaked their wrath upon him. If convicted he would face many years in a filthy English prison, and if he emerged at all, he would be a broken man. Even if he were to prove his innocence, such as it was, there would be no return to the life of hopes and dreams and vaunting ambition.

If there was one consolation, it was that he was not entirely alone in his ordeal. Erné Boulton and Fred Park were in New-gate too, though there were bitter feelings in his heart towards Erné, once his ravishing and beloved Laïs and Antinous in one, now the spring and the source of this terrible nightmare in which he found himself trapped. Even cautious, clever, charm-ing Louis Hurt had been arrested at the same time on the same charges and was also in Newgate. They made a strange quartet. They were tied together by dark and invisible threads of lust and love and they would stand, or most likely fall, together.

Dead or Disappeared

We have it on the authority of a usually well-in-
formed daily contemporary, that peers of the realm
are implicated with the dirty proceedings that will
shortly come prominently before the public in a
court of justice.

Reynolds's Newspaper, 26th June 1870

Very few people were surprised when the warrant for Lord
Arthur Pelham-Clinton's arrest was finally issued in early
June, five weeks after the arrest of Fanny and Stella. Indeed, the
only surprise was that it had taken so long, given that Lord
Arthur had been so publicly implicated in the scandal of the
Young Men in Women's Clothes from the very start.

As the weeks went by, there had been mounting public indignation over what was seen as deliberate foot-dragging on
the part of the authorities in bringing Lord Arthur to justice.
Rumours began to circulate that powerful forces were at work
on his behalf. As the son of the fifth Duke of Newcastle, who
had been Secretary of State for War, and as godson to Mr Gladstone, the current Prime Minister, the recently retired Honourable Member for Newark, it was said, was being shielded from
prosecution.

As the evidence unfolded, it was clear to everybody that
Lord Arthur was up to his aristocratic neck in the scandal. He
knew both Boulton and Park: he had performed in public with

Boulton and lived with him in private, apparently and aston-ishingly as man and wife. There were compromising letters, suggestive photographs, and at least two dozen sworn state-ments that put Lord Arthur at the dark heart of this wicked sodomitic conspiracy.

But the powers that be still hesitated, still delayed. Why? There were mutterings that Lord Arthur was being given time to settle his affairs and make good his escape; that he was about to flee abroad; indeed, that he had already flown and was now safely beyond the clutches of the Metropolitan Police.

Some newspapers, like the *Pall Mall Gazette*, were con-vinced that Lord Arthur knew too much. If he was arrested and brought to justice, there was a danger that he would impli-cate others – peers and politicians and personages – in the vast spider's web of sodomy and scandal, and that the cankerous corruption at the heart of the ruling class would be exposed. 'Peers of the realm are implicated with the dirty proceedings' was the unambiguous verdict of *Reynolds's Newspaper*, which prided itself on taking up the cudgels for ordinary folk against the bastions of birth and privilege.

The *Pall Mall Gazette* called for steely 'resolution on the part of the Government' not to yield to the influence of 'the highest classes of society' who were 'on the side of hushing up a scandal of this magnitude'.

The suspicions of those who believed that the Government was intent on hushing up the scandal were strengthened, rather than diminished, when, on the day that the long-looked-for warrant was belatedly issued for his arrest, Lord Arthur Clin-ton was nowhere to be found. He had vanished off the face of the earth, leaving not a trace.

The last person to have seen Lord Arthur was a cabman. At around two o'clock on the afternoon of Saturday, 28th May, Lord Arthur hailed a cab and told the cabman that he would need him to drive him around upon a variety of errands until that evening.

'I took up my fare at the Opera Hotel, Bow-street,' said the cabman, 'and on depositing him at the same hotel at night I was sent to Long's Hotel with a letter addressed to a gentleman stopping there. But the gentleman had gone abroad (so I was informed), and when I got back to the Opera Hotel to report the result, and to get my money, I was informed that Lord Arthur had gone also.'

And that was the last sighting of Lord Arthur Pelham-Clinton, at least as far as Inspector Thompson and his detectives could establish. The ports were being watched and his description had been circulated. But where he had gone was a mystery.

For those with a suspicious turn of mind, like Inspector Thompson, there was something not quite right about Lord Arthur's six-hour cab journey around London. Why would a man who was about to disappear, seemingly in a puff of smoke, go to the trouble of bilking a cabman for a fare of £1? And why, if you were going to bilk a cabman, would you be at pains to reveal that your name was Lord Arthur Clinton and that you were residing at the Opera Hotel, Bow Street?

Inspector Thompson could smell a rat. He had a nose for such things. He suspected that this seemingly aimless, six-hour cab journey was nothing more and nothing less than a diversion, a clever and cunning attempt to lay a false trail. The police would be trying to trace the movements of the man claiming to be Lord Arthur from the time the cabman deposited him at the Opera Hotel around eight o'clock. But what if the real Lord Arthur had crept away hours or perhaps even days before?

Speculation was rife. 'We understand the police believe that Lord Arthur Clinton has gone to America,' the *Weekly Times* reported. The *Observer* agreed, but added that 'there are people who have affirmed that His Lordship has been seen in London, and notably at Ascot'.

Rumours of the death of Lord Arthur Clinton first began to filter through to Fleet Street during the afternoon of Saturday 18th June, just in time for the final editions of the evening papers. Facts were in short supply but it appeared that the troubled Lord Arthur had died in the remote village of Muddeford in Hampshire. Or was it Huddeford, as the *Illustrated Police News* reported? Or Nuddeford, as the *Weekly Times* had it?

There was speculation – hope even – that, as an officer and a gentleman, Lord Arthur had done the decent thing and shot himself through the head with a single silver bullet. Such a course of action was very much to be desired. It would have been Lord Arthur's admission of guilt and a demonstration of his remorse. A clean and contrite conclusion to a sodomitic conspiracy which had caused a convulsion of the national mind. No washing of aristocratic dirty linen in public. No risk of further revelations. No need for a damaging and debilitating trial to further sap the nation's sense of strength and virility.

But such sanguine – not to say sanguinary – hopes were dashed when it emerged that Lord Arthur had died of natural causes just a few days short of his thirtieth birthday. 'The rumour which was current late on Saturday regarding the death of Lord Arthur Clinton is confirmed,' the *Daily Telegraph* reported two days later. Lord Arthur, it appeared, 'had been in the neighbourhood of Christchurch for some time, on a fishing excursion, passing under the title of Captain Edward Gray'.

Over the following week, more details of Lord Arthur's final days and hours emerged. 'We are in a position to give a trustworthy account of Lord Arthur Pelham Clinton's fatal illness,' the *Lancet* confided to its readers (though quite why the *Lancet* should take such an interest in Lord Arthur's untimely death was curious, to say the least).

On Monday, 13th June, doctors attending Lord Arthur 'found him suffering from sore throat and other symptoms of Scarlet Fever, which has been widely prevalent in the neighbourhood', the *Lancet* continued. 'Lodgings in the village were procured for him, and thither he was safely removed. The disease, though virulent, ran a normal course, and the patient appeared to be gaining ground.' But complications set in on the morning of Thursday, 16th June, and Lord Arthur was unable to void urine. 'The patient', the *Lancet* reported, 'had sunk very low, and, in spite of the free administration of stimulants, failed to rally. Telegrams were immediately despatched to his friends, and at five minutes past one on Saturday morning he died.'

Among those 'friends' of Lord Arthur who were telegraphed when his condition worsened was the ubiquitous and unsavoury Mr W. H. Roberts, his solicitor, who arrived in Muddeford early on the Friday morning to find his client still conscious and still rational, but in a state of 'utter prostration'.

Just hours after Lord Arthur expired, Roberts took the extraordinary step of releasing a letter purportedly dictated by him from his 'bed of sickness'. It was a deathbed denial of the accusations of sodomy made against him. 'Nothing', Lord

Arthur declared, 'can be laid to my charge other than the foolish continuation of the impersonation of theatrical characters which arose from a simple frolic in which I permitted myself to become an actor.'

If Mr Roberts and the late Lord Arthur (wherever he may be, looking down hopefully, or up, more probably, given the general dissipation of his short life) thought that this deathbed declaration of innocence would, to use a vulgar phrase, 'wash' with a hostile and sceptical public, they were much mistaken. The letter was greeted with universal incredulity and howls of raucous laughter.

On the 'sad and wasted' life of Lord Arthur Clinton, the *Daily Telegraph* confined itself to a few choice words. 'There was nothing specially notable in his Lordship's career,' it wrote, 'and it is expressing only the bare truth to say, that what was known reflected on him no credit whatever.' Under the banner headline 'A MIS-SPENT LIFE', *Reynolds's Newspaper* denounced him as 'dissolute, debauched, reckless, and brainless', 'the disreputable scion of the Newcastle family' and 'a blackguard Lord'.

'Lord Arthur's inclinations', the *Porcupine* wrote, 'seem to have led him into the worst society, into the maelstrom of London dissipation, and he ended in being charged (wrongfully, let us hope) with one of the most abominable of crimes.' The *Porcupine* concluded its moral spasm with a homily which might have been taken directly from the pages of the Old Testament. 'Verily,' it intoned piously, 'those of us who are apt to envy the lot of high-born personages may take the lesson of Lord Clinton's life and death profitably, though painfully, to heart.'

Lord Arthur's funeral took place on what would have been his thirtieth birthday. 'The funeral was unusually plain,' the

Weekly Times reported, 'and the grave, though in a secluded spot was a common one.' The main mourners present were Lord Arthur's older brother, the present Duke of Newcastle, his uncle, Lord Thomas Clinton, and the ever-present Mr Roberts.

It was, in the opinion of many, a decidedly hole-and-corner affair, conducted with a mere nod to ceremony and with almost indecent haste. Lord Arthur's family, it seemed, were falling over themselves to bury both his memory and his mortal remains as deep in the Hampshire earth as they possibly could.

Lord Arthur's corpse was enclosed in no fewer than three coffins, one of them rumoured to be made of lead, a precaution for the prevention of contagion which struck some observers as really quite excessive. Engraved under the figure of Our Blessed Lord on the silver breastplate of Lord Arthur's outer coffin was the simple text: 'He hath borne our griefs and carried our sorrows.' Opinion was divided as to whether this text was a reference to Christ in his capacity as Redeemer, or whether it was the family's sad and poignant commentary on Lord Arthur's short and dissolute life.

Even before the coffin was lowered into the yawning and hungry grave, there were those who openly doubted whether Lord Arthur was dead at all. The *Nottingham Daily Guardian*, which might be thought sympathetic to the Clinton family because of the local connection with the family seat of Clumber, reported that certain 'persons of the critical and legal cast of mind profess to doubt the authenticity of Lord Arthur Clinton's death'. 'Is Lord Arthur Clinton really dead and buried?' the *Porcupine* asked, speaking for many. 'It is no secret that persons of a suspicious mind have been heard to say that the death of Lord Arthur is "all moonshine".'

The sudden and strange disappearance and death of Lord Arthur Clinton raised more questions than answers. Why had he gone to ground in the small town of Christchurch, taking the *nom de guerre* of Captain Edward Gray? If he was, as he proclaimed, as innocent as the day is long, then why misdesignate himself in this way? It was a suspicious thing to do and plainly suggested that he did not wish to be found.

And why Christchurch? Mr Roberts's assertion that Lord Arthur had gone there for a fishing holiday was unconvincing. Though the fishing in and around Christchurch was reputed to be excellent, anybody who knew Lord Arthur would swear that his passions were theatrical, and emphatically not piscatorial. Indeed, it was said that he did not know one end of a rod from the other and he thought that a reel was an Irish jig.

For stern logicians like Inspector Thompson, the whole affair was baffling and bewildering. 'It is understood', the *Daily Telegraph* confided, 'that Inspector Thompson has been specially employed to inquire into the circumstances of Lord Arthur Clinton's decease.' Clearly there were doubts, strong doubts, within the Metropolitan Police, within the Treasury, and quite possibly within 10 Downing Street, where Lord Arthur's affectionate godfather, Mr Gladstone, still held sway.

But there were certain immutabilities that Inspector Thompson could grip hold of. Either Lord Arthur Clinton was dead or he was alive. If he was dead, he had died of natural causes, or he had taken his own life, or he had been murdered. Of these three possibilities, Inspector Thompson discounted murder. With the exception of poisoning, which could be tricky to detect, murder usually meant blood and gore and signs of violence. And there was not a scrap of evidence to suggest that Lord Arthur had been done away with.

Natural causes or suicide were both possibilities, but Inspector Thompson was unpersuaded. In his experience, the Lord Arthurs of this world did not willingly resign themselves to death or to doing the decent thing. And if Lord Arthur had planned to take his own life, why had he gone to the bother of disappearing and living under an assumed name? Why not simply blow his brains out in the comfort of his own home?

No. There were too many inconsistencies, too many contradictions. In Inspector Thompson's experience, death was starkly factual and rarely admitted to the confusion and fancy footwork which characterised this particular case. Nothing was quite right, nothing seemed to fit: the strange six-hour cab ride, 'Captain Edward Gray', the posthumous letter, and the three coffins, one of lead – to make assurance triply sure? It might be supposed that this latter was a certain means to prevent poisonous miasmas leaching out from the corpse and spreading the contagion. On the other hand, it might equally be a clever means of keeping prying eyes out of the coffin and keeping Nosy Parkers, like himself, at bay.

Lord Arthur had died in Prospect Cottage in Muddeford, attended, at the hour of his death, by only a boy. It was odd, too, that the death was notified to the authorities by this boy, Sambrooke Newlyn, the son of a coal merchant-cum-hotel proprietor. It seemed a heavy responsibility for one so young. No fewer than three doctors had attended the gentleman in Prospect Cottage suffering from scarlet fever. But curiously, not one of them could say that they actually saw him die.

Inspector Thompson's instinct told him that it was a put-up job, that Lord Arthur had not died, but merely staged his own disappearance. He doubted that the theatre-loving Lord had the necessary low cunning to carry out so audacious a plan. But

Mr Roberts was, in his opinion, more than capable of conceiving and executing such an elaborate scheme. Roberts was here, there and everywhere, with a finger in every pie and a perfect – too perfect – answer to every question. He was the spider at the centre of this very strange web of lies and deceit.

Short of exhuming the body encased in its three coffins, Inspector Thompson would never know whether Lord Arthur Clinton was dead, whether he had left for America or Paris or Buenos Aires, or indeed, whether the coffin was filled with a sack of sawdust. In any event, an exhumation based on a hunch would never be permitted.

Lord Arthur Clinton had evaded the law. He had escaped with help from his family and from his friends in high places. There was a forlorn hope that justice might still be done. Lord Arthur might make a mistake. He might one day return and be recognised in the street, in the theatre, or at Ascot.

Inspector Thompson smiled to himself. He could wait.

I n his offices in Moorgate only a day or so after Lord Arthur's funeral, Mr Roberts also smiled to himself as he sealed the envelope addressed to Mr Ouvry, the Pelham-Clinton family solicitor. Mr Roberts specialised in trouble. It was his stock in trade, his meat and drink. He was never very far from trouble, it followed him and found him out. He delighted in trouble, in solving trouble, in making trouble disappear, and making troublesome peers vanish, as if by magic. Lord Arthur was gone, and though not quite forgotten, would soon gently fade from memory like a watercolour left in the sun.

Mr Ouvry tut-tutted to himself when he opened Mr Roberts's missive. He was, he had to confess, a little taken aback by the promptitude – a promptitude verging on indecent haste – of Mr Roberts's bill for £251 of 'expenses' incurred on behalf of Lord Arthur Clinton. Not even a week had passed since Lord Arthur's interment. But Mr Roberts's claim was special, not to say unique. Mr Ouvry immediately advanced the sum of £50 but was unable to settle the bill in full because, as he explained in a private letter to Mr Gladstone, now Lord Arthur's executor, 'nothing was coming to Lord Arthur's estate'. Unfortunately, Lord Arthur's debts had not died with him and his estate was besieged on every side by angry creditors.

But in Mr Ouvry's opinion, this bill was a debt of honour that must be met by the family. 'It is impossible that the family should allow Mr Roberts who has really behaved most kindly in this matter to be out of pocket,' he wrote confidentially to Gladstone. Lord Arthur's father, the late and unfortunate Duke of Newcastle, Mr Ouvry said, 'would have paid for getting him abroad, and I would have thought would not have hesitated to meet this claim'.

There it was, in black ink on white paper, in the crabbed hand of the respected and respectable Mr Ouvry. There could be no doubt about it. Mr Roberts had got Lord Arthur abroad, he had spirited him out of the country to start a new life free from debt, free from taint, and free from the best endeavours of Inspector Thompson and his detectives. All for the not inconsiderable but still very reasonable sum of £251.

And the beauty of it all, at least from Mr Roberts's point of view, was that everyone – or almost everyone – believed that at that very moment the worms of Hampshire were feasting upon what remained of Lord Arthur's fleshly being.

This Slippery Sod

The management of the case for the prosecution on
the part of the police is entitled to the utmost
praise. Inspector Thompson, of Bow-street, has
displayed throughout an acuteness, tact, and
shrewdness reflecting the greatest credit on that
officer. 'Involuntary' witnesses have been ferreted
out, subpoenaed, and placed in the box, with a
celerity that perfectly astounded them.

Reynolds's Newspaper, 29th May 1870

M r Charles Ferguson of Abbey Green in Lanarkshire gave
an involuntary start when he heard the doorknocker so
vigorously engaged. It was not yet nine o'clock and he was not
expecting visitors, especially at so uncivilised an hour. He had
not yet breakfasted and was still *en déshabille*. Visitors were the
very last thing he wanted or needed today or, indeed, any day.

If Fanny and Stella's troubles were not enough to be going
on with, enough to worrit him and fret him and make him feel
ill, John Safford Fiske and Louis Hurt had been taken into custody four weeks ago. The net seemed to be closing, the noose
was tightening, and he could not help wondering how many
more friends, how many more acquaintances, would be rounded up, let alone whether he would be among their number.

The mere thought of nets and nooses gave him palpitations
and made him feel faint. He had not been sleeping at all well

– in truth, hardly at all – and he was at a loss to know what to do or where to go. Should he stay? After all, there was no reason why the police should ever pay a call upon Mr Charles Ferguson of Abbey Green: the respectable, retiring, irreproachable Mr Charles Ferguson of Abbey Green who travelled a great deal on business and who was hardly known by his neighbours except as a young man who kept himself very much to himself.

Or should he flee? Pack a valise with his clothes and his papers and abandon Abbey Green for ever. And go where? With the hue and cry raging in London, and the police sniffing the scent like bloodhounds in Edinburgh, the two places where he had friends and family were closed to him. But there were any number of other places he could go to. Out-of-the-way places, ordinary, very slightly dreary places, like the small town of Abbey Green (or the unpronounceable Lesmahagow, as the locals would have it), which he had chosen so carefully because no one, other than its denizens, had ever heard of it.

Or there were the cities. The best places to hide, he had been told, were the large cities, like Leeds and Manchester and Liverpool, cities where a solitary young man could settle himself quietly in a small hotel or in a suite of rooms; where his presence would be unremarkable and unremarked; where he might come and go as he pleased until the dogs were called off and he could think more clearly.

Or then again there was Paris. Arthur and Louis and Stella had so constantly sung its praises, had so constantly recounted their adventures there that he had a great longing to visit this city where the streets were paved with erotic gold. And what did it matter that his French was so poor? Love was a universal language, and he had always prided himself on having the gift of tongues.

Sometimes he would be on the point of going, his bags packed and at the door, and then he would hesitate. Something always held him back. He could not explain it. It was a strange combination of fear – fear of leaving, fear of starting afresh – and optimism: was there really any need to up sticks and travel to the ends of the earth – to Paris, at least – to escape a fate that was by no means certain? There was no reason to run. No one here knew him as anyone other than Charles Ferguson. The money from his father had always come by a highly circuitous route. It would be impossible to trace him that way. And even if the police found any of his letters, they would be hard-pushed to find him as he had always been so scrupulous about never writing down his address – though Fanny and Stella, and one or two others, of course, knew where to write to him. No, it would take a very skilled hunter to beard him in his lair.

This terrible business with Fanny and Stella and John and Louis had brought it all back. Everything he had tried to forget, everything he thought he had forgotten. All back with terrible, terrifying clarity. Asleep and awake. Every detail, every sensation played out again and again. Cold sweats. Heart pounding. Nausea in the pit of his stomach. The sensation of having been punched violently in the gut. He trembled at the very thought.

He was barely seventeen the first time it had happened, with that foolish Italian boy. He had naively fallen into the trap. It was all too good to be true and he was surprised when the boy demanded money, and kept demanding money. When he had no money left to give, the boy, true to his word, had gone to the police. Much to his shame and chagrin, he had been very publicly arrested in his father's house in Wimpole Street, and every servant in the street had talked about it for a year and a day.

Fortunately, he had been acquitted. It was his word against the boy's. The well-spoken word of a well-educated young gentleman, the son of a respected and respectable judge, against the accusations of a young Italian immigrant who had no business to be here and who seemed to be entangled in all sorts of dubious endeavours.

Mr Charles Ferguson loosened his cravat and poured himself a drink. He had been drinking rather heavily, more heavily than usual, since Fanny and Stella's arrest, and it was not the first time these past weeks that he had breakfasted upon a glass of whisky or a brandy and soda. It calmed his nerves but clouded his judgement.

Drink had been the cause of his downfall eight years before in the early hours of April Fool's Day. He was eighteen and had been drinking heavily all evening as he scoured the streets and the public houses of London looking for a man, with a signal lack of success. Sometimes it was like that. You could go for hours with nothing doing. Other times, it was there on a plate, just waiting to be eaten.

Of course, if he had wanted to pay for it, there were any number of Mary-Anns on the pad in the warren of alleys around Leicester Square who would go with him for a few shillings – plump and prosperous Mary-Anns; hungry, desperate Mary-Anns with haggard and drawn faces; handsome, dangerous Mary-Anns who were not real Mary-Anns at all, but ruffians and blackmailers who would rob you as soon as look at you.

But he did not want Mary-Anns that night. He wanted real men, strong men. Soldiers, sailors, porters, working men. Men who smelt like men. Men who fucked women. Men who would treat him as a woman. Men who would make him gamahuche them until he choked. Men who would fuck him. Brutally. No quarter given. And none expected. Men who would make him pay for the privilege.

The night had been an unmitigated disaster. In the early hours of the morning, drunk and exhausted, he had finally admitted defeat and was on his way home to Wimpole Street when he noticed the policeman standing at the top of Weymouth Mews looking at him. Staring him out of countenance. Not another soul was abroad. He may have been drunk but not drunk enough to mistake what it was the policeman wanted. It was obvious. Obvious from the way he spoke to him, obvious from the way he so manifestly adjusted his crotch, obvious from the trembling intensity of his voice. There could be no doubt about it. He could feel it. He could smell it. It was like a great galvanic wave of electricity passing between them. Wordlessly they walked into the sheltering, darkness of Weymouth Mews.

S omewhere between three and four o'clock in the morning, Police Constable George White was, he said, walking his regular beat in Weymouth Street, just north of Oxford Circus, when a clean-shaven young man of 'a rather effeminate appearance' accosted him.

'Policeman, I want to speak to you,' he said.

'I walked with him to the corner of Weymouth Mews,' Constable White recalled, 'which was only a few yards off, and went down.

'I expected that the prisoner was going to give me some important information about a burglary,' White continued. 'Instead of doing so, however, he got his arm around my neck, kissed me, and pinned me against the wall with his left knee. Then he exposed his person and otherwise acted improperly.'

Constable White responded by charging the youth with 'disgusting conduct' and said he was going to take him into custody.

According to White's testimony in court, the boy had looked as if he was about to faint. 'Oh! pray don't arrest me!' he had exclaimed. 'Have mercy on me; it nearly broke my father's heart when a charge was made against me on a former occasion. I'm sure it will be the death of him now.'

The young man struggled ineffectually to escape, White claimed, but by now another policeman, Acting Sergeant Edwin Dibdin, had appeared to lend a hand. The young man tried another tack. 'Come with me to my father's house in Wimpole Street and he'll give you twenty pounds apiece and my watch and chain,' he said in a wheedling, pleading voice. But the bribe was refused – at least according to the testimonies of White and Dibdin – and the terrified boy, white as a sheet, trembling and sobbing, was marched to Marylebone Police Station where he gave his name as Charles Ferguson, aged nineteen, and was formally charged with 'having indecently exposed himself and trying to incite a Police-Constable to commit an indecent offence'.

Charles Ferguson appeared before Mr Yardley, the magistrate, the next day, whereupon he shamefacedly admitted that his real name was Edward Henry Park, the son of Judge Alexander Park. 'I am ashamed to say,' he told Mr Yardley, 'but I never was more drunk in all my life. I have no recollection of anything that passed.'

It was a clever defence. A young man, blind drunk, larking around, clumsy and stumbling, needs to empty his bladder urgently, exposes his person in front of a passing police constable and accidentally falls upon said police constable. A clever defence which was to fail dismally. Harry Park was committed for trial. With the evidence against him he could expect a hefty prison sentence. Bail was set at the enormous sum of six hundred pounds. But it was a price worth paying, Judge Alexander Park reasoned, if it meant his beloved son's freedom.

No sooner was Harry released than he forfeited bail and disappeared from the face of the earth, and was to remain disappeared for eight long years.

I nspector Thompson permitted himself a rare smile of satisfaction, gazing out of the window of the train as it chugged northwards through a landscape of soot-blackened red-brick factories and chimneys belching forth giant clouds of mephitic vapours.

Thompson had every reason to be satisfied. He had four in the bag, which was not a bad day's work, all things considered. He knew that dozens, perhaps even hundreds more had been arrested up and down the land, and those who had fled abroad or gone to ground would not dare to flaunt themselves in public again any time soon. He had, as yet, failed to apprehend Cumming and Thomas, but there was plenty of time to turn his attention to those young men. Only Lord Arthur Clinton, the biggest prize of them all, was beyond his reach after conveniently – rather too conveniently, he thought – dropping dead of the scarlet fever.

This one he was after now was by way of a bonus. An unexpected but nevertheless most satisfying catch who had cleverly evaded detection for eight long years. By tomorrow this slippery sod would be safely in custody and, if Inspector

Thompson got his way, he would go to prison for a very long time.

Inspector Thompson turned his attention to his travelling companion, who was an altogether unprepossessing specimen. George White looked as if he was in his forties, but was probably younger. He was tall, burly and running to fat now. But eight years ago, when he would have been a little slimmer, a little more upright in his smart police uniform with gleaming buttons, the Margeries and the Mary-Anns must have seen him as a fine figure of a man.

Inspector Thompson did not know, and did not wish to know, exactly what it was that White had done. All he knew was that he had left the police force under a cloud. It must have been something bad because, even under the new broom, corruption was still rife and still tolerated. No doubt White had been stupid or greedy, or both, and got caught red-handed.

It was that one letter, one among many hundreds of letters, that had caught Inspector Thompson's eye and led him to this forlorn and forgotten corner of Lanarkshire in vigorous pursuit of his prey. It was in a trunkful of papers belonging to Lord Arthur Clinton which the fearsome Miss Ann Empson, Lord Arthur's splenetic former landlady, had commandeered until the rent was paid in full. Miss Empson was still spitting pins when she got in touch with him and said she had important information about those funny He-She Ladies (though, in *her* humble opinion, they were very far from being ladies).

That one letter had stood out from all the rest:

> Dear Stella,
>   You can easily imagine how dull I am and disinclined to write. I hope you will have much fun tonight and both

you and Dan must send me news as soon as is
convenient. I left the two ladies a few moments after you
departed but met them again at 12. Bob never turned up
but Stenney came at 3 o'c. I forgot all about the photos
and he never mentioned them – he saw me to the Station.
I came from Holytown with George and James
Tudthorpe.

Today is Glasgow Fast. I will positively write again
soon but at this present I *cannot*,

Love to Fanny

Yours ever

Harry

PS: Of course I have as ever left a few little things
behind such as the Glycerine – *that* don't matter but I
cannot find (oh horror!) those filthy photographs nor
Louis's likeness. I do hope they are not lying about your
rooms.

No address, no date and signed only 'Harry'. Inspector
Thompson knew that any letter addressed to 'Stella' was most
likely written by a fellow votary of the Hermaphrodite Clique.
The postscript gave the game away: it was obvious what
'Harry' meant when he referred to 'those filthy photographs'.
'Oh horror!' indeed. Inspector Thompson was only too painfully aware of the vast trade in indecent and obscene photographs that went on under the very noses of the police, including photographs of the most depraved and disgusting acts of
sodomy between men.

Rather more recondite was the reference to 'Glycerine'. At
first sight it seemed innocuous enough, but to any policeman
like himself, with a working knowledge of sodomy and sodom-

ites, it spoke scarlet volumes. From plain old-fashioned spittle to cold cream, lard and butter, he knew they needed these lubricating agents in furtherance of their filthy games. Glycerine was the very latest thing, he had been told. It was quite the rage amongst them. He shuddered at the very thought.

Whatever the shortcomings of the Metropolitan Police Detective Force – and they were legion – it excelled at the administrative apparatus of criminality, at keeping lists, records, photographs of suspected and convicted criminals alike. These records revealed that Park had an older brother, Edward Henry Park, also known as Charles Ferguson, who had been charged with attempted indecency upon a police officer eight years ago.

Henry or Harry? Was it possible? No address. No date. No surname. But adrift in the tumultuous sea of paper in Lord Arthur's trunk there was an envelope and upon that envelope there was a postmark. He had never heard of Abbey Green but he understood it to be somewhere in Lanarkshire. A telegram to Glasgow. Discreet enquiries undertaken. They were looking for a Mr Park or a Mr Ferguson (or any other young Englishman of effeminate appearance aged around twenty-six) living in or around Abbey Green. It was a long shot, but it had proved to be a lucky shot, a very lucky shot.

M r Charles Ferguson of Abbey Green was not entirely sober. Truth be told, he was some considerable distance from sobriety, but he carried his drink very well and could muster enough gentlemanly self-possession to instruct the girl to show his visitors in. He felt a familiar churning in the pit of his stomach as he recognised the unmistakable presence, the unmistakable smell of a policeman, though neither of his two visitors were dressed as such.

George White spoke first.

'Mr Edward Henry Park?' It was as a much a statement of fact as it was a question.

'Will you have something to drink?' Charles Ferguson countered, fumbling with the decanter.

George White nodded to Inspector Thompson. Yes, they had the right man.

'You are wanted for absconding from bail,' Inspector Thompson said calmly, 'while awaiting trial for serious offences.'

Harry Park turned to face his visitors.

'Not likely,' he replied. 'It's so long ago. They had the "tin", had they not?'

Inspector Thompson turned and looked at George White disdainfully. He knew full well what Harry Park meant by the 'tin'. It meant money paid for sex, money extorted after sex. So that was it. George White and Edwin Dibdin. They were in it together. A racket. White would entice the sodomites. Something disgusting would take place. Money demanded with menaces. Money handed over. And then the poor sod would still be arrested. He almost felt sorry for Harry Park and for the others – for there would have been others, you could be sure of that.

Three days later, on the day Fanny and Stella were released on bail, Harry Park, 'a tall, stylishly-dressed young man, who had an effeminate aspect, no beard or whiskers, slight moustache, and hair carefully parted in the centre', was back in Marylebone Police Court. 'The bench and court were densely crowded with persons anxious to hear the trial,' the *Illustrated Police News* reported. Harry Park had nothing to say for himself, except his name and his address and that he left the case entirely in the hands of his solicitor.

In court, Mr Sergeant Parry was eloquent in his plea of mitigation.

'I am here at the earnest request of a broken-hearted father. Where Park has learnt such degrading practices it is utterly impossible to surmise or guess, and the father's anguish must be the greater in thinking that all his care and anxiety should meet with this sad result.

'Many persons are of the opinion that the perpetration of such offences in itself shows something wanting in mind and feeling which indicates that the offender is not in full possession of his faculties, and that such cases would be far better treated in a lunatic asylum than in a court of Justice.'

But Mr Sergeant Parry's oratory fell on deaf ears. The magistrate, Mr D'Eyncourt, was not to be swayed by pleas for mercy or intimations of insanity. He sentenced Harry Park to twelve months' imprisonment with hard labour, the heaviest sentence he was able to impose under the law, he said. Harry Park remained impassive as the sentence was handed down, but his frail-looking father, Judge Alexander Park, was seen to stagger under the weight of the blow.

'Pestiferous and Pestilential'

What words can paint the infamy of such Hellish
proceedings on the part of men towards those of
their own sex?

Extraordinary Revelations, 1870

At the time of Fanny and Stella's arrest in April 1870, the
subjects of Queen Victoria could be forgiven for thinking
that their world was under siege from an army of threats: internal and external, visible and invisible, actual and imagined.
Things seemed to be getting worse rather than better, and
many thought that they could hear the not-so-distant thunder
of the hooves of the Horsemen of the Apocalypse: pestilence,
war, famine and death.

The nation was in a state of flux, of transformation. The
world seemed to be changing almost daily. New ideas, new
inventions and new ideologies were everywhere. There were
threats of war, revolts and revolutions at home and abroad. The
Fenians were bringing terror to the streets of London, Liverpool and Manchester, and nobody knew where they might
strike next. And there were no less important revolutions of the
mind, revolutions which seemed to shake and shatter the old
certainties. Mr Charles Darwin seemed to be suggesting that
Man was not created by God in His own image, but was actually descended from the bestial ape, and might very well revert
to that bestial state.

Contagious diseases had become virtually endemic, and frequently erupted into epidemics: smallpox, consumption, cholera, typhus, typhoid, scarletina, diphtheria, influenza, measles and the whooping cough killed off large swathes of the population, especially infants and children, and debilitated those who survived.

And there were other contagions, no less dangerous, no less threatening to the nation's health. There were the multiple and interlinked contagions of poverty, crime, disorder, immorality and vice. Especially vice. Prostitution was everywhere, with some experts positing that there were no fewer than a hundred thousand prostitutes working in London, or one prostitute to every ten men. Marriage was on the wane, and yet the numbers of children born – especially to the very poor – just grew and grew. As the poor became more numerous, the slums of the cities expanded, becoming the breeding grounds for all the spoken and unspoken ills of society.

The certainties and clarities of a divinely ordered hierarchical society where all men – and women – knew their station had been replaced by an anarchic world driven by instinct and appetite, by lust and by greed; a random, rudderless and unfixed world where the old bastions of religion, law, custom and morality were buffeted and besieged by forces so dark and so primal they could barely be apprehended, let alone understood.

Doubt – a corrosive, contagious and cancerous doubt – had entered into the heart and soul of the nation. Fears, anxieties and uncertainties seemed to swirl about the landscape of the national psyche like a London pea-souper, casting strange new shapes and shadows upon a once familiar landscape. Much of this doubt seemed to coalesce and dwell upon the human body, upon its sexual frailties and deviations, and upon the concomitant afflictions which – many thought – were visited upon the land as divine retribution for sins of the flesh.

Of all these sexual contagions, syphilis – silent, creeping, invisible and ultimately deadly – was the most feared. Many believed that syphilis was causing degeneration in the wider population. If syphilis continued to spread unchecked, then future generations would be enfeebled and made even more prone to disease and early death. Mr William Henry Sloggett, a noted surgeon, was in deadly earnest when he told a Royal Commission that he was convinced that 'the effect of venereal disease is to deteriorate and sometimes to produce the gradual *extinction* of a race, as is the case of the South Sea Islanders'.

Everyone was agreed that something had to be done to stem the rising tide of filth, immorality and disease that threatened to inundate and destroy Britannia and all that she stood for. What was needed was 'a grand movement . . . to improve the social and moral condition of the inhabitants of this country', a newspaper editorial rousingly declared. It was to be a vast sanitary and social engineering endeavour, a modern crusade, designed not merely to reclaim Jerusalem from the infidel, but to remake it, to build a new Jerusalem for the modern world.

Innumerable commissions of the great and the good were established to enquire minutely into every aspect of life, most especially into the lives of the poor: into their housing, their sanitation, their children, their diet, their health, their leisure, their habits and their work. There were grand plans afoot to clear slums and eradicate overcrowding; to provide sewers and clean drinking water; to set standards of hygiene in common lodging houses; to have compulsory education and compulsory vaccination for children; to regulate working conditions in factories; reform the legal system; and stop the adulteration of food. Innumerable charities were established with the stated aim of reclaiming prostitutes, encouraging temperance and promoting sexual continence.

If the lives and habits of the poor could be regulated and controlled, if they could be sanitised, the entire nation would benefit. Just as the children of the poor would be vaccinated against disease, society would be inoculated against the evils of crime and disorder, plague and pestilence, revolt, revolution and degeneration.

Sex between men had long been a target for those who wanted to cleanse society of its vices. And sodomy with its clear associations with excrement lay at the very confluence of potent fears, both old and new, about sex, dirt, disease and death which haunted the national psyche.

Sodomy was both an old and a new vice. It was as old as sin, as old as the Old Testament itself, as old as the horrible fate of the Cities of the Plain, Sodom and Gomorrah, destroyed by fire and brimstone.

From the Middle Ages onwards, there was a widely held belief that sodomy, even the least toleration of sodomy, would bring down divine retribution upon an entire nation. Sodomy was, as the illustrious jurist Edward Coke wrote, '*contra ordinationem Creatoris et naturae ordinem*', contrary to the commandments of God and the order of Nature.

Even to speak the very word was dangerous. Sodomy was the '*crimen inter Christianos non nominandum*', the crime not to be named among Christians. To say the word was to invoke the diabolical deed and bring calamity in its wake. In 1642 Governor Bradford of New England spoke of sodomy and buggery as 'things fearful to name'.

Sir Robert Heath, the Attorney-General who, in 1631, prosecuted the Earl of Castlehaven in a state trial in Westminster Hall for committing sodomy with his servants, warned that the Earl's crimes were 'of that pestiferous and pestilential nature that if they be not punished they will draw from Heaven heavy judgements upon this Kingdom'.

'Pestiferous and pestilential' was more than mere rhetoric on the part of Sir Robert Heath. He meant exactly what he said: sodomy was literally plague-bringing. If even a single case of sodomy went unpunished, the Kingdom would be collectively and divinely punished by plagues, contagions and pestilences. 'By these abominations the land is defiled,' he declared, 'therefore the Lord does visit this Land for the iniquity thereof.'

In his masque *Sodom*, John Wilmot, Earl of Rochester and celebrated Restoration rake, wrote of the imaginary Kingdom of Sodom ruled by King Bolloxinion and Queen Cunitigratia. Advised by Borastus, his 'Buggermaster-General', and encouraged by Buggeranthos, General of the Army, Bolloxinion decrees, in a fit of pique, that sodomy is to be the new order of the day:

> Henceforth, Borastus, set the Nation free,
> Let conscience have its force of Liberty,
> I do proclaim, that Buggery may be us'd
> Through all the Land, so Cunt be not abus'd.

The Kingdom of Sodom is turned upon its head. All is in 'hugger-mugger': topsy-turvy, upside-down and inside-out. Death and disease stalk the land; children are stillborn; crops fail; and the people are 'raving and mad'. Sodom totters on the edge of a dark abyss. A despairing Flux, the King's Physician and 'Man of Philosophy', beseeches Bolloxinion to reverse his decree in an effort to cure the 'epidemical' and 'tortur'd pains your Nation doth endure'. But Flux's pleas falls on deaf ears. 'I'll reign and bugger still,' a defiant Bolloxinion proclaims, provoking a horrible chorus of 'firy demons' to rise up in a cloud of 'fire, brimstone and smoke'. It is Hell upon earth.

When, in February and March 1750, two earthquakes shook London, Thomas Sherlock, the Bishop of London, declared them divine retribution for the rise of sodomy in the city:

> The unnatural Lewdness, of which we have heard so much of late, is something more than Brutish and can hardly be mentioned without offending chaste Ears, and yet cannot be passed over entirely in Silence, because of the particular Mark of Divine Vengeance set upon it in the Destruction of *Sodom* by Fire from Heaven. Dreadful Example!

In the 1840s and 1850s there had been shocking revelations about the prevalence of sodomy and the rape of boys in the convict barracks of New South Wales and in the mines of Van Diemen's Land. Questions had been asked in Parliament.

By the 1860s, sodomy was a vice that was once again beginning to exercise, to agitate, to vex society. Hardly a week passed without some veiled – and often not so veiled – references to unnatural or abominable crimes in local and national newspapers.

In January 1866 the journalist James Greenwood anonymously published three articles in the *Pall Mall Gazette*. 'A Night in the Workhouse' was Greenwood's sensational account of the night he passed in the casual ward of the Lambeth workhouse, the locked male ward where the dispossessed and the dislocated could pass the night; all the vagrants, trampers, ex-convicts and assorted riff-raff who had fetched up hungry and homeless and hopeless on the streets of Lambeth.

It was a shocking revelation of human degradation; of poverty, dirt, disease and, most shockingly of all, of raw and unrestrained – almost feral – sodomy between men and between men and boys. As he witnessed naked 'great hulking ruffians' and 'dirty scoundrels' seeking bedmates for the night, as he lay in the dark listening to the 'infamous' sexual noises of the night, Greenwood 'could not help thinking of the fate of Sodom'.

There was new knowledge of old sins; new scientific facts were being formulated. In *Hard Times*, Charles Dickens's novel of industrial life, Thomas Gradgrind, the cruel factory owner, is a man obsessed with facts:

> 'Now, what I want is Facts,' said Mr Gradgrind. 'Teach
> these boys and girls nothing but Facts. Facts alone are
> wanted in life. Plant nothing else, and root out
> everything else. You can only form the minds of
> reasoning animals upon Facts: nothing else will ever be
> of service to them . . . Stick to Facts, sir!'

Facts, facts and more facts were the intellectual *lingua franca* of the nineteenth century. Victorians were obsessed with facts and the classification of facts. Taxonomy, or the science of 'classification, of putting things in their proper order', according to an anonymous lexicographer in 1839, first made its appearance in relation to botanical and mineral samples in the early part of the nineteenth century. By the 1850s, taxonomy had become not so much a method of classification as a potent guiding principle. The Victorian world-view was dominated by a need – a need verging on a compulsion – to order, to classify, to list and to designate; to establish relationships, formulate hierarchies and assign values. Nothing escaped this minute taxonomic enquiry. Everything was grist to the great mill of knowledge which ground out the meal of the modern world.

And now this great taxonomic enterprise was turning its attention to sodomy and sodomites. Learned tomes on medical jurisprudence began for the first time to describe the symptoms of sodomy. Articles and books started to appear – in France and Germany at first, but soon imported to Britain – which attempted to define and classify the sodomite, by his ways, his wiles and his physical characteristics. Experts included Casper in Germany, translated into English in 1864, and Tardieu in France (whose 1857 treatise on sodomy would find its way into the eager hands of Dr Paul). There were new names for old sinners, like 'Uranian', first coined in 1864, and 'homosexual', invented in 1869. There were even the slow, steady rumblings of medical and legal debate about the rights and wrongs of sex between men.

In 1867, three years before the arrest of Fanny and Stella, the *Medical Times and Gazette* had published an article by an anonymous 'alienist', a new breed of doctor who sought to bridge the physiological and the psychological, the sexual and the social. Entitled 'Aberrations of the Sexual Instinct', the article was a comprehensive catalogue, a complete taxonomy of unnatural behaviour, singling out for especial concern and condemnation the linked vices of masturbation, androgyny and sodomy.

By the 1860s, the dangers of masturbation had become a

national obsession verging on mass hysteria. Masturbation in girls and women – or 'peripheral excitement' as the distinguished obstetric surgeon Isaac Baker Brown termed it – was thought to be responsible for a raft of female ailments including painful menstruation, melancholia, hysteria, epilepsy, nymphomania, dementia and death.

Boys who masturbated or who were deemed at risk of masturbating were isolated and variously beaten, clamped, bound, bathed, exercised, physicked, hectored and lectured. Not only did masturbation lead to a bewilderingly wide variety of diseases from spermatorrhea to blindness, it also sapped vitality, weakening and destroying the healthy male body. But most seriously of all, masturbation inexorably led by paths secret and mysterious to sodomy.

Masturbation also sapped virility, making men biologically and psychologically less manly, more androgynous, more effeminate, dangerously closer to that weaker vessel, woman. 'Androgynism', the *Medical Times and Gazette* declared, 'may be taken to mean the intrusion of either sex, voluntarily or not, into the province of the other; to wit, when a woman dissects a dead body, or a man measures a young woman for a pair of stays.'

There was growing concern and complaint about the increasing visibility of masculine women and effeminate men. 'There is not the slightest doubt', a carefully worded editorial in the *Englishwoman's Domestic Magazine* announced, 'that England is hastening towards the border which divides the sexes; already persons have over-stepped and stand alone, hated and despised.' The *Pall Mall Gazette* launched a lengthy diatribe against the 'unsexed' masculine woman who seeks to 'usurp' the place of men:

She has probably learned to smoke, and she takes kindly
to a little strong drink; she talks slang, perhaps she bets,
perhaps dabbles in the share market. She pants for
excitement of a fierce and manly kind – for excitement
that will stimulate her, that will satisfy her – for
excitement that will unsex her.

As early as 1857, *The Times* was fulminating about a new
breed of smirking and 'respectable young men who serve in
drapers' shops': 'For our own part we would far rather see any
son of ours wielding the saw or the trowel, or even standing
side by side with navvies on parade, than mincing and bowing
and rubbing his hands to "carriage people" during the best
days of an effeminate life.'

'Smirking, mincing and effeminate': it was clear that the
Thunderer's ire was directed at what it saw as the emergence
of a new class or type of young men, men who were neither one
thing nor the other, neither fish, nor fowl, nor good red meat,
not men and not women, in-between men, 'mistakes', androgynous, effeminate men, sodomites by instinct and inclination,
young men in fact very much cast in the mould of Fanny and
Stella.

It was not for nothing that in 1851 the Registrar-General
described the shortage of men over twenty years of age as 'unnatural'. Marriage was waning, healthy young men were in
short supply and yet androgynous, epicene young men seemed
to be on the increase. Something was wrong. Very wrong.

There was a widespread feeling of unease that sodomy was
spreading. 'The increase of these monsters in the shape of men
commonly designated as Margeries, Pooffs, &c, of late years, in
the great metropolis, renders it necessary for the safety of the

public, that they should be made known,' *The Yokel's Preceptor* warned in the 1850s.

After the arrest of Fanny and Stella, simmering public anxiety and indignation at the spread of sodomy reached a crescendo. Fanny and Stella were, it seemed, the tiny, visible tip of a vast iceberg. For every sodomite 'who is known, innumerable persons unknown offend in a similar way', reported the *Daily Telegraph*. The *Saturday Review* heartily agreed. 'It is certain that the numbers are far more numerous than it is pleasant to imagine.'

Not only was sodomy on the increase, but rather more seriously, sodomites were becoming more visible, and more flagrant. 'A certain form of iniquity has, within the last year or two, been thrust more openly than of old on the attention of the public,' claimed the *Daily Telegraph*. Sodomites were organised and confederated. They were a gang; they were part of 'a doubtful fellowship'; they formed a 'clique', and, most worryingly of all, a class.

The newspapers worried where it all might end if left unchecked. 'Vice,' the *Daily Telegraph* warned, 'emboldened by impunity, will at length stalk forth boldly from its secret haunts, and flaunt about in public places in a way that must compel attention.' *The Times* went even further: 'There is no saying how far things might go in a year or two,' it prophesied. '"Drag" might become quite an institution, and open carriages might display their disguised occupants without suspicion.'

What was to be done, what could be done in the face of this tidal wave of sodomy? *Reynolds's Newspaper* drew an explicit comparison with Sodom and Gomorrah. 'This London of ours is as foul a sink of iniquity as were certain Jewish cities of old, which, for their flagrant wickedness, met with retributive destruction by fire from heaven.' Clearly, the fate of London, of Britain, and of its empire-in-all-but-name hung by a sodomitic thread. The only solution was to root out and destroy sodomy before 'fire, brimstone and smoke' engulfed the nation.

That the contagion of sodomy had spread, was spreading, and had infected all levels of society was not in doubt. The question was how far had it already spread, and how much further might it spread. There was, the *Pall Mall Gazette* thought, a strong sense of 'organisation and concert' involved in this sodomitic 'conspiracy'. Sodomites were essentially vampiric. In order to survive, they were driven and compelled to corrupt the innocent and, in so doing, create even more sodomites. 'It is essential for its continuance that it should go on enlisting fresh members,' the paper warned.

It was this idea of a deliberate and purposeful conspiracy to spread the contagion of sodomy, to infect – and by infecting, re-cruit – new sodomites which so frightened the authorities. The very words used in the indictment against Fanny and Stella – conspiring, confederating, combining, agreeing 'with divers other persons whose names are unknown' – revealed the fear of a contagion that was turning into an epidemic, a veritable plague.

As sodomites, especially as effeminate sodomites, disguised as women, and prostituting themselves, Fanny and Stella and everything they stood for touched some of society's deepest and darkest fears of dirt, degeneration, syphilis, excrement, poverty, violence and effeminisation.

Sodomites had to be identified and stopped, though where to start? The arrest of Fanny and Stella was just the beginning. With the sanction of religion, law and custom, and with the support of a modern and powerful police, the lines of battle were drawn. It was nothing less than a crusade, a great and grand design to discover, defeat and destroy the dark Kingdom of Sodom, to banish it, once and for all, from this green and pleasant land.

26

The Ship of State

'Herald, read the accusation!' said the King. On
this the White Rabbit blew three blasts on the
trumpet, and then unrolled the parchment scroll,
and read as follows:

    'The Queen of Hearts, she made some tarts,
    'All on a summer day:
    'The Knave of Hearts, he stole those tarts,
    'And took them quite away!'
    'Consider your verdict,' the King said to the jury.

Alice's Adventures in Wonderland, 1865

'To judge from the crowd assembled in Westminster Hall at an early hour,' the *Daily Telegraph* reported, 'there has been no falling-off of the public interest in this twice-told tale.' It was almost a year to the day since the arrest of Fanny and Stella in drag outside the Strand Theatre, and a large crowd had gathered in Palace Yard this brilliant May morning to catch a glimpse of the defendants as they arrived. Many of them were hoping to squeeze into the public gallery to watch what they hoped would be the trial of the decade, if not the century.

The trial of the Young Men in Women's Clothes was a trial that some had predicted would never take place, especially after the Attorney-General himself had suddenly and dramatic-ally intervened in early July 1870 and withdrawn all charges of sodomy against Ernest Boulton and Frederick Park. Fanny and Stella (along with Louis Hurt and John Safford Fiske, against whom charges of sodomy had also been withdrawn) were released on bail quietly and without fanfare, and it was generally assumed that that was that and the entire dismal and disturbing affair would gently fade from public memory, like a photograph left out in the sun. The *Porcupine* was confident that 'the public are not likely to be troubled much further in this matter'. The *Penny Illustrated* agreed: 'It is thought nothing more will be heard of the Young Men in Women's Clothes.'

To all intents and purposes, Fanny and Stella had vanished off the face of the earth. There had been neither sight nor sound of them since they were released on bail in July 1870. The months had gone by and not a squeak, not a whimper, not a whisper had been heard from them or about them. It was, perhaps, too much to hope that they were dead. Too much to hope that they had done the decent thing and died by their own hand. Or that they were dead from natural – or rather, *un*natural – causes, from the foul contagions that their course of life must necessarily have inflicted upon them. Or – vain hope! – that they had died from shame and remorse (though neither of them had yet exhibited the least bit – not a morsel, not a scrap, not a crumb – of these worthy Christian virtues).

If not death, then it was profoundly to be hoped that their disappearance was for good (in every sense of the word), that they had had the sense to flee these islands, never again to return and so disturb and upset the nation's equanimity. More prosaically and more probably, they had gone to ground and were merely lying low. Even if they wanted to flee, or 'scarper' as their slang talk had it, good Inspector Thompson and his team of detectives were no doubt alert to that possibility and would be watching their every move, just as they had watched their every move for a year or more before their arrest.

All that might be said by way of mitigation and by way of compassion was that the families of Boulton and Park had exercised and demonstrated the most Christian charity and forbearance in giving these hunted and cornered beasts shelter and food, though a sound birching and a fatal dose of prussic acid might have been more to the point.

So it had come as a shock and a jolt after all these months to discover that Fanny and Stella and their confederates – eight of them in all – still had a case to answer and were to answer that case in the Court of Queen's Bench, the highest court in the land, before the highest judge in land, the Lord Chief Justice, and a special jury.

Just before ten o'clock Fanny and Stella made their way with some difficulty through the crammed courtroom towards the plain and simple wooden bench where defendants and counsel alike would sit for the duration of the case. Both Fanny and Stella had flowers – 'a bouquet of flowers' – in their button-holes and both were dressed, according to one of the witnesses, 'somewhat more tastily' than was quite common with young men.

'Boulton was scarcely altered in looks since his appearance at Bow Street and, except for the faint shade of a moustache, he might still easily have been taken for a girl in boy's clothes,' the *Daily Telegraph* breathlessly reported. 'Park, on the other hand, has grown stout, and his large whiskers have so altered his face as completely to deprive it of the feminine look which it wore a year ago.'

If Fanny and Stella were nervous, they did not show it. But they were subdued. Indeed, their demeanour was quite different from that bravado, that defiant jocularity which had so characterised – and in the opinion of many, so disfigured – their many appearances at Bow Street a year ago. Now, they had every appearance of being sober, serious and dignified young men. Fanny's stoutness and luxuriant dark whiskers proclaimed her masculinity, and even Stella had made her nod to maleness with the 'faint shade of a moustache' that dear, dull Louis Hurt had begged her, in vain, to grow.

Gone, too, were those 'campish' ways of theirs: the constantly darting eyes, the cocked eyebrows, the pursed lips and the theatrically expressive faces. There was no more playing to the gallery. There was no more giggling or flirting or ogling or chirruping. There were no more hissing sibilants; no more contemptuous snorts; no more withering looks; no more tossings of actual or imaginary curls; no more flutterings of eyelashes; no more swishings of metaphorical bombazines. Every detail of Fanny and Stella's outward appearance in the Court of Queen's Bench that morning proclaimed them to be elegant, educated and civilised young gentlemen. This transformation, this miraculous migration from vicious effeminacy to virtuous manhood, was the work of one man: their new solicitor, Mr George Lewis.

Mr George Lewis was a very different kettle of fish from the beleaguered Mr Abrams who had single-handedly and with great gallantry acted as the Forlorn Hope of Fanny and Stella's defence from the moment of their arrest, but who, it had quickly become apparent, was floundering badly in the face of the magnitude and complexity of the charges levelled against them. Mr George Lewis was ferocious and formidable. He was a force to be reckoned with, provoking fear and love in equal measure. He was an implacable prosecutor and a determined defender, and he had a growing reputation as the man to turn to when scandal threatened. The Prince of Wales himself had consulted him when he was named as a lover – as one of several lovers – of Lady Harriet Mordaunt in the sensational action for divorce brought by her husband, Sir Charles Mordaunt. Mr George Lewis had advised His Royal Highness to go into the witness box and had, by all accounts, so perfectly coached him in what to say and how to say it that he was credited with saving not only the Prince's tattered reputation, but also the institution of the Monarchy itself.

Mr George Lewis was a different sort of a solicitor from the commonality of solicitors. More of a general: a Marlborough or a Wellington or a Napoleon. He was obsessed with each and every detail of a case. Nothing, however small, however insignificant, escaped his notice, and yet he always kept his eye on the great game. He would tell his clients what to wear, what to say, how to act – in court and outside court. His clients were his puppets, they were putty in his extraordinary hands.

In person, Mr George Lewis was quiet, polite, unassuming. Indeed, most of those present in Westminster Hall for Fanny and Stella's trial hardly noticed this young-looking, slightly built man, prematurely grey and with abundant Dundreary whiskers who accompanied them into court. He looked like a clerk and he liked it that way. He did not want to stand out from the crowd. He liked to be unobtrusive and self-effacing. He liked to beaver away behind the scenes, delving and digging, dissecting and directing.

Mr George Lewis was nothing if not rigorous. Rigour was the beginning, the middle and the end of his work as a solicitor.

He left nothing to chance. He would devour depositions and scour witness statements looking for errors, anomalies, contradictions. And he made sure that he read everything himself. Indeed, shortly after taking on the case of the Young Men in Women's Clothes, he had presented himself at Mr Pollard's office at the Treasury and insisted on reading through each and every deposition and document, each and every letter and note and report connected with the case.

Mr George Lewis wanted to find out everything there was to know, and more besides. His methods were said to be as unorthodox as they were audacious. He had an extensive and unrivalled network of informants – 'a spider's web of narks and spies', as one disgruntled observer put it – which he would use to devastating effect in turning up new evidence that the police would never have found in a month of Sundays. He revelled in theatrical flourishes, producing surprise new witnesses, like a magician pulling rabbits out of a hat.

Mr George Lewis disliked injustice in any shape or form. The case of Boulton and Park, friendless, despised and beleaguered, and with all the apparatus and power of a merciless State ranged against them, may have touched a chord of sympathy and compassion within him and prompted him to offer his services. That and the fact that the case was widely regarded not just as unwinnable, but also as toxic, a case that would infect and poison all those who had dealings with it. Whatever the reason, now that he had taken the case, Mr George Lewis let it be known to one and all that he would fight for Fanny and Stella with every fibre of his being. He would fight and he would win.

Of the eight men whose names were listed in the Indictment, only four were present in court. Lord Arthur Clinton was dead and buried, supposedly of scarlet fever, but there were many who thought he was merely playing dead, that he was comfortably ensconced abroad, cocking a snook at the police and at the public morals. Three of the defendants, Martin Luther Cumming (the Comical Countess), William Somerville and Cecil 'Sissy' Thomas, had never been interviewed, let alone apprehended, and were to be tried in their absence. That left just four defendants who were there in the flesh: Ernest Boulton, Frederick Park, Louis Hurt and John Safford Fiske.

Many if not most of those who had managed to push and squeeze themselves into the small courtroom found themselves not a little baffled and bewildered by the charges. It appeared that none of the defendants were charged with *actual* acts of buggery or sodomy, nor even with acts falling short of buggery or sodomy. No, they were charged with 'conspiracy to solicit, induce, procure and endeavour to persuade persons unknown to commit buggery'. It struck many present that morning, from the highest to the lowest, that such a charge was somehow incomplete and rather lopsided. Was it really possible to convict persons for the thought but not for the deed? It was like bread without butter, cakes without ale, pie without mash. How could you prove the intention without the act? And where would it all end? If minds were now to be read, if private thoughts and whims and wishes and fancies were now constituted crimes, who then was safe from the long arm of the law?

Fanny and Stella (and the absent Comical Countess) were also charged with a second offence: that they 'unlawfully and wickedly did conspire, confederate, combine' to 'openly and publicly pretend and hold themselves out and appear to be women and thereby to inveigle, induce and incite divers of the male subjects of Her Majesty improperly, lewdly and indecently to fondle and toy with them as women and thereby openly and scandalously to outrage public decency and to offend against public morals'.

(Not that anyone could ever have been fooled – even for a moment – by the Comical Countess. Miss Martin Luther Cumming might publicly pretend and hold herself out to be a woman until she was blue in the face, but, in her case, wishes were emphatically not kisses. She was and would always be a clownish and clowning fat young man, blowsily and badly dressed as a woman, an object of fascination, repulsion, ridicule and – strangely – sometimes pity.)

Here again, some of those present in Westminster Hall had the unworthy thought that when all was said and done, this second charge of conspiracy and confederation amounted to not much more than dressing up in drag and flirting with gentlemen.

Not to put too fine a point on it, the case against the four young men was all at sea. Everything was upside-down and inside-out and back-to-front. The judicial cart was being put before the horse. Instead of being tried for the crimes they had committed, these four young men were on trial for crimes they had yet to commit, for crimes they might have thought about, or talked about, or imagined for a moment in their mind's eye – or not, as the case may be. No wonder that some were reminded of nothing so much as the strange topsy-turvy trial of the Knave of Hearts for stealing the tarts in Mr Lewis Carroll's curious and entertaining book, *Alice's Adventures in Wonderland*.

All the might and main of the great Ship of State had been brought to bear upon the Young Men in Women's

Clothes. Every cannon had been primed and loaded and trained and targeted upon Fanny and Stella, ready to fire a deadly broadside. The Attorney-General himself was to lead the charge, which was a rare and notable occurrence, usually reserved for only the gravest of grave cases, for the most serious of seditioners and for the highest of high treasoners. And even then, it had been many a long year – long beyond the memory of most there that day – since the Attorney-General had stripped down to his long drawers and stepped into the ring for a bare-knuckle, bloody fight, ably seconded by the Solicitor-General brandishing a sponge soaked in vinegar. And it had been centuries, quite literally, since an Attorney-General had personally prosecuted a case of sodomy – two hundred and forty years, almost to the day, in fact, since Sir Robert Heath, Attorney-General to Charles I, had stood up in Westminster Hall to denounce the Earl of Castlehaven for multiple acts of sodomy with his servants.

Defending Fanny and Stella (and Louis Hurt and John Safford Fiske, who might just as well have been numbered among the absentee and absconded defendants for all the notice anyone took of them) was the flower of the British Bar, if that was not too great a stretch of the imagination to describe the half-dozen or so overstuffed, barrel-chested, bewhiskered and bewigged barristers who formed the thin red line bravely holding back the massed and powerful armies of an outraged Britannia.

Any prosecuting counsel worth his salt (and the Attorney-General was generally allowed to be well worth his salt) knew only too well that his opening address to the jury could make or break the case. A good opening speech was half the battle won, it was the first and most deadly salvo, ripping through the defence with devastating accuracy. A clever prosecutor was like a skilled general, carefully choosing his ground, exploiting the topography and marshalling his forces to maximum advantage. Indeed, a clever prosecutor could often outwit his adversary and win his case by the brilliance and vigour of his opening address.

But today, as he stood up to deliver his opening speech, it was clear that the Attorney-General was not his usual self. He was not comfortable, he was not confident and he was not easy. It was plain to all that Sir Robert Collier would rather be anywhere than in the Court of Queen's Bench in Westminster Hall leading the prosecution in a trial about which he clearly had his doubts. For all the rhetorical flourishes and folderols of his opening address, it was evident that his heart was not really in it. His speech was weak and colourless, the thinnest of thin gruel, insubstantial to the point of incorporeality. It was not so much what Sir Robert said, or even the way he said it, it was simply that he lacked conviction. And, because he lacked conviction, his words fell on stony ground.

It did not take long before the causes of his unease became apparent. 'This is a prosecution that I open with peculiar *reluctance*,' Sir Robert began rather unpromisingly, going on to explain that he had 'no choice' in the matter. With much beating about the bush and with a great deal of umming and aahing and ahemming, Sir Robert let it be known that the prosecution was at the request and at the behest of the Home Secretary, Mr Henry Bruce. That worthy gentleman, Sir Robert said, had 'felt it his bounden duty to undertake the most searching investigation in order to ascertain as far as possible whether an apprehension – a popular apprehension – that a crime held in peculiar detestation in this country had been committed was a well-founded apprehension'.

Sir Robert had bewildered and confused the court almost before he had begun. No one in court was quite sure of his exact meaning. 'An investigation to ascertain whether an apprehension that a crime had been committed was a well-founded apprehension.' It did not seem to make any sense. And that was putting it politely. Who, or rather what, was on trial here? Was it the perpetrators of the crime itself, the crime 'held in peculiar detestation in this country' (by which, presumably, Sir Robert meant sodomy)? Was it Boulton and Park and Hurt and Fiske, and all the divers other sodomites, named and unnamed, alive and dead, known or unknown, who were on trial? Or was it the 'popular apprehension' of sodomy that was on trial? Was it Sir Robert's task to test the truth of the widespread belief that sodomy had gained a foothold – more than a foothold – in England? Was he there to prove that sodomites were daily becoming bolder and more brazen? That they were daily becoming proselytisers? That by their tricks and their ways and their wiles, and especially by their dressing and passing as women, they were daily deceiving, corrupting and recruiting the flower of English manhood? That their sodomitic stalking-ground, mission field and battlefield all rolled into one was England's green and pleasant land?

The answer appeared to be that everything and everyone was on trial. Sodomy in thought and sodomy in deed was on trial. Sodomites in particular and sodomites in general. Effeminate men and men who dressed as women. England's manhood and England's morality and England's masculinity. They were all on trial. So the trial was not really a trial at all but an investigation and a deliberation, and the defendants were not really defendants but symbols and representatives of the fearful sodomitic threat that hovered darkly over fair Albion.

It was clear that Sir Robert Collier hoped, perversely, that the evidence would lead to an acquittal. 'Perhaps I am not going too far,' Sir Robert declared, 'when I say that you and I and all of us will experience a sense of relief if we come to the conclusion that the popular apprehension was unfounded.' If Boulton and Park and Hurt and Fiske were found to be not guilty then there could and would be general rejoicing that our island nation, our granite fortress sailing serenely in a silver sea, had repelled the piratical and parasitical sodomitic boarders, that it had fought off the sodomitic threat from without.

'But,' Sir Robert gravely warned the Jury,

> if the evidence leads you to the conclusion that the
> prisoners are guilty, you will not hesitate to perform a
> public duty than which nothing can be more important.
> You will do what in you lies to stop this plague which, if
> allowed to spread without check or hindrance, might
> lead to a serious contamination of our national morals.

A guilty verdict would mean that sodomy had broken forth in the land, that the contagion had been unleashed and was spreading silently, infecting and contaminating all who came into contact with it. A guilty verdict would mean that all of them – Fanny and Stella, Louis Hurt and John Safford Fiske, the absconded Comical Countess, Miss Sissy Thomas and the mysterious Mr Somerville, even the dead-and-buried Lord Arthur Clinton, even the 'divers others' and the 'persons unknown' of the indictment; all the sodomites and all the buggers and all the Mary-Anns; all the He-She's and the She-He's; all the effeminate men and masculine women; all the young men in women's clothes and all the young women in men's clothes; all the androgynes and all the hermaphrodites and the in-betweens – all of them must be punished. All of them must be purged. All of them must be prevented from spreading the taint and poison of sodomy. A guilty verdict would mean the preaching of a new national crusade to hunt down and extirpate the sodomites from the nation's midst.

It was almost too terrible a prospect to contemplate, and it was no wonder that all those present in the Ancient and Honourable Court of Queen's Bench felt a sudden and collective shudder of horror, as if someone or something had walked across their graves.

The Most Sensational Event

By sometimes dressing in female costume, sometimes in male costume, with a studied air of
effeminacy, powdering their necks, painting their
faces, by amatory airs and gestures, the Defendants
endeavoured to excite each other's passions, and to
make themselves objects of desire to persons of
their own class.

> Opening speech of the Attorney-General, 9th
> May 1871

W ho was the strikingly handsome young man who made
his way into the court in the company of the eminent
and silver-tongued barrister Sir John Karslake on the second
morning of the trial? Was this dark and soulful-looking young
man one of the missing defendants in the case? William
Somerville, perhaps? Or Cecil Thomas? Or Martin Luther
Cumming?

Rather more sensationally, might it be a contrite Lord Arthur Clinton, back from the dead; back from foreign parts; back
from whichever hole he had crawled into to hide after leaving
his catamite to face the music? Such a spectacular resurrection
and return of this missing-declared-dead peer and politician
would greatly add drama and piquancy to a trial that already
seemed to be listing and foundering under the freight of its own
expectations.

Much to the disappointment of some, Mr Simeon Solomon was neither an absconded defendant nor a revivified Lord Arthur. He was an artist and a man of self-confessed 'irregular affections', and his presence in the Court of Queen's Bench that morning could be attributed to an admixture of vulgar and prurient curiosity to see Lady Stella Clinton and Miss Fanny Winifred Park in the flesh, a strong sense of solidarity in adversity with them, and an overwhelming fear that his own name, or the name of his intimate friend and fellow sodomite – or 'Dolomite', as they were fond of calling each other – Mr Algernon Charles Swinburne, the infamous young poet, might come up.

'Boulton is very remarkable,' Simeon Solomon wrote to Swinburne. 'He is not quite beautiful. But supremely pretty, a perfect figure, manner and voice. Altogether, I was agreeably surprised at him.' Solomon was less impressed by John Safford Fiske, 'the writer of those highly effusive letters', who 'looks rather humdrum'.

In his preliminary canter through the evidence, the Attorney-General had made much of the mass of epistolary evidence available to him in this case and insisted on reading aloud, and in full, no fewer than thirty-one letters. Many of these letters had already been aired in Bow Street a year earlier and subsequently widely reproduced in the newspapers, much to the dismay of Mr Collette of the Society for the Suppression of Vice, who fretted that evidence of such 'a very revolting nature' might inadvertently be read by ladies at the breakfast table.

But if Sir Robert Collier hoped that these letters would be the first deadly salvo in the battle to come, that they would leave the lines of the defence rent and tattered, he was disappointed. Many, if not most, of the letters seemed to fall some-what short of the mark or to miss their target completely. It was surprising how quickly the host of 'My Dears' and 'My Darlings' and the endless and ardent declarations of love had lost their power to shock. Most of those present had heard it all or read it all before. And, regrettably, Sir Robert's sonor-ous style of recitation hindered rather than helped matters. Sir Robert was no Mr Poland. He lacked that rotund gentleman's vulgar quality of showmanship and his ability to lubriciously underscore and point up certain phrases in the letters, which had added greatly to the gaiety of nations.

Sir Robert's slow and deliberate readings added a good hour to the length of his address and, though the case had barely begun, there was already a distinct air of ennui and a palpable sense of impatience in the court. When would the Attorney-General get to the point? When would he get to the meat and drink of the case? It was all very well to listen to these endless ejaculations of love and friendship, but it was sodomy and buggery that were the order of the day and where were they? The tedious wait reminded those present of the fabled dinner where guests were first tantalised and then tortured by the delicious smells of a promised feast that never materialised.

It was true that Sir Robert had up his sleeve a few new letters which, like the vigorous application of birch twigs on the pos-terior parts, helped to stimulate – momentarily – the flagging passions of the court. There was the intriguing letter to 'Dear Stella' from Mr Edward Henry Park – or 'Harry' as he signed himself – the older brother of Frederick or Fanny Park, a letter which seemed to suggest that he was no stranger to sodomy. He had written, in that incautious postscript, of the 'Glycerine' and 'filthy photos' he had left with Boulton, but surprisingly,

Sir Robert Collier made no attempt to amplify the meaning nor explain – let alone exploit – the significance of these comments, much to the frustration of his auditors.

Then there were two letters from the absconded defendant Mr William Somerville, addressed to his 'Dearest Stella' and signed 'Willy' with his 'fondest love' and 'many kisses'. 'You imagine I do not love you,' he had written. 'I wish to God it was so, but tell me how I can prove it and I will willingly do so.'

These letters from Harry Park and Willy Somerville served only to illustrate one of the very central contradictions of the case: why was it that some young men were indicted on the slightest of slight evidence while others, against whom the evidence seemed much stronger, were not? Willy Somerville had been named as a conspirator in this plot to inveigle the flower of the nation's manhood to knowingly or unknowingly engage in sodomy – and yet the only evidence offered against him was these two letters, the letters of one lovesick youth to another, of so bland a character as to send everyone soundly to sleep.

In sharp contrast, Harry Park's name had not figured in the indictment. And yet it was clear, crystal clear, that Harry Park was up to his elbows in this sodomitic conspiracy. He had spoken of 'Glycerine' and 'filthy photographs' and even the purest of pure minds could not fail to apprehend (at least in part) his meaning. Besides, as everyone knew only too well, Harry Park was currently detained at Her Majesty's pleasure, having been convicted of indecently assaulting Police Constable George White. So why had his name not been added to the roster of conspirators? It seemed an inexplicable omission.

And then there was the presence of Mr Cecil 'Sissy' Thomas on the indictment. No letters from him or to him were presented as evidence. Indeed, the only 'evidence' against him was hearsay. It was alleged that he was the young man in the company of Fanny and Stella on the night they were arrested, the young man who had, in the sodomitic slang, 'scarpered' when the police reared their ugly heads. And he had supposedly dressed in drag once or twice at Wakefield Street with his intimate friend Amos Westropp Gibbings, known to his friends as 'Carlotta'.

If Sissy Thomas was part of this alleged conspiracy, then why had Carlotta Gibbings not been fingered too? The morning after the arrest of Fanny and Stella, Carlotta had cleared the rooms at Wakefield Street of incriminating materials and fled to France, clutching two pairs of her favourite stays. Then she had come back and stood up in Bow Street and declared that she had been out and about 'in drag' on many occasions, to theatres, to restaurants and, famously, to the Boat Race, complete with parasol and picnic. She had even thrown a ball for twenty-four couple at Haxell's Hotel where Heaven knows what had gone on in the Ladies' Retiring Room, in darkened corners and in back passages.

The trio of letters from Miss Fanny Winifred Park to Lord Arthur Clinton were by far the most revealing and the most entertaining of the letters read out by Sir Robert Collier. They were also the most bewildering and required a considerable stretch of the imagination on the part of the twelve Jurymen to think themselves into the upside-down, back-to-front, inside-out world of these young men. Everything was at once familiar and yet at the same time strange. Black was white, and white was black. Men were women, wives and sisters, with lovers, husbands and brothers. Ernest, or rather Stella, was the 'sister' of Frederick or Fanny. Stella was the 'wife' of Lord Arthur Clinton, which made her Lady Stella Clinton, and which in turn made Miss Fanny Winifred Park Lord Arthur's 'sister-in-law'. It was an altogether unsettling experience, like gazing into a distorting mirror. It was a world within a world, hidden, unsuspected and compelling.

The court was frankly baffled by some portions of Miss Fanny Winifred Park's letters. 'My cawfish undertakings are not at present meeting with the success which they deserve,' she had confided to Lord Arthur, 'whatever I do seems to get me into hot water somewhere but *n'importe*, what's the odds so long as you're happy?'

'Cawfish?' It was an odd word to use, unless it was a misspelling for crawfish, and was a reference to the small lobster-like decapod commonly called a crayfish or a crawdad. Was Miss Fanny Winifred Park exhibiting signs of a growing (and manly) interest in angling? Or was she appealing, shamelessly, to one of Lord Arthur's sporting passions?

Mr Straight, who was assisting Mr Sergeant Parry in Miss Fanny Winifred Park's defence, was of the opinion that the word was 'campish', but Mr Sergeant Parry overruled him peremptorily. 'It is "cawfish" in my copy,' he declared emphatically. 'What "campish" means I cannot understand, but if he had written "scampish" he would not, I think, have been using an improper word.'

The Lord Chief Justice felt that matters were drifting dangerously off the point. 'Whatever it may mean it is certainly "campish",' he decreed firmly.

The Attorney-General had marshalled no fewer than thirty-one witnesses for the prosecution, an impressive array by any standards and one which held the promise of exciting and extraordinary revelations. First to go into the witness box was Mr Hugh Mundell, who had barely changed in the course of a year, except that he blushed and stammered and swallowed and hesitated more than ever. Why the Attorney-General had chosen this bumbling young man, who seemed rather younger than his years, as his star witness whose testimony would encapsulate and exemplify all the sodomitic evils of Fanny and Stella was beyond comprehension.

He was there, in theory at least, to confirm the very worst suspicions about 'Miss Stella' and 'Mrs Fanny', as he insisted on calling them. He was there to state in no uncertain terms how Miss Stella and Mrs Fanny, sometimes dressed as women and sometimes as men, had by 'painting their faces' and 'powdering their necks', by their 'studied air of effeminacy' and by their 'amatory airs and gestures' conspired to induce and inveigle him to fondle and toy with them, conspired to dupe and deceive him into committing sodomy. In theory at least.

But Hugh Mundell turned out to be a witness for the defence. Miss Stella and Mrs Fanny had, he said, for the avoidance of doubt, informed him repeatedly, verbally and in writing, that they were men dressed as women, but he had wilfully refused to believe them. And far from inducing and inveigling him to fondle and toy with them, when, unprompted and with no encouragement, he had attempted to take indecent liberties with Miss Stella, she had most firmly rebuffed him.

From the way his eyes shone when he spoke, it was apparent to everybody that Mr Hugh Mundell was still more than half in love with Miss Stella and would not hear a word said against her, let alone speak ill of her himself. It was a dismal, not to say disastrous, beginning to the case for the prosecution, and it was universally agreed that Sir Robert Collier would have to work very hard if he was to save his ship from crashing onto the rocks.

There was a surprising number of new witnesses, among them some eminent medical gentlemen and a positive phalanx of new witnesses from Scotland, including Mrs Agnes Dickson, Louis Hurt's landlady, and Detective Officer Roderick Gollan of the Edinburgh City Police, who had discovered the cache of compromising photographs and *cartes de visite* hidden in the chambers of Mr John Safford Fiske.

There was Police Constable Thomas Shillingford who, in 1867, had arrested – or more properly, rescued – the young and very beautiful Miss Stella Boulton and her companion, the young and not-at-all-beautiful Martin Luther Cumming, from a mob of battle-scarred and very angry whores in the Haymarket. Both Stella and the Comical Countess were in drag and had aroused the rightful ire of the Haymarket whores by daring to trespass on their hallowed pads and patches.

Mrs Jane Cox, the widow of Mr Francis Kegan Cox, the gentleman who had so unadvisedly and so passionately kissed Ernest Boulton full on the lips in his office in the City, had bravely agreed to stand in her shamed spouse's shoes, and her dignity in the witness box as she listened with a stricken face to her late husband's deposition elicited many fitting murmurs of sympathy.

Miss Eleanor Colton, a most ladylike attendant at the Lyceum Theatre, told how Stella, dressed in mauve satin, had used the convenience in the Ladies' Retiring Room to relieve herself while Fanny stood guard at the door. Miss Colton's testimony aroused feelings of righteous indignation and utter revulsion. It was one thing to dress up as a woman and dupe and deceive unsuspecting men, but to violate and pollute so sacred a sanctum as the Ladies' Retiring Room made the blood of every true Englishman boil over with anger. 'If every *roué* can by assuming feminine garb enforce his way with impunity into the chambers set apart for our countrywomen,' one editorialist declared, 'then we call upon Law and Justice to aid us in exposing these outrages on decency.'

Mr William Kay, of the long-established firm of Outfitters and Dressmakers that bore his name in Russell Square, was called to give his expert opinion on the costumes confiscated at Wakefield Street. A number of portmanteaux, baskets and boxes were brought into court and disgorged a dazzling array of feminine attire. There were no fewer than seventeen dresses and gowns; quantities of skirts and petticoats; bodices and blouses; cloaks and shawls; shoes and boots and gloves; a bewildering assortment of ladies' unmentionables; a single muff; seven chignons, two long curls, ten plaits and – sitting rather oddly like a cuckoo in this nest of femininity – that artificial grey beard.

By the time everything was unpacked and laid out for the consideration of the Jurymen, the court resembled nothing so much as a fripperer's shop in one of the less salubrious parts of the city. After their long incarceration in those assorted portmanteaux, baskets and boxes, the clothes showed 'the crush and spoil of age', as Mr Digby Seymour, defending counsel for Stella, most poetically put it. They were fusty and frowsy, and there was that decidedly unpleasant smell that always pervades shops dealing in second-, third- and fourth-hand clothing, a smell of unwashed bodies and unwashed linen, of dirt and want and overcrowding, of cheap scent and cheap sex, of unfulfilled dreams, disappointments and death.

Mr Kay had, he said, 'thoroughly' examined each and every item of clothing and declared them 'very much tumbled about' and 'not as clean as they might have been' (which was a polite way of saying they were filthy). In consequence, they were of little or no value. 'I wouldn't have them as a gift,' he declared contemptuously.

A cheap and theatrical stunt it may have been, but this display of tawdry feminine finery did its work well. 'A thrill of horror ran through the jury box,' reported the *Daily Telegraph*, as the clothes were unpacked and displayed. To be told that Fanny and Stella had dressed as women and walked the streets was one thing. To see the very clothes they had worn while so promenading was quite another. All the letters of love and longing in the world could not state the case so concisely and so compellingly as these tumbled-about women's clothes had done.

Then there were those witnesses who had already appeared at Bow Street Magistrates' Court and who were now obliged to stand again in the witness box, like Slow Eliza from Norfolk and Sharp-eyed Maria, the bickering housemaids of 36 Southampton Street, where Lord Arthur and Stella had lived as man and wife. Mr John Reeve, the taciturn and gloomy staff supervisor at the Royal Alhambra Palace, spoke to the scandalous and shocking behaviour of Fanny and Stella and of the accompanying gaggle of other like-minded painted and powdered young gentlemen when they regularly descended upon the Alhambra and wreaked moral havoc with their oglings and their chirrupings and their tongue-wagglings.

And then there was Miss Martha Stacey who, in company with her elderly mother, ran the infamous house of accommodation in Wakefield Street where Fanny and Stella and Carlotta and Sissy had lodged and dressed, and where, it was strongly suspected, they 'entertained' – for want of a better word

– 'gentlemen' – again for want of a better word – even though nobody could prove it. If Miss Martha Stacey knew of the gentlemen callers at her establishment, she was most certainly not saying so. She was not saying very much at all, and her frequent glances towards Mr George Lewis sitting inconspicuously at the bar might have suggested – to a suspicious mind – that that gentleman had coached her in what and what not to say.

Martha Stacey exemplified a curious feature of this trial. To the very evident frustration of the Attorney-General, the testimony of several witnesses for the prosecution seemed to have changed subtly. What had been established facts and adamantine certainties at Bow Street a year earlier were now something less than established, something less than adamantine. A small and almost imperceptible degree of doubt had crept into the testimonies of Miss Martha Stacey, Mrs Louisa Peck (the chatelaine of Southampton Street) and Mr Arthur Gladwell, the occupier of the second-floor front in Southampton Street (and now the proud husband of Mrs Peck's sister, Sarah Jane). None of them had done anything as obvious as retract or change their evidence, but now they seemed fractionally more hesitant, more ready to believe in the possibility that they may have been mistaken in their observations. It was enough to unsettle and undermine the case for the prosecution and to lead to the unworthy thought that the £5,000 so generously put up for Fanny and Stella's defence (reputedly by the wealthy Miss Carlotta Westropp Gibbings) had been well spent by Mr George Lewis on bribes.

There was, however, no such hesitation, no such doubt on the part of the formidable Miss Ann Empson. Back by popular demand, Miss Empson delighted her audience by reprising her role as the fearsome and fire-breathing Dragon of Davies

Street. She fumed and smouldered with indignation, she scowled and snorted with rage, and she so frequently spat out small balls of fire and brimstone in the general direction of Fanny and Stella that those two young gentlemen must surely have felt themselves fortunate not to go up in flames like the citizens of Sodom and Gomorrah. When Miss Empson turned her eye upon any particular gentleman in the courtroom, he was seen to step back and stumble, and even the Lord Chief Justice himself appeared to recoil from Miss Empson's Gorgon-like gaze.

But 'the most sensational event of the day', according to the *Daily Telegraph*, 'was the cross-examination of the ex-beadle of the Burlington Arcade'. It was a barnstorming *tour de force* by the policeman-turned-beadle-turned-loafer, a man who had begun his career with high and manly ideals and who, over the years, had progressively sunk to his present unfortunate state, a slave to the demon drink, living off the largesse of his mother-in-law at best, and at worst, off the immoral earnings of prostitutes.

His performance melded tragedy and comedy in equal measure and was full of self-delusion and self-pity. One minute he was the cock of the walk, a braggart and a blusterer, his chest puffed out like a pigeon's with manly self-importance; the next, his voice was choking with emotion, and tears were running down his reddened cheeks as he was made to confront the depth and depravity of the abyss he had fallen into.

Mr George Smith was a liar. An habitual liar. He lied, and he lied, and he lied again. He lied to cover up his lies. He lied so much that he forgot what he was lying about, and then would accidentally reveal the startling truth his lies were designed to conceal. There were 'roars of laughter' as he was caught out – again and again and again – in deceit and dishonesty, as 'one damaging confession after another was wrung out of him' in cross-examination.

It seemed that Mr George Smith had taken money in the form of tips and bribes from almost everyone: from the gay ladies in the Burlington Arcade he was supposed to keep out; from the wealthy gentlemen he introduced to those selfsame gay ladies; from the shopkeepers in the Burlington Arcade who tipped him to encourage those gay ladies and their gentlemen followers to patronise their establishments; from his mother-in-law and from his friends; from Inspector Thompson; from the Treasury Solicitor; and from anyone else who was prepared to pay him. Indeed, the only persons that Smith had not taken money from were Fanny and Stella, or so he said.

It was left to the Lord Chief Justice to bring Mr George Smith's devastating cross-examination to an end. 'Do you think it is possible', he asked Mr Sergeant Parry with withering irony, 'to prove this witness to be less credible than you have shown him to be already?'

It was a disaster, there was no other word for it, a downright disaster. Even if Smith was telling the truth about the haunting of the Burlington Arcade by Fanny and Stella, by Sissy Thomas and the Comical Countess, and by all the other painted and powdered young men looking for wealthy gentle-men, no one would believe him, no one could believe him.

The case for the prosecution was in tatters. Apart from the *coup de théâtre* of producing Fanny and Stella's extensive ward-robe of feminine finery in court, the Attorney-General had yet to make any sort of a case against them or the other six defend-ants, present, absconded or dead. His star witness, the hapless

Hugh Mundell, had effectively been a witness for the defence. Martha Stacey, Louisa Peck and others had cleverly sown seeds of doubt about their own testimony, and George Smith had, quite literally, been laughed out of court.

It was clear that the tide was beginning to turn. When Fanny and Stella emerged from Westminster Hall at the end of the second day's proceedings, the large waiting crowd in Palace Yard cheered and clapped them, drowning out the feeble chorus of boos and hisses.

After spending the day observing the trial, it was not surprising that Simeon Solomon was in no doubt about the outcome. 'Of course they will be acquitted,' he told Swinburne.

As Fanny and Stella were whirled away in their cab, Stella, wreathed in smiles and looking radiant, blew kisses to all and sundry.

28

A Rout

The conception of criminal justice which the atmosphere of Scotland Yard fosters is pretty much the
same as that which has existed for countless ages in
the empire of China. If a crime has been discovered, the majesty of the law must be vindicated
by the punishment of somebody. But it is a minor
consideration who that somebody shall be. The police have in a great measure lost the faculty of seeing
things as they are, and not as they wish them to be.

The Times, 25th July 1871

The Attorney-General knew that his last and best hope of
a conviction in this case was the evidence of the two
medical men: Dr Richard Barwell and Dr James Paul. Never
mind that five of the six doctors who had so minutely examined
the parts of Boulton and Park in Newgate Gaol were of the
opinion that there were no signs of sodomy present. Those five
doctors had examined the young men only after they had been
in custody for almost six weeks, six long weeks during which
the worst of their sodomitic injuries, if the Attorney-General
could so phrase it, would have had the opportunity to heal and
fade from view.

But Dr Barwell had treated Frederick Park for chancre of
the anus at Charing Cross Hospital when that young man had
come in using a false name and disguised as a respectable clerk

from the poorer classes. He had seen him week in and week out over a period of three months and he could and would speak authoritatively to the extraordinary state of sodomitic disease that obtained in this young man's posterior parts.

Dr Paul was the police doctor who had examined Fanny and Stella in a dingy room at the back of Bow Street Magistrates' Court on the morning after their arrest. He had been shocked and horrified – indeed he had been turned quite pale – by the gaping anuses and the deformed and elongated penises of these young men, signs and symptoms which, according to the texts on the subject, could only have been caused by persistent sodomitic indulgence on a scale which beggared belief.

Both these medical gentlemen had seen the signs and symptoms of sodomy written in scarlet upon the bodies of these two young men in exceptional and in intimate detail. Surely a jury of twelve Englishmen good and true would be obliged to give credence to the testimony of Dr Paul and Dr Barwell over that of five doctors who had examined Boulton and Park only long after their sodomitic crimes had been forcibly ceased?

For his part, Dr Barwell was indignant. Indignant still, a year on, that he had been forced, under threat of a summons, to testify in this case against his wishes and against what he considered to be his professional duty of confidence to his patients, even patients like the three young sodomites who had attended his clinic in as many weeks. And newly indignant that his word as to the identity of the young man he had treated for the syphilitic affliction of the anus was now being so heavily challenged by counsel for the defence. Those legal gentlemen thought themselves very clever, so very clever (and no doubt they were) in the way they sowed their seeds of confusion and uncertainty in the minds of the Jurymen; so very clever in the way they tried to trip him up; so very clever in the way they tried to make out that *he* was confused, mistaken or misled – if not actually lying under oath. And he was well aware that the more indignant and the more insistent he became, the less credible he appeared. But *he* knew, beyond any doubt, that the young man Park standing in the dock – though stouter now, better dressed and sporting manly whiskers – was the same young man who had stood trembling before him in his room at Charing Cross Hospital with an affliction of the anus and mutely pleading for help.

When his turn came, Dr Paul stood up in Westminster Hall manfully and repeated his shocking findings as to the state of the orifices of evacuation and the organs of generation of Ernest Boulton and Frederick Park. There was no denying that his account was clear, concise and compelling. He had been the first doctor to examine these youths just hours after they were taken from the streets and it was clear that they had both recently engaged in sodomitical activities. So far Dr Paul was proving to be a strong witness, perhaps the strongest witness for the prosecution, and the Attorney-General was well pleased.

'What is that book in your pocket?' demanded Mr Digby Seymour. It was a curious and abrupt way to open a cross-examination.

'This?' replied Dr Paul, pulling the book from his coat pocket and feeling surprised and not a little flustered by the question. 'This is a work of Tardieu's.'

The book in question was Professor Ambroise Tardieu's *Étude médico-légale sur les attentats aux mœurs*, a famous work of scientific observation upon the ways and wiles of sodomites in Paris, a manual intended for doctors, especially police doctors like Dr Paul, on how to read the unmistakable signs of sodomy which the good professor believed were forensically engraved upon the bodies of sodomites.

'Have you been studying Tardieu lately?' Mr Seymour enquired, with an ever so slight and sarcastic emphasis on the word 'studying'.

'I have read it today,' Dr Paul replied, reddening. 'I have had it fifteen months.'

Fifteen months? Indeed? Mr Seymour seized on this like a ferret. 'That would be about the time you bought it with reference to this case?' he suggested.

Dr Paul opened his mouth to reply but no words came forth.

'Not so long ago as fifteen months,' he said after an embarrassingly long pause. 'I never heard of it until I had given evidence in this case.'

'Who told you of it?'

'An – an anonymous letter that I received,' he stuttered out after another pause.

It was clear to all that Dr Paul was lying. But why had he lied under oath, on such a subject, and lied so palpably, and so badly? And why had he come up with the barely credible story that an anonymous admirer had written to alert him to the existence of the book? Surely the date when he actually read the book was of little or no moment? February or May 1870. Two months before the arrest of Fanny or Stella. Or two months afterwards. Did it really matter all that much?

It mattered a great deal. If Dr Paul's first answer was true – if indeed he had acquired his copy of Tardieu in February 1870, a full two months before the arrest of Fanny and Stella – then it meant that something was amiss. It meant that there was more to the arrest of Fanny and Stella than met the eye.

It meant that Dr Paul had, in short, been priming himself and preparing himself for the day when he would examine Fanny and Stella for signs of sodomy.

There was more.

Mr Sergeant Parry, defending Fanny Park, dragged from a very reluctant Dr Paul the curious admission that he had met with Inspector Thompson on the Sunday *before* the arrest of Fanny and Stella.

'Just attend to me,' Mr Sergeant Parry instructed Dr Paul, whose attention appeared to be wandering. 'You say Inspector Thompson called on you on the Sunday before. This is before these young men were apprehended?'

'Exactly,' Dr Paul replied with a certainty he clearly did not feel.

'Did he tell you he was on the watch for them?'

'Certainly not.' Dr Paul's reply was just a little too emphatic, a little too shrill, to be convincing.

'He did not communicate with you on that subject?' Mr Sergeant Parry enquired with a note of evident surprise.

'Not in the least.'

'Then he called to pay you a *friendly* visit?' Mr Sergeant Parry's sarcasm was undisguised.

'No, it was something about the attendance on some man,' Dr Paul replied falteringly, conveniently forgetting that he had just said he saw Inspector Thompson every day – or almost every day – at Bow Street and that it was as unlikely as it was inconvenient that Inspector Thompson would journey halfway across London on a Sunday to discuss Dr Paul's attendance on 'some man'.

'It was not in reference to this case at all?' persisted Mr Sergeant Parry.

'Not in the least,' Dr Paul answered with as much certainty as he could muster.

It was again clear to everyone present that Dr Paul was lying, and that Inspector Thompson's highly unusual house call was in some unfathomable way connected with the arrest four days later of the Young Men in Women's Clothes.

And was it really a coincidence, Mr Sergeant Parry wanted to know, a mere accident, as Dr Paul tried to suggest, that he just happened to be passing, just happened to be loitering without intent, outside the entrance to Bow Street Magistrates' Court at exactly one o'clock in the afternoon on Friday, 29th April, the day after Fanny and Stella's arrest, at precisely the same time as Fanny and Stella were leaving Mr Flowers's courtroom? And again, was it really a coincidence that, at that very moment, he was spotted by an unnamed and lowly police constable who just happened to have been sent by Inspector Thompson to see if he could find Dr Paul to ask him to come and examine the Funny He-She Ladies?

And what of the examination itself? On this thorny subject the wretched Dr Paul was subjected to a devastating catechism and chastisement at the hands of Mr Digby Seymour, who questioned the legitimacy, and indeed the legality, of such an examination.

'Had you received any Magistrate's order or any authority to make this examination?' Mr Digby Seymour enquired.

'I was in the street and the policeman came and told me that Inspector Thompson wanted me,' Dr Paul answered shakily. 'When I got there Inspector Thompson said, "Sir Thomas Henry has ordered that you are to examine these men."' Sir Thomas Henry was the senior Stipendiary Magistrate at Bow Street.

'Have you ever stated before that there was any order from Sir Thomas Henry?' asked Mr Digby Seymour. 'Have you not always said that you acted upon your own responsibility?'

Dr Paul mumbled a confused reply to the effect that he had never been allowed to explain himself properly.

'Did it occur to you', Mr Digby Seymour concluded, 'that it would be a matter of simple fairness to have a medical man representing Boulton present when this examination was going on?'

There was another long and unfortunate pause.

'No,' Dr Paul replied in a stricken voice.

It was left to the Lord Chief Justice to destroy what little credibility remained to Dr Paul. 'You should be more careful in future or you may find yourself involved in very unpleasant consequences,' he warned Dr Paul sternly. 'I am not aware that the mere fact of your being Surgeon to the Police Force entitles you to send a man behind a screen and examine him for any purpose you may think necessary. You had no more authority to call upon these young men to undergo this revolting examination,' he continued, 'than if you had sought a man in the street and asked him to unbutton his breeches.'

Something very curious was happening. As one conspiracy seemed to melt away like the morning mist, a new and very different conspiracy was emerging from the shadows. The steady stream of damaging revelations and admissions from other prosecution witnesses, taken together with Dr Paul's transparent lies, strongly suggested that the police, the politicians and the powers that be in the Treasury had conspired together in preparing the arrest and prosecution of Fanny and Stella.

Mr George Smith, the ex-Beadle of the Burlington Arcade, had boastfully claimed that he had been 'getting up evidence for the police in this little affair', a most unfortunate choice of words. And he had admitted to meeting with Inspector Thompson fully four days *before* the arrest of Fanny and Stella, which to a suspicious mind might suggest that the arrest was planned and premeditated.

More damaging still was Smith's claim that Inspector Thompson had promised to 'pay him for his trouble'. That and the fact that he received the sum of fourteen shillings from Mr William Pollard, the Assistant Treasury Solicitor, who had so energetically and assiduously interviewed all the witnesses in this case before they appeared in court (which was in itself a highly unusual proceeding). To make matters worse (if they could be made any worse), the loquacious Mr Smith had hinted that some sort of promise had been held out to him of 'a situation at the Treasury', a prospect which Smith declared he would most certainly 'not object to'.

Then there were the admissions from certain police officers of 'E' Division that Fanny and Stella had been under continuous and extensive police surveillance. 'I have watched them for a year past,' Detective Officer Chamberlain had asserted. 'I have seen them at the Casino in Holborn, and I have seen them in Brunswick Square, and in Southampton Row.' Stella's return from Edinburgh, three weeks before the arrest, had triggered day-and-night surveillance of Martha Stacey's house of accommodation in Wakefield Street by Police Constable Charles Walker, who said he had watched the house for a marathon twenty days and twenty nights.

Surveillance by plain-clothes officers was a new weapon in the armoury of the police. Sir Richard Mayne, the zealous and authoritarian Commissioner of the Metropolitan Police, had established an unofficial special branch in the 1860s to engage in spying and surveillance. Plain-clothes detective officers were sent all over London to report back to the Commissioner on those considered a threat to the nation's security, threats which ranged from the serious to the faintly ridiculous.

Anything or anyone that had the potential to threaten the state was relentlessly surveilled. The Trade Unions were regularly spied upon, as were 'meetings of the unemployed', both seen as potential hotbeds of revolutionary change. One detective had filed a report on a meeting he attended in Soho Square on the subject of 'Maladministration of the Law'. Another reported on 'a speech made by Mr Bradlaugh at the New Hall of Science, Old Street, on Percy Bysshe Shelley'. Charles Bradlaugh was a declared atheist and was thus seen as a threat to the status quo.

Day-and-night surveillance was expensive and was usually restricted to master criminals, anarchists, Fenian conspirators and foreign spies. It seemed decidedly odd to place the activities of two feather-pated young men like Fanny and Stella, barely out of their teens, on a par with the Fenian bombers. Their frivolous chitter-chatter and their endless forays in drag might be immoral (most would say disgusting, unmanly and un-Christian to boot), but it was not – as yet – a crime to dress up as a woman.

Mr Digby Seymour and the entire defence counsel were at very considerable pains to stress the youthfulness and the boyishness of Fanny and Stella. They were 'young Mr Boulton' and 'young Mr Park'; they were 'boys' or 'little more than boys'; they were 'youths' and 'young men'; they were 'dainty lads' and 'pleasing boys': unformed and unfinished, prone to larks and high spirits, as all boys are. And certainly, they were sometimes foolish, sometimes thoughtless, and sometimes heedless of the consequences of their actions – as all boys are. But foolishness should not be confused with wickedness, nor folly conflated with vice.

And even if there had been goings-on, sodomitical shilly-shallyings, between these two foolish young men and others in their circle, what of it? Did their sordid sexual misadventures really merit such lavish attention from the Metropolitan Police? Hardly a week went by without one or more prurient reports of trials for 'abominable' and 'unnatural' offences between men committed throughout the length and breadth of the land. So, what, if anything, was special about Fanny and Stella?

There were more uncomfortable disclosures. Mr William Pollard confirmed that the Treasury Solicitor, Mr John Greenwood, had from the very beginning taken personal charge of the prosecution until his untimely death two months earlier. Surely this very eminent and very important gentleman had bigger fish to fry? Surely he had better things to do than busy himself with the doings of two young men who liked to dress as women?

And how was it that the conspiracy charges against Fanny and Stella were ready and waiting for them on the morning after their arrest? In the normal course of events, such an indictment would have taken weeks, if not months, to prepare. Reports of surveillance would have had to be written and submitted, summaries of evidence prepared and considered, and senior police officers like Inspector Thompson – and perhaps even the Commissioner himself – quizzed before the final indictment could be drafted.

Such a serious prosecution would certainly require the knowledge and approval not only of Mr John Greenwood himself, but quite probably of the other senior Government law officers, the Solicitor-General and the Attorney-General, and perhaps even beyond. Sir Robert Collier had already let slip that the Home Secretary had taken a strong personal interest in this case and was driving the relentless prosecution of these two young men.

Then there were the secret and not-so-secret payments to witnesses for the prosecution. George Smith freely admitted that he had received fourteen shillings, even though there was no record of this payment in the Treasury Register. But the Treasury Register *did* record payments to Francis Kegan Cox and to Maria George, *née* Duffin, via Inspector Thompson: '679 – Dec 1870 – R. v Boulton and Park – Direct payment to Inspector Thompson of amounts paid to Maria Duffin – I authorise further advances as may be necessary.'

It was all very worrying. Why should Mr Cox receive payment for doing his public duty and testifying to criminal acts? And why was Inspector Thompson making payments, payments *plural*, to Maria George, *née* Duffin? There was indisputable evidence that three witnesses were being paid. How many more witnesses were being paid? And for what? Something was wrong.

More worrying still was the entry in the Treasury Register detailing payments to the three policemen most closely connected with this case: '492 – Dec 1870 – R. v Boulton and Park – To pay £5 – £3 – £2 to Inspector Thompson, Sergeant Kerley, and Detective Officer Chamberlain.'

It was almost unheard of for officers of the Metropolitan Police to receive a gratuity in the ordinary course of their duty.

Gratuities were only ever given upon retirement from the force. There might be exceptional circumstances when the Commissioner might advance a small sum to relieve hardship, but such payments were rare. Why, then, was the Treasury doling out these 'rewards', as Mr Digby Seymour contemptuously termed them, to salaried officers of the Metropolitan Police? It was all very irregular.

Spying, surveillance, bribery, collusion, corruption and political interference at the highest levels. What on earth was going on? Could it be that this prosecution was in some way political? Had it something to do with the late Lord Arthur Clinton? Or was it an ill-conceived and badly executed attempt to extirpate the scourge of sodomy from the land by holding a solemn state trial which would serve as a terrible example and warning to any and all young men tempted to indulge in this criminal folly?

Whatever the motives, the prosecution was in utter disarray. It was a rout, there was no other word for it. All that remained was the ugly stench of conspiracy and corruption and the abhorrent spectacle of justice being seen to be *un*done.

'This Terrible Drama of Vice'

> She watches, if his cheek grows pale,
> She watches, if his glad smile fail,
> She watches, if a sigh he breathes,
> And if he sorrows, then she grieves;
> She watches for his safe return,
> Through life, the mother watches on.
>
> Fanny Fales, 'A Mother's Love', 1853

Mrs Mary Ann Boulton was the object of the greatest curiosity and the greatest compassion as she stepped into the witness box to speak in defence of her beloved and beleaguered son.

Mrs Mary Ann Boulton looked frail and she looked old, though she could not have been much more than fifty, if that. That there had been trials in her life – quite apart from this latest great and grand trial – was evident from the lines etched upon her face. She looked worn out by cares and worries. Nevertheless, she was sombrely and respectfully dressed in deference to the solemnity of the occasion, though she had taken care to follow Mr George Lewis's sage advice not to wear black in case it looked as if she were already in mourning for Ernest. Her eyes were red and swollen as if from recent tears, and her voice was a little hoarse as though she were labouring under great emotion.

But here she stood, proud and unafraid. She was not here to apologise or to explain. She was not here to beg or to plead. She was here to speak truth to power, to tell the highest judge in the land in the highest court in the land that Ernest was innocent of the terrible crimes and dark conspiracies imputed to him. She was here to tell the world about her son, about her 'own beloved Child'. The thought of him made her eyes prick again with hot tears and her chest swell with a mother's love.

It was obvious that Mrs Mary Ann Boulton was not a well woman, that she was some sort of invalid, though the nature of her affliction was not known. Her doctor had, of course, warned her not to appear. She badly 'wanted strength', he had said. The ordeal would be too much for her. It could set her back. But she had dismissed his concerns and ignored the butterfly flutterings of her heart and steeled herself to fight for her child, like a tigress defending her young. And so when Mr Digby Seymour asked, 'Are you the mother of Mr Ernest Boulton?' she had answered in a clear voice replete with strength and pride and love.

'I am,' she declared.

It was a powerful beginning.

But where was Mr Thomas Boulton? That was the unspoken question on everyone's lips. Surely as a husband and a father he should have been in court in the stead of his wife in this hour of need. Why must Mrs Mary Ann Boulton endure such a terrible ordeal alone and unprotected? But if there was a ripple of indignation it was quickly followed by a wave of sympathy for the bravery and courage of this frail woman so ready and so willing to fight in hand-to-hand combat for her beloved son.

Which was exactly what Mr George Lewis had had in his

mind when he persuaded Mrs Mary Ann Boulton that she, and she alone – unencumbered by her husband – was Ernest's best hope of acquittal. A mother's love, a mother's loyalty was more powerful and more potent in the eyes and in the hearts of a jury of twelve Englishmen good and true than all the legal arguments in the world.

So Mr Boulton had been despatched to the Cape of Good Hope on some ship-broking errand which would brook no delay. He was, in consequence, safely out of the way, leaving the stage clear for what promised to be the greatest performance of Mrs Mary Ann Boulton's entire life.

Mrs Mary Ann Boulton still clung to the sweetly pretty fashions of her youth and wore her hair in the same girlish bunched ringlets which had so captivated Thomas Boulton during their courtship. In those distant, happier days, her ringlets softly shook like the May blossom on the trees when she laughed or when she sang. And even though, today, these same ringlets trembled with suppressed pain, passion and emotion, Mrs Mary Ann Boulton still recalled to the minds of those present a happier and more certain age, a less cynical and less sordid age of bluer skies and brighter promise.

Who could not but be impressed by the admirable Mrs Mary Ann Boulton? She was all courtesy and all attention. She had a very particular and refreshingly pleasing way of inclining her head in mute respect and deference to her gentlemanly interlocutors, as if bowing to their superior knowledge. When questions were put to her, she listened hard (and was seen to listen hard), and when she replied to those selfsame questions she did not so much answer as wholeheartedly agree. 'Exactly so', she would answer. 'Entirely so', 'Quite so', and 'Certainly', she would say with a reassuring nod and an eager smile.

And sometimes when it fell to her to recall the happy days and the sad days, a tear would glint like a diamond in her eye, and there would be a fresh rush of sympathy and love for this frail but strong Mother among Mothers. Counsel for the prosecution and the defence alike, even the Lord Chief Justice himself, treated her with kid gloves. Consequently, she got away with murder, or as good as. Difficult questions that really demanded a clear and direct answer were brushed aside or answered instead with a fondly recalled family anecdote.

If all else failed, Mrs Mary Ann Boulton could rely on her memory, or rather, her lack of a memory. 'I have not at all a retentive memory,' she would say. 'I cannot remember', 'I do not remember at all', 'I may have forgotten', 'I should be afraid to say exactly' and 'I could not say positively' were endlessly combined and confederated and given out with such charming conviction that it would have been hard – not to say heartless – to insist on pursuing the fox to the kill.

Mrs Mary Ann Boulton had a very confiding and a very including manner of expressing herself, a manner that drew people in, and once she had begun to speak she could not stop. She told Ernest's life story (and much of her own) in a series of sweetly charming vignettes which she acted out before the court. She would recall and repeat entire conversations and then pause and look about her to see the effect of her words. She conjured up the past so naturally, so guilelessly, that the entire court was transfixed and transported. When she swelled with pride or shuddered with dread, the court swelled and shuddered with her. When she smiled or she laughed, or was indignant or angry, the court smiled and laughed, and was equally indignant, equally angry.

Ernest: A Story of Sweetness and Light. It might have been

the title of a sentimental tract upon the sanctity of a mother's love for a son. And a son's devotion to his mother. A tract upon courage and fortitude in the face of suffering. A tract upon hope, faith and perseverance. Most of all it was a tract upon innocence – innocence of heart, innocence of deed and innocence of thought.

Ernest. A much-wanted and much-loved child, weak and sickly from birth. So weak and so sickly that Mrs Mary Ann Boulton had had to fret and fuss over her boy. A delicate, fragile boy who delighted in dressing up and in acting. And yes, they had rather encouraged it, as it seemed to make him happy. (And who could deny a sickly child those few precious moments of happiness?)

Ernest. Such a clever, funny child. A little boy who had dressed up as the maidservant and waited at table, even fooling his Grandmamma. Ernest, with the voice of an angel, who would make grown men weep when he sang.

Life had not been easy. Mr Boulton's business affairs, never on the firmest of footings, had gone from bad to worse, and they had experienced great reverses. Not that she had ever allowed any shadow to fall on her two boys. *She* would go without – indeed she had gone without – rather than let her sons suffer in any way.

Ernest had gone out to work, but his health could not cope with the rigours of the London and County Bank. So *she* had put her foot down, and Ernest had resigned, to devote himself to performing. He had performed at charitable benefits in town, and toured the county of Essex with Mr Pavitt, where his reception had been something wonderful. Bouquets, some dozens of bouquets, had been thrown upon the stage. He had performed professionally in Scarborough with Lord Arthur

Clinton. And yes, she had kept every single programme, every single newspaper clipping and every photograph of Ernest in character. What Mother worthy of the name would not swell with pride at her son's successes?

Then a shadow had fallen. Her worst fears had been realised. Ernest's health deteriorated. He got worse and after a year of the *greatest* anxiety they were told that he must have an operation to save his life. She had never known such dread. But she had put a brave face on it. She had smiled and laughed and told Ernest to take no notice of his silly old Mamma weeping over a trifle.

It was all most affecting, and there were tears in Mrs Mary Ann Boulton's eyes as she spoke, and lumps in the throats of many of those present in court.

'Ernest has been a most dutiful and affectionate son,' she proclaimed, smiling radiantly across the courtroom at him. 'The *only* fault he ever had was a love of admiration which has been fed by the gross flattery of *some* very foolish people.' She would go no further than that. She would not name names. *They* knew who they were and that was enough. It was because of *them* that her dear darling boy was standing where he was today.

There was barely a dry eye in the house, and if the Ancient and Honourable Court of Queen's Bench had been a theatre (which in a way it was), then Mrs Mary Ann Boulton would most certainly have received a standing ovation, and bouquets – some dozens of bouquets – would have been thrown. As it was, there was an appreciative hum, with much noisy clearing of throats and many blowings of noses.

Mr Digby Seymour bore more than a passing resemblance to a well-fed cat. He was sleek and smooth and shiny with

luxuriant white whiskers. Though rotund, he was surprisingly
nimble on his feet, and his voice, with just a touch of his native
Irish brogue, was soothing and calming and altogether reassuring. But his eyes were sharp and ever watchful, and he could
turn in an instant to snarl and scratch and rend and tear, as the
unfortunate Dr Paul had discovered to his cost.

Mr Digby Seymour rubbed his hands together and positively purred. He had taken Mrs Mary Ann Boulton by the
hand and with the greatest courtesy, charm and solicitude
guided that good lady through her testimony. It had all gone
very well. Better than he had dared to hope.

Mrs Mary Ann Boulton had held the court spellbound. Her
account of Ernest's life had been as compelling as it was con-
sistent, and it had swept all before it. No matter that it was
sugary and sentimental, almost to the point of sickliness. No
matter that it was partial and incomplete. No matter that her
memory had so consistently and conveniently failed her. She
had risen above the morass and mire of claim and counter-
claim, of truths, untruths and half-truths, of opinion, conjecture and speculation, and revealed the higher and the greater
truth of a mother's love for her son. Mrs Mary Ann Boulton
had convinced herself of the truth of her testimony, and in consequence she had convinced everyone else.

Mr Digby Seymour knew that the lacklustre performance of
his esteemed colleague and friend the Attorney-General had
signally failed to prove the case for the prosecution. But it did
not necessarily follow that the trial would result in an acquittal. Juries were fickle, frightened creatures who turned this way
and that depending on the direction of the wind and the scent
in their nostrils. They needed certainty and they needed con-
vincement: commodities which, fortunately for the defence,

Mrs Mary Ann Boulton had provided in spades with her Authorised Version of Ernest's life. From now on hers would be the gold standard of truth against which every other scrap of evidence must be weighed and measured and judged.

Mrs Mary Ann Boulton was invoked at every possible opportunity by Mr Digby Seymour: 'We know as a fact from Mrs Boulton,' he would say. 'We have it proved by Mrs Boulton' and 'Mrs Boulton swears' and so on and so forth. For every alleged crime and misdemeanour, for every fact and circumstance that told against her son, Mrs Boulton's seemingly guileless, garrulous testimony was a perfect and complete antidote. She was a universal panacea, a potent remedy of last resort.

Almost every plank of the case for the prosecution was upended and demolished by the asseverations of Mrs Mary Ann Boulton. All was open and above board. She knew about everything and everyone, and everything and everyone had met with her approval. She knew nearly all the defendants in this alleged conspiracy. She knew Mr Frederick Park as her son's intimate friend and fellow enthusiast for the theatre. Frederick often stayed with them and had stoically and devotedly helped to nurse Ernest back to health after his terrible surgical ordeal. She approved of the friendship between these two young men, and why on earth should she not?

Mr Louis Hurt was 'a friend that we esteemed'. He had been a frequent guest at their home. It was not at all a secret that Mr Hurt and her son corresponded – in fact, Ernest always read Mr Hurt's entertaining letters aloud to her and there was never so much as a *hint* of impropriety in them. She had encouraged Ernest to accept Mr Hurt's kind invitation to spend a few weeks recuperating in the bracing air of Edinburgh after his operation. She had supplied Ernest with more than adequate

funds for this visit. Indeed, Ernest had always been well supplied with funds. (So why, Mr Digby Seymour was at pains to
point out to the Jury, would there be any need for him to prostitute himself to men for money?)

Mrs Mary Ann Boulton had been no less approving of
Ernest's friendship with the late Lord Arthur Pelham-Clinton.
The acquaintance had been formed in circumstances of the
utmost respectability. She herself had been present on the
occasion of a dinner given by Mr and Mrs Richards at which
Lord Arthur was also a guest. He had become a friend of the
family and visited them in Dulwich on occasions too numerous
to mention.

Yes, she was fully aware that Ernest personated women in
private theatricals, on the amateur stage, and latterly on the
professional stage. Ernest had her full sanction and approval.
Indeed, she had even given him one or two of her old dresses.

If Ernest Boulton's own mother did not object to these theatrical *jeunesses*, to these burlesques, to these dressings-up in
women's clothes, so Mr Digby Seymour's persuasive argument
ran, if *she* could not see the harm in this play-acting and panto-
miming and make-believe, then was it not reasonable to assume
there was no *real* harm in the behaviour of these young men?

Mrs Mary Ann Boulton knew, too, that her Ernest's friends
and fellow enthusiasts for all things theatrical – Mr Park, Mr
Cumming, Mr Thomas, the late Lord Arthur Clinton and
others whose names she could not presently recall – used to
call her son 'Stella' by way of a nickname. There was nothing
sinister or secret about it. It was merely a jest and a joke among
boys and she had laughed along with them.

Now, Mr Digby Seymour argued, if there had been anything
untoward, anything unsavoury, anything indicative of unnatur-

al vice in the use of this nickname (as the prosecution had most odiously suggested), then surely Mrs Boulton would have recoiled from its use, as if from the serpent's kiss itself?

As to the photographs of young Mr Boulton attired in female costume, what of them? The Attorney-General had made much of them, suggesting that they were in some way indicative of a tendency towards unnatural vice. 'But there is nothing indecent or indelicate in these photographs, nothing to shock the most critical morality, nothing to disturb the most refined taste,' Mr Digby Seymour protested. Had not Mrs Boulton been shown each and every one of these photographs of her son so attired? 'My son sent me every one,' she had said, more than once. And had she not collected them in an album and kept them, along with the theatrical programmes, the newspaper notices and other related ephemera as memoranda of her son's growing success and fame?

If these photographs were what the Attorney-General so filthily suggested, was it conceivable that a son would dare to expose them to the gaze of his mother, or that Mrs Boulton could have borne to look at (let alone collect and keep) such photographs without revulsion?

And this led Mr Digby Seymour on quite naturally to the whole subject of openness and concealment which went to the very heart of the matter. He did not and could not constitute himself an expert in the ways and means of the dark vice imputed to the defendants, but it struck him forcibly, most forcibly indeed, that the very openness of Boulton and Park's conduct told strongly in their favour. There was no concealment, no attempt at concealment. On the contrary, there was flaunting and there was display – in theatres, in casinos and in public places. These young men went to any and all lengths to draw attention to themselves, to advertise themselves, to announce themselves to the world.

'You would expect a different kind of conduct,' said Mr Digby Seymour, 'you would expect a secret hiding from the sight of men and women. They would try to avoid exciting the suspicions of others. They would shrink and hide away and draw over themselves and their horrible deeds a pall of darkness.' 'Would young men engaged in the exchange of wicked and accursed embraces put on the dresses of women and go to theatres and public places for the purpose of exciting each other to the commission of this outrageous crime?' he asked theatrically.

'Gentlemen,' he answered himself solemnly, 'the very *absurdity* of the suggestion is its own refutation.'

Lastly and with the greatest reluctance, Mr Digby Seymour was obliged to turn to the medical part of the evidence.

'Ernest Boulton comes accused of being the principal actor, or rather, Gentlemen, the principal *sufferer* in yielding to the habitual embraces of others in this terrible drama of vice,' he began. But a majority – five out of six – of the eminent medical men, 'men of the highest position in their profession', who examined the state of this young man's parts in Newgate Gaol, 'were strong and emphatic that there is not one trace, from beginning to end, not one particle of evidence in favour of his guilt'.

'Not one trace and not one particle,' he repeated.

That left just two medical gentlemen, Dr Richard Barwell and Dr James Paul, whose testimony suggested that young Mr Boulton had indulged in these 'vile and wicked practices'. But under cross-examination Dr Barwell had reluctantly admitted that he could not be absolutely certain that the condition of the parts of Ernest Boulton was the consequence of unnatural acts.

His was a conjecture merely, a speculation, no doubt arrived at with the best of intentions, but still a conclusion that was subjective and open to contest and to challenge.

And then there was Dr Paul. Well, the less said about *that* gentleman the better. And with that, Mr Digby Seymour assumed an expression of dignified contempt. 'Dr Paul who gave us a story so absurd, after an examination so unsatisfactory, that I shall not say another word about it.'

Besides, Mrs Boulton had given a compelling account of the very serious illness suffered by her son which culminated, after many months of severe – the severest – pain, in an operation to save his life. No one who had listened to her deeply affecting account could be in any doubt as to its veracity.

Mr Digby Seymour wished to deal with and dispose of the medical evidence once and for all. Throughout the entire period when, according to the Attorney-General, young Mr Boulton was the willing pathic, if he could so term it, of Lord Arthur Clinton, of Mr Louis Hurt and Mr John Safford Fiske, throughout the period when he was, apparently, being sodomised by dozens – perhaps even hundreds – of unknown and unnamed men, it was an indisputable and an undeniable fact that he was suffering from (or latterly recovering from) the terrible and painful affliction of *fistula in ano* and was, in consequence, 'morbidly sensible to pain'.

Was it conceivable, was it credible, that this young man, already in agony in those delicate parts, would consent to further add to that agony, to further augment it, by allowing himself to be sodomised – as the Attorney-General alleged – at every possible opportunity, when such acts must have created 'the most exquisite torture'?

Mr Digby Seymour threw himself upon the common sense

of the Jury. 'Surely, Gentlemen,' he reasoned, 'you will say that Ernest Boulton was the very *last* being alive as to whom you would entertain the suspicion that he would be the suffering and the yielding party to the perpetration of such an offence? I put it before you almost as a *physical impossibility*.'

Mr Digby Seymour had made his point well. There were murmurs and nods of agreement, and the Gentlemen of the Jury shifted uncomfortably on their hard benches, their eyes positively watering at the very thought of such exquisite torture.

Mr Digby Seymour knew that he bore a heavy burden of responsibility. Perhaps the heaviest burden. The Attorney-General had roped together, as it were, all the defendants, which meant that if one fell, they all fell. And if one was found innocent, all were innocent.

But it was *his* client, young Ernest Boulton, who bore the brunt of the prosecution. He was at the dark heart of this spider's web of sodomy and corruption. He was the lynchpin and the king-post of this conspiracy. All roads led to him and all roads led from him. Stella, the shining star to whom all were drawn. Stella, the glittering sun around whom all orbited. Four of the defendants were Ernest Boulton's paramours, the remaining three his friends and fellow female personators. Without Ernest Boulton there could be no conspiracy. Without Ernest Boulton there was no case. All the evidence, all the evidence that really mattered – the letters and photographs; the tittle-tattle of servants and landladies and ladies' retiring-room attendants; the observations and insinuations of Dr Paul – all of it was focused and concentrated on Ernest Boulton. Acquit Ernest Boulton, and all would be acquitted.

There were what looked like tears in Mr Digby Seymour's

eyes and there was a break in his voice as he imploringly invoked the image of Mrs Mary Ann Boulton one last time. He beseeched the Jury to acquit this mother's child, this mother's most dutiful and most affectionate son. A young man who could so inspire the love and loyalty and admiration of this Mother among Mothers could surely not be 'capable of plunging at his young age into the depths of this terrible defilement'.

'Pronounce by your verdict that there may be folly, but not guilt,' Mr Digby Seymour enjoined, his oratory beginning to soar like a lark on the wing. 'Pronounce by your verdict that there may be extravagance; that there may be madness, if you please, in the indulgence of this fancy on the part of my client. But you will require stronger evidence than this before you come to the conclusion that these men are guilty of the terrible charge made against them.'

Mr Digby Seymour paused and took a deep and portentous breath before his final peroration.

'I say that, in a case like this, I trust your verdict will establish that the moral atmosphere of England is not yet tainted with the impurities of continental cities, and from our island position we are insulated from these outrages upon Decency, Morality and Nature itself.

'I trust that you will pronounce by your verdict that London is not cursed with the sins of Sodom, or Westminster tainted with the vices of Gomorrah.'

And with that powerful and patriotic rallying call to reject and renounce the very idea of sodomy and sodomites stalking England's green and pleasant land, Mr Digby Seymour abruptly and dramatically sat down.

I t was a few minutes before five o'clock when the Jurymen filed back into the Ancient and Honourable Court of Queen's Bench. It had taken them just fifty-three minutes to consider their verdict. Such a short deliberation was extremely unusual, especially in a case so complex and important.

According to the collective wisdom of the counsel assembled in Westminster Hall that afternoon, such a perfunctory consideration meant one of two things: either the guilt of the defendants was so evident, or their innocence so shining, that little or no discussion was needed to reach a verdict.

'Gentlemen, are you all agreed?' the Clerk of the Court asked the Jurymen. 'Do you find the defendants guilty or not guilty?'

'*Not* guilty,' replied the Foreman emphatically, at which there was an outbreak of wild cheers and whistles and loud cries of 'Bravo!'

'Upon all counts of the indictment?' the Lord Chief Justice asked, struggling to make himself heard above the din.

'Yes, my Lord. Not guilty on *all* the counts.'

As all eyes turned towards the defendants, Stella, with perfect timing, swayed melodramatically, and fell into a dead faint.

30

Clouds and Sunshine

Rose of the garden,
Blushing and gay. . .
E'en as we pluck thee,
Fading away!

Anne Fricker, 'Fading Away', 1854

MR ERNEST BOULTON begs to thank those managers
who have offered engagements, but intends to resume the
Drawing-Room Entertainment in which he originally
appeared. He is desirous of meeting with a gentleman
who is musical, has a good voice, and who could take one
of the leading parts in the entertainment — Address, &c.

Reynolds's Newspaper, 6th August 1871

J ust two months after her sensational acquittal at Westminster Hall, Stella was eager to be back in the theatrical
saddle. Though the trial had taken a very considerable toll
upon her fragile health and strength, she was nevertheless resolved to return to the stage at any and at all costs.

Besides, what choice did she have? A respectable life was
closed to her for ever. Who would marry her now? The stench
and taint of sodomy was upon her and she was now so notorious that even going on the pad was unthinkable. She would be
recognised at once and hauled straight back to court.

Of course, she could always scarper abroad, as so many of her friends and acquaintance had done, like rats fleeing a sinking ship. But Miss Stella Boulton was made of sterner stuff. She had not come this far, through tribulations and through trials, through fire and through flame, to turn and run, to hide herself away from the light of day and live a haunted and hunted life.

No matter that she was notorious. No matter that her name was on everyone's lips – for all the wrong reasons. Miss Stella Boulton was defiant. She would snatch victory from the jaws of defeat. She would steal fame from infamy. She would take up where she had left off, return to the stage and be a shining star. The world had most certainly not heard the last of Miss Stella Boulton.

But Stella had a problem. She needed a leading man.

Lord Arthur Clinton was dead and buried (though that strange story had more than its fair share of doubters and disbelievers). Dead or alive, Lord Arthur was, in any event, no longer at liberty to play Sir Edward Ardent to her Fanny Chillingtone.

So Stella took the bold and unusual step of advertising for a leading man. She had no idea how many – if any – applicants there would be. But at least one, Mr Louis Munro, a gentleman in the prime of life, rose to the challenge, and by the early autumn of 1871 Stella and her dashingly handsome new leading man (off stage as well as on stage) were embarked on an ambitious tour of the Midlands and the North.

'Mr Ernest Boulton in his Drawing-Room Entertainment,' the advertisement in the *Liverpool Mercury* proclaimed. 'Mr Ernest Boulton in his unrivalled impersonation of the Female Character. As played before the Mayors of Oldham, Macclesfield and Other Towns to Crowded Houses.'

According to a gushing review in that organ, 'Mr Boulton displayed considerable ability, particularly in the character of the four female cousins, in which the rapidity of change of dress and the alterations of voice, gesture, and general appearance were very striking. There was a numerous audience, and the entertainment gave the most unqualified satisfaction.'

Not all towns and cities were as enthusiastic as Oldham, Macclesfield and Liverpool, however. Towns in the South of England were considerably less enamoured of the theatrical and womanly charms of Ernest Boulton. In May 1872 the following announcement appeared in the *Hampshire Telegraph and Sussex Chronicle*:

PORTLAND HALL, SOUTHSEA
FOR TWO NIGHTS ONLY
Mr Ernest Boulton, assisted by Mr Louis Munro, will have the honour of giving his Select, Varied and Refined Drawing-Room Entertainment in which he will appear in those Wonderful Impersonations of Female Character which have won him world-wide celebrity.
The Entertainment will commence with a Fashionable Sketch, entitled 'A CHARMING WIDOW' (with the celebrated song 'Fading Away' sung by Mr E. Boulton)
To be followed by an Original Operetta (in ten minutes) composed expressly for Mr Boulton, and entitled 'THE POWER OF GOLD'
To conclude with the Domestic Person Entertainment, entitled 'CLOUDS AND SUNSHINE'.
(Constance, Mr Ernest Boulton, Ferdinand, Mr Louis Munro)

It was a dismal flop. 'The beauty of the song, "The Fair Gipsy Maid", was entirely destroyed by Mr Boulton, who, of course, was the Fair Gipsy Maid, singing far too loudly and without the slightest attempt at pathos,' a scathing notice in the *Hampshire Telegraph* read. Mr Louis Munro 'sang in a very wretched manner', and taking everything together, the *Telegraph* concluded, 'this is an entertainment which is scarcely one we can recommend'.

Other newspapers were even more damning. 'This so-called "entertainment" is one of which we feel we cannot too strongly disapprove,' the *Hampshire Advertiser* opined sternly in an editorial. 'It is a class of performance pandering to a vitiated taste, and ought therefore to be discouraged in every possible way.'

Things went from bad to worse. Two months later a performance had to be abandoned amid scenes of near riot:

> Ernest Boulton, of Boulton and Park notoriety, was to have given an entertainment at Aldershot on Monday evening but was prevented by a number of officers and others, who determined they would not hear him, and a regular row ensued, in the midst of which the gas was turned out, and the principal performer was glad to make his escape as best he could.

There were simmering private and professional tensions, too, and a few weeks after the debacle of Aldershot, Stella and the dashingly handsome Mr Louis Munro acrimoniously parted company.

As far as Stella was concerned it was good riddance. There would be no difficulty in replacing Louis Munro. Her good-looking and manly brother, Gerard, was shaping up very nicely and would be the perfect foil to her leading lady.

Stella and Gerard continued to tour the North of England, generally to great acclaim, though there were periodic ejaculations and expostulations of surprise and ire that the notorious Ernest Boulton was continuing to perform in drag and seemingly making a good living from it.

> Beams of the morning,
> Promise of day,
> While we are gazing,
> Fading away!

Despite Stella's many professional triumphs, the past always came back to haunt her. When she was appearing in York, the *Pall Mall Gazette* fulminated against 'the impudence of aged sinners' performing in a cathedral city. And whenever any young man was arrested in drag, the name of Ernest Boulton was always brought up.

Stella was weary of it. And so at the end of 1873, she made two momentous decisions. She would change her stage name to Ernest Byne and she would go to America to find the fame and fortune that still eluded her in England. Besides, she was missing Fanny dreadfully and wanted to see her.

When Judge Alexander Park had stood up in Westminster Hall to give evidence on Fanny's behalf, it was painfully obvious to everyone that he was a very sick man, and it came as no surprise when he died just six months later. Fanny and Harry, who had been released from prison in July 1871, were with him to the end.

Now there was nothing to keep either of them in England.

America would be a fresh start. They would make a new life for themselves, where no one knew them, where they would be free, in so far as it was possible, of the past. They had money, more than enough money, to live comfortably, and if the stories Fanny had heard about America were true, there would be no shortage of handsome American beaux for Harry and herself.

Much as she loved Stella, Fanny had always felt overshadowed by her sister's beauty and by her talent. It was not that she resented Stella. She most certainly did not. But it was hard sometimes not to feel a little piqued when Stella was so determinedly hogging all the limelight, and she herself so constantly standing in the wings. In America she would have the chance to make her own way, to prove herself on the New York stage and find fame and fortune.

As Fred Fenton, 'comedian', Fanny carved out a modest career for herself in the 'small business' of the theatre: walk-on parts and character roles, nearly always in drag. She excelled, as she always had, at playing elderly and eccentric English dowagers, and for a short and glorious period she was resident at the famous Fifth Avenue Theater in New York. It was the closest she ever came to stardom.

S tella and Gerard arrived in New York in the spring of 1874. One of their first engagements was at the Theatre Comique where they reprised their successful English comedietta *The Four Cousins*, attracting favourable notices: 'Ernest Byne in the character of Ellen, a domestic young lady, sang with much effort "A Pretty Girl Milking Her Cow", and at the close of the piece, with Gerard in a duet entitled "Now With Joy My Bosom Bounds".'

'Two gentlemen who sat next to us', the reviewer for the *New York Clipper* breathlessly confided, 'discussed in audible tones the merits of Ernest Byne, believing him to be a woman. After enjoying their conversation, we took the liberty of informing them of the sex of the supposed lady, and handed them a programme to substantiate it, whereupon they were completely *astonished* and *confused*.'

Colonel T. Allston Brown, one of New York's most flamboyant – and shrewdest – agents and managers, took Stella on and mounted a vigorous press campaign to announce his newest signing: 'ERNEST BYNE, pronounced by the entire press of New York, Boston and London to be the most WONDERFUL impersonator of female character ever before the public, and whose debut in New York has met with such unparalleled SUCCESS.' A selection of 'OPINIONS OF THE PRESS' followed, including an entirely fictitious quote from '*The Times of London*' which declared that 'anything more marvellous and clever than Ernest Byne's impersonations cannot be conceived, the difficulty being in believing that he is not acting real life'.

In New York, Stella was a star, perhaps not of the first magnitude, but celebrated enough to have her likeness taken by the society photographer Napoleon Sarony, the brother of Oliver Sarony, the Scarborough photographer who had taken no fewer than thirty-four studies of herself and Lord Arthur after they had performed *A Morning Call* to great acclaim in that genteel spa.

In 1876, the *New York Clipper* was moved to hymn Ernest Byne in doggerel:

> Your airs and graces make us all
> Believe you must be feminine:
> Your arts, though you're no *Harlequin*,
> Do well deserve a *column*, *Byne*.

As well as the joy of seeing Fanny and Harry again, it was quite possible – probable even – that in New York Stella was reunited with Lord Arthur Clinton, apparently back from the dead.

Ever since Lord Arthur's sudden and convenient death from scarlet fever just days before the police closed in on him, there had been sightings of him here, there and everywhere. He was shooting in Scotland or racing at Ascot. He had been spotted in town, at the theatre, in fashionable restaurants, strolling in Hyde Park. Or he was living abroad, under an assumed name, in Paris, in Sydney, in New York. Especially New York. According to *Reynolds's Newspaper* in October 1872, the dissolute peer was alive and well and living there: 'Lord Arthur Clinton who was mixed up in the Boulton and Park business, and was reported dead, has been recognised several times at some of the New York Theatres and clearly identified.'

Three years later, in September 1875, the *Northern Echo* in Darlington reported that Lord Arthur Clinton was amongst the mourners at the funeral of his sister, Lady Susan Vane-Tempest, and the following year the *Morning Post* said that he was present in Dublin 'at the Installation of the Duke of Connaught as Great Prior of the Irish Masons'.

In 1879, the grandly named Australian newspaper the *Clarence and Richmond Examiner and New South Wales Advertiser* proclaimed that 'My Lord Arthur Clinton' was not dead at all. He had, in fact, 'only temporarily died to oblige his family', the paper revealed, and now, after an absence of some years, he 'has just appeared in the arena of London society alive and hearty' having spent the past eight years in hiding in Australia.

Stella and Gerard returned to England in early 1877 and resumed touring as 'The Wonderful Bynes'. With 'Elegant Parisian Clothes and Costly Appointments', the Wonderful Bynes offered a varied programme of 'Songs, Eccentricities, Duets, Operettas &c'. All in all, it was 'a most marvellous entertainment', the theatrical bible the *Era* declared. 'The Bynes are the talk of Grimsby'.

But the past could still catch up with Stella. In April 1879, 'AN INDIGNANT NONCONFORMIST' in Cardiff wrote to the *Western Mail* to complain about some 'disgustingly suggestive' posters placarded across the town announcing the forthcoming engagement at the Stuart Hall of 'The Wonderful Bynes Company' featuring 'Mr Ernest Byne, the Unequalled Impersonator of Lady Characters': 'Will either Mr. John or Mr. Richard Cory, who are part-owners of the Stuart-hall, kindly inform the public who this "unequalled impersonator of lady characters" is, and also whether "the Wonderful Bynes Company" include Boulton and Park, or either of that notorious pair?'

In 1881, the Wonderful Bynes were in London. According to the census taken that year, Ernest Byne, 'actor', was living in lodgings at 21 Euston Street in Somers Town. Stella was thirty-two but she defied the advancing years by the simple expedient of knocking five years off her true age and proclaiming herself to be twenty-seven. She was still a fine figure of a woman and if she could get away with it, why should she not?

Spring's fairest blossoms.
Summer's bright day . . .
Autumn's rich cluster,
Fading away!

Just five days before Stella passed herself off as a still-blooming twenty-seven-year-old, Mrs Fanny Winifred Graham (*née* Park) breathed her last in Newark, New Jersey, where she had been looked after for some years past by Mr Oliver Hagen, a watchmaker, and his wife, Catherine. No cause of death was listed on her death certificate, a tactful omission which usually meant that syphilis and its fearsome complications were responsible.

The syphilitic sore on Fanny's bottom, the sore that would not go away, the sore that had forced her to seek grudging treatment from the forbidding figure of Dr Richard Barwell at the Charing Cross Hospital, had finally caught up with her. Dr Barwell had managed to heal the sore, but he could not eradicate the syphilis from her body. As the years passed, the syphilitic poison slowly but surely gnawed away at Fanny's body and Fanny's mind until, at the last, half-mad and half-blind, racked with pain and paralysed, Fanny died aged thirty-four.

Dear garrulous, gossiping, glorious Fanny. Fanny: stout of heart, stern of feature and sweet of nature. Fanny: with her campish ways, her braying laugh and her low cunning. Fanny: not beautiful, certainly; frequently foolish; uncommonly lewd; invariably lustful. Fanny: always kind, utterly charming and generous to a fault, especially with her favours.

In her short span, Fanny had perfectly realised her true self. She had fashioned herself from the most unlikely and the most unpromising of clays. She had formed herself and shaped herself with nothing but the ingenuity of her own hands. She had stitched and sewn, knitted and glued, pinned, tied, taped and laced herself to miraculously contrive the strange and gaudy creature that was Mrs Fanny Winifred Graham (*née* Park).

Not for Fanny the uncertainties and the insouciances of youth or beauty. There was no delicate, blushing springtime, no clustering blossom – other than artificial – on the bough. Fanny had been delivered of herself in her prime. She was a woman of a certain age, a woman of the world. Clever, knowing, witty and wise, it was no wonder she played principally dowagers and duchesses. She *was* one.

Defiant, determined, brave and fearless, Fanny did not flinch and she did not flee. 'How *dare* you address a Lady in that manner, Sir?' Fanny had challenged Detective Officer Chamberlain with superb aplomb and frigid hauteur on the night of the arrest. Her courage never failed her, even in her darkest hours.

So Mrs Fanny Winfred Graham (*née* Park) lived and died. '*N'importe,*' she would often say. 'What's the odds as long as you're happy?' It could have been her epitaph.

Fanny was laid to rest in Rochester, New York, alongside her beloved brother, Harry, who had died five years earlier in October 1876. A year's imprisonment with hard labour in the House of Correction in Coldbath Fields was generally considered to be a sentence of death by another name. Appalling food, lack of sanitation and back-breaking work – designed to subjugate the strongest will – reduced even the most robust of men to physical wrecks. Harry died a broken man, but it was no small consolation that he died a free man.

At the time of her death, Fanny was neither rich nor poor, but comfortably placed and living off the income from her capital. Her estate was to be divided between the widow of her older brother Alexander and the devoted Catherine Hagen, who had nursed Fanny through her last, long illness. There was one other bequest: 'I give, devise and bequeath the sum of £500 and also my Topaz ring now worn by me unto my friend Henry B. Warner, now of the City of San Francisco, California.'

Who was Henry B. Warner? Was he that handsome American beau that Fanny had hoped to meet, that ardent swain she had been searching for all the days of her life and thought she would never find? Was he the great love of her life? Had Henry B. Warner perhaps given Fanny the topaz ring as a love token? The ring was clearly important. It was the ring 'now worn by me', as Fanny had so scrupulously written in her last will and testament. Two years later, in the St James Hotel in St Louis, the legacy was given over to Henry B. Warner who signed a receipt for it in a shaky hand, as though he were labouring under great emotion.

> Song of the wild-bird,
> Heart-stirring lay. . .
> E'en as we listen,
> Fading away!

The year after Fanny's death, Stella and Gerard became Ernest and Eden Blair, and for the next twenty-two years would tour as The Brothers Blair, with a staple of two short drawing-room comediettas, *My New Housekeeper* and the 'Society absurdity' *Complications*. It was a tried and tested formula. To Gerard's handsome male lead Stella would appear in various comic female incarnations: an argumentative Irish washerwoman, a giddy young widow and a haughty and acidulated peeress of the realm. 'The performer who undertakes the female characters is very good, without being vulgar in the slightest degree,' the *Era* noted in 1891.

Touring the length and breadth of the country was arduous. Bookings were steady rather than spectacular, and reviews were lukewarm rather than lavish. 'The Brothers Blair are artistes of a high order,' the *Belfast News-Letter* wrote in 1896, 'and their drawing-room sketch caused much amusement.' They found themselves performing mostly in provincial music halls, often in small, out-of-the-way places like Douglas on the Isle of Man and Margate in Kent. Occasionally they got a booking in London, which was useful for Gerard as by this time he was married with a wife and son living in Camberwell.

It was not quite hand-to-mouth, but it was an erratic, irregular existence, punctuated by worrying periods with no work. The bright promise of Stella's youth, the bright promise of her beauty and her talent, had slowly tarnished with the passing years. The brilliant future that she had envisioned for herself had faded, faded away.

Stella rarely complained now. The dark moods and thunderous faces of her younger self were gone, replaced by a quiet joy and a deep sense of gratitude. She was grateful for the life she had; grateful that she was not rotting in some dark and dank prison cell; grateful to be working in the theatre; grateful to be alive. And if, for a moment, she was ever ungrateful or disappointed or dissatisfied with her lot, if she was ever sharp or impatient or petulant, she had only to turn her thoughts to poor dear Fanny so cruelly taken from them in her prime.

Of course there were still followers and beaux and gentleman callers (though to be strictly accurate, only a very few of her gentleman callers were gentlemen, or anything much approaching gentlemen).

Still they came, though she was no longer young and no longer beautiful. But she was, after all, Miss Stella Boulton-Byne-Blair and she could no more stop followers from following, beaux from coming and gentleman callers from calling than she could stop the rain from falling or the wind from blowing.

Still they came, like the endless waves breaking upon the shore: young men and old, fat men and thin, tall men and short. Shy working men in stiff collars and Sunday-best suits, who spoke in strange accents and came to ask her to walk out with them. Callow youths who blushed and stammered and poured their love out in a scalding torrent of words, and cocky, cheeky youths who flirted with her violently.

Soldiers and sailors, vagabonds and ruffians. Men of middling rank and men of no rank at all. Poor men aplenty and rich men (though in truth, these days rich men were at something of a premium). Still they came, to fete Stella, to admire her, to desire her, to court her, to fall in love with her, and sometimes, sweetly and seriously, to propose marriage to her.

Stella loved them all. And she was kind to them all. What else could she do? How else could she be? She must be tender. She must give them comfort and she must give them love. She must tend to their bruised and broken hearts. She must fledge them and make them strong. She must teach them courage and she must teach them to endure against all hazard and against all hardship, just as she herself had learned these bitter lessons.

She must give them hope, even when hope could hardly be imagined, let alone grasped. Most of all she must transmit to them the strange and secret joy that was special to their kind and to their commonwealth. The same strange and secret joy that poor dear Fanny had found. The small, flickering flame of joy that must be painfully and carefully nursed from feeble, sickly ignition into clear and vigorous combustion.

It was her mission and her purpose. Stella knew that the path stretched out endlessly before her. Not in her lifetime, certainly. Nor in the lifetimes of those that followed. But perhaps in the lifetimes of their children's children, the first glimmerings of this burgeoning flame of joy would pierce the dark and cruel night, like the breaking of a rosy dawn on a summer's morn.

> Hope's fairy promise,
> Charms to betray,
> All that is earthly,
> Fadeth away . . .

S tella had seen in the new century and she had outlived the old Queen. In the autumn of 1903, she fell ill, seriously ill, with an affliction of the brain. The doctors said it was a cerebral neoplasm, a growth in the brain, and most probably a consequence of syphilis. It was a long illness, bravely born. After a life of quite extraordinary incident, Stella passed away peacefully a year later, aged fifty-four, with Gerard by her side.

There was just enough money to bury Stella, but not enough to raise a headstone to mark her grave. Only a handful of mourners were there to witness her passing.

> But there's a land,
> Where nought shall decay,

Where there's no sorrow,
No fading away!

The sky was bright with heavenly light as they gathered above Stella's unmarked grave. All of them. A great celestial host of bougers, bowgards and buggers, of catamites and Ganymedes, of ingles, pathics and poofs, of Mollies, Margeries and Mary-Anns. All the sad young men and all the sad old men. All the he-she's and the she-he's; all the effeminate men and all the masculine women; all the young men in women's clothes and all the young women in men's clothes. All the androgynes and the hermaphrodites and the in-betweens. All the generations of numberless and nameless sodomites, of martyrs, outcasts and outlaws, of the lost, the lonely and the unloved. All of them, in serried ranks, gathered together, a great and joyful host, there to raise her up, to throne her and to coronate her, with gladsome laudings and praisings, as Stella, Queen of Queens, Star of the Heavens.

Epilogue

On Wednesday 15th June 1870, the *Echo* reported a sighting of Martin Luther Cumming.

> Mr. Cumming, against whom a warrant has been issued in connection with the charge of personating women, went to Brussels immediately after the arrest of Park and Boulton, and put up at one of the best hotels. As, however, he had no papers, and could not give evidence as to his means of existence, he was requested to leave the country. When he was called upon he had his hair in curl papers, and portraits in which he and a friend were represented in women's clothes were found in his rooms.

And that was the last time that anyone saw or heard of the Comical Countess.

Dr James Paul, who had squirmed with shame and embarrassment at the Lord Chief Justice's stern and stinging criticisms of his conduct in the case, continued to be gainfully employed as Surgeon to 'E' Division of the Metropolitan Police until his premature death in 1877.

Malcolm Johnston, the Maid of Athens, was arrested in Dublin in 1884 after the exposure of a sodomitic scandal in Dublin Castle, the seat of English rule in Ireland. He was tried and sent to prison for sodomy and was never heard of again.

Jack Saul, the infamous male prostitute, was also caught up in the Dublin Castle Scandal of 1884 but managed to avoid prison. In August 1890, Jack was interviewed by Inspector Abberline of the Metropolitan Police in connection with the Cleveland Street Scandal. 'I am still a professional Mary-Ann,' he told Inspector Abberline. 'I have lost my character and cannot get otherwise.' Later that year, Jack Saul testified in court that he had been picked up in the street by no less a personage than the Earl of Euston and gone back with him to the male brothel at 19 Cleveland Street. 'Lord Euston was not an actual sodomite,' Jack deposed. 'He likes to play with you and "spend" on your belly.'

Miss Carlotta Westropp Gibbings took up with Louis Munro, Stella's short-lived leading man, and together they scraped a precarious living touring the South Coast with 'A Drawing-Room Entertainment' almost identical to that offered to the public by Stella. In 1873, Carlotta and Louis were arrested and charged with 'uttering a fictitious cheque' for a watch they later pawned. By a miracle they were acquitted. Penniless and friendless, Carlotta had no choice but to return to Cheltenham and live with her forbidding Mamma. Carlotta died in 1890, aged forty-one, from 'congestion of the lungs'.

The dogged and determined Inspector Thompson continued to serve in 'E' Division of the Metropolitan Police until his retirement in 1890. He died seven years later, aged sixty-two.
Both Detective Sergeant Frederick Kerley and Detective Officer William Chamberlain retired early from the Metropolitan Police and became private detectives. In 1895, Kerley put his knowledge and experience of London's sodomitic under-

world to good use when he was employed, alongside the famous Inspector Littlechild, by the Marquis of Queensberry to find male prostitutes willing to testify against Oscar Wilde.

George Lewis's career continued to prosper. In 1895, he was employed to defend Queensberry against a charge of criminal libel brought by Wilde. Lewis worked tirelessly for reform of the divorce laws and he was instrumental in the creation of the Court of Criminal Appeal. He was knighted in 1893 and died in 1911 at the age of seventy-eight.

Two years after attending Fanny and Stella's trial in Westminster Hall, the young Pre-Raphaelite painter Simeon Solomon was arrested with George Roberts, a sixty-year-old stableman, in a public lavatory in Oxford Street. They were charged with attempting to commit sodomy. Roberts was sentenced to eighteen months' imprisonment with hard labour, while Solomon's sentence of eighteen months' imprisonment with light labour was reduced on appeal to a term of police supervision. A year later, Solomon was arrested with another man in a *pissoir* in Paris and sentenced to three months' imprisonment.

'Cecil Graham', the false name given by Stella to Inspector Thompson on the night she was arrested, reappeared in 1892 as the name of a character in Oscar Wilde's first society comedy, *Lady Windermere's Fan*. Wilde's Cecil Graham is a sharp, brittle and witty man about town who easily mixes in high – and in low – society. Wilde insisted that Cecil Graham wear a green carnation on stage on the first night. Although Wilde later claimed that the mystic green carnation was his own idea – 'I invented that magnificent flower,' he said – he had, in fact, merely borrowed the idea from the sodomites and cross-dressers of Paris who wore the green carnation as a badge of their sexuality. Was Wilde's fey and effeminate Cecil Graham a secret homage to Stella Boulton? Wilde certainly knew of Fanny and Stella, having read the explicit account of some of their sexual exploits in Jack Saul's *The Sins of the Cities of the Plain* (1881). But had they met? Wilde lived in London between 1878 and 1895, years in which Stella and Gerard regularly performed in the capital, and it is entirely possible that the famous Oscar Wilde encountered the infamous Miss Stella Boulton in London's sodomitic underworld and listened with rapt attention and shining eyes to Stella's account of her scandalous life and extraordinary trials.

Hugh Mundell, Stella's Hapless Swain, renounced the world together with all its snares and temptations and became a chiropodist instead. He was still practising this useful profession in 1901, at the age of fifty-four, in the parish of St George's, Hanover Square. He never married.

Miss Ann Empson, the Dragon of Davies Street, remained true to her Vestal Vows and never married. A year after the trial of Fanny and Stella, she retired to Croydon to keep house for her half-brother, Mr Alexander Sidebottom, where she died, aged sixty.

Cecil 'Sissy' Thomas became an underwriter at Lloyd's. He never married and lived for most of his life with his sister in circumstances of the utmost respectability.

John Reeve left the Alhambra and became the landlord of the

Union Flag, a public house on the Lambeth Road. The Union Flag also became a theatrical boarding house, accommodating music-hall turns as diverse as a French trapeze artiste, a low comedian and a pantomime dame.

Charles Pavitt spent most of the rest of his working life writing comic songs for music halls. Among his most popular were 'The Gretna Green Galop' and the ever so slightly *risqué* 'I've Got a Peep-Show', the refrain of which ran:

> For I've got a Peep-Show, a Peep-Show, a Peep-Show,
> I've got a Peep-Show, a penny for a peep.

Mr Edward Nelson Haxell, the jovial hotel keeper, built himself a castellated gothic fantasy of a house in the pretty rural village of Kingsbury on the outskirts of London. He died in 1899, at the age of seventy-nine. In the 1920s, Haxell's Hotel, the scene of Carlotta's famous drag ball, became part of what is now the Strand Palace Hotel.

Dr Richard Barwell's career prospered and he continued to work until he was nearly seventy. In his retirement he was an enthusiastic skater and remained hale and hearty into his late eighties. He died in Norfolk, the county of his birth, in December 1916, aged eighty-nine.

Maria George (*née* Duffin) married and buried two husbands. In 1911, she was a widow and living in Hampstead with her younger sister, Hannah, a council lavatory attendant. Maria died in 1931 aged eighty.

Mrs Mary Ann Boulton, Mother of Mothers, died peacefully on a summer's day in 1889 aged sixty-seven. To the very end she continued to assiduously collect every playbill, every newspaper clipping and every photograph of her darling boys, and she would boast about them and their career on the stage to anyone and everyone who would listen. Mrs Mary Ann Boulton died in the sure and certain knowledge that she had done her duty by her sons and never, as she had so proudly proclaimed in court, 'allowed any cloud to fall upon my children'. And when the time came, Stella was laid to rest beside her.

John Safford Fiske took himself off to Europe where he spent most of the rest of his life painting, writing and cultivating his 'large and beautiful garden' in Alassio, in north-west Italy, 'where the rose blooms the whole winter'. In 1905 he wrote, 'I think I may claim that, in an unpretending way, I have shaped for myself a life that is agreeable enough in the living.' He died in 1907, aged fifty-seven. He left his carefully catalogued library of four thousand volumes, including Oscar Wilde's *The Picture of Dorian Gray* and an edition of Walt Whitman's poems, to Hobart College in New York State. His carefully concealed photographs of Stella (and one or two of Fanny, as well), which were unearthed by Detective Officer Roderick Gollan of the Edinburgh City Police on the morning of 9th June 1870, were taken into custody and pasted into the Linlithgowshire Rogues' Gallery, where they can still be seen today in Edinburgh City Archives.

Dear, dull Louis Hurt left London immediately after his acquittal and spent the next five years wandering Europe, visiting

Paris, St Petersburg and Rome before eventually settling in Vienna in 1876. He was appointed Professor of English at the Wiener Handelsakademie and also taught at the Theresianum, a semi-military school for royalty and aristocrats where, according to his obituary in the *Wirksworth Parish Magazine*, the last Khedive of Egypt, Abbas Hilmi Pasha II, and Ferdinand of Coburg, later King of Bulgaria, 'passed through his hands'. He died in Vienna in 1936, at the remarkable age of ninety-one.

After a flurry of real and imagined sightings of Lord Arthur Clinton in the 1870s, nothing was heard of him ever again. Was he dead? Or had he, like Louis Hurt and John Safford Fiske, taken himself off to the kindlier climes of Europe? In the will of Henry, seventh Duke of Newcastle, drawn up in 1927, there is a curious and beguiling reference to 'my uncle, Lord Arthur Pelham-Clinton (a person reputed to be dead and as to the proof of whose death some question might arise)'. *Some question might arise.* Was this cryptic legalese the closest that the family would ever come to admitting that Lord Arthur had not died of scarlet fever in 1870, but had been helped to escape the ends of justice? The clause in the seventh Duke's will effectively disinherits Lord Arthur – and (improbably) 'any of his male issue' – 'as if the said Lord Arthur Pelham-Clinton had died in my lifetime'. Either Lord Arthur had died in the seventh Duke's lifetime, or he had not. If he was still alive in 1927, as the seventh Duke's will seems to hint that he was, he would have been eighty-seven.

Gerard Boulton gave up the stage after Stella died and moved to Winchester with his wife, Matilda, and their son. Gerard kept the name 'Eden Blair', and for many years he was the manager of the Regent Theatre in Winchester. 'His charming manner earned him the respect of all, and especially of children,' his obituary in the *Hampshire Chronicle* recorded. In his later years he was a stalwart of the Spiritualist Church in Hyde Abbey Road. He died on 26th January 1940 aged eighty-six. Gerard was just sixteen when the scandal of the Young Men in Women's Clothes erupted in 1870, and with him died the last living memories of Fanny and Stella.

Notes

Every word of the sensational six-day trial of Fanny and Stella in May 1871 was assiduously taken down by a team of short-hand writers from Messrs Walsh and Son of Little George Street, Westminster. The entire trial was then transcribed in longhand in at least a dozen clerkly hands (of varying legibility), and bound together in one enormous volume. *The Queen v Boulton and Others before the Lord Chief Justice and a Special Jury: Proceedings on the Trial of the Indictment* is a remarkable document, not least because it has survived intact when so many other transcripts of major Victorian trials have been lost or destroyed. The trial transcript is in the care of the National Archives in Kew, along with the bundle of thirty-one depositions given by witnesses at Bow Street Magistrates' Court in April and May 1870 and some thirty letters, just a tiny fraction of the two thousand documents handed over to Inspector Thompson by Miss Ann Empson, the Dragon of Davies Street.

Much of the material in this book is drawn directly from the trial transcript (DPP 4/6), the depositions (KB6/3) and the letters (KB6/3, part I) in the National Archives, and designated in the notes as 'Trial', 'Deposition' and 'Letters'. I have relied heavily on contemporary newspaper reports of the trial and its aftermath, all of which can be consulted at British Library Newspapers in Colindale, London.

1 *Leading Ladies*

1 'When they were seated' – 'The Funny He-She Ladies', *Curiosities of Street Literature, Comprising Cocks and Catchpennies* (London, 1871).

2 'the very fairest' – *Echo*, 3 May 1870.

2 'The general opinion' – *The Lives of Boulton and Park: Extraordinary Revelations* (London, 1870).

3 'There was a young man' – *The Pearl*, November 1879.

3 'lasciviously ogled' – *Extraordinary Revelations*.

4 'no harm in it' – *Pall Mall Gazette*, 6 March 1881.

5 'sterner features' – *Evening Standard*, 2 May 1870.

6 'charming as a star' – Quoted in the opening speech of Sir John Karslake, Trial.

6 'Stella, Star of the Strand' – *Extraordinary Revelations*.

7 'I'm a police officer' – *Daily Telegraph*, 30 April 1870.

7 'How *dare* you' – *Evening Standard*, 2 May 1870.

7 'Look here' – Deposition of Detective Sergeant Kerley/*Reynolds's Newspaper*, 14 May 1871.

9 'Your name and address?' – Trial testimony of Inspector Thompson.

10 'There were flannel petticoats' – Trial testimony of Detective Officer Chamberlain.

10 'One of the police' – Deposition of Hugh Mundell/*Daily Telegraph*, 7 May 1870.

11 'a cruel sell' – 'The Funny He-She Ladies'.

11 'so brave' – Trial testimony of Detective Officer Chamberlain.

2 *The Hapless Swain*

12 'These young men' – *Extraordinary Revelations*.

12 'the nightly resort' – Jim Davis and Victor Emeljanow, *Reflecting the Audience: London Theatregoing, 1840–1880* (Hatfield, 2001).

12 'a few pilgrims' – *All the Year Round* (19 May 1877) quoted in Davis and Emeljanow, *Reflecting the Audience.*

12 '23 years and a half' – *Daily Telegraph*, 7 May 1870.

13 'very little experience' – Deposition of Hugh Mundell.

13 'an "idle" sort of a life' – *ibid.*

14 'Those two are women' – *ibid.*

14 'I took them to be women' – *Daily Telegraph*, 7 May 1870.

14 'We think you're following us' – Trial testimony of Hugh Mundell.

15 'these monsters' – 'H. Smith', *The Yokel's Preceptor: Or, More Sprees in London!* (London, *c.*1850).

16 'I talked to them' – *Daily Telegraph*, 7 May 1870.

16 'only be too happy' – Deposition of Hugh Mundell.

16 'never anything improper' – *Daily Telegraph*, 7 May 1870.

17 'our private box' – Trial testimony of Hugh Mundell.

17 'Dear Mr Mundell' – *ibid.*

17 'It's a good joke' – *ibid.*

18 'In what way' – *Daily Telegraph*, 7 May 1870.

18 'I shall ask for Mrs Park' – Trial testimony of Hugh Mundell.

19 'a bit of brown' – 'Walter', *My Secret Life* (Amsterdam, *c.*1880).

19 'back-door work' – *The Pearl*, 1880.

20 'I said I had' – Trial testimony of Hugh Mundell/*Daily Telegraph*, 7 May 1870.

21 'They were talking' – *Extraordinary Revelations.*

21 'principally dowagers' – Deposition of Amos Westropp Gibbings.

22 'Who *are* they?' – *Daily Telegraph*, 7 May 1870.

22 'I have my doubts' – Trial testimony of Hugh Mundell.

23 'I am not a lady' – *ibid.*

23 'There was a great deal of confusion' – *The Times*, 7 May 1870/ *Extraordinary Revelations.*

23 'quite in a myth' – Trial testimony of Hugh Mundell.

23 'led on' – *ibid.*

3 The Slap-Bum Polka

24 'a cute detective chap' – 'The Funny He-She Ladies'.
25 'He asked whether two gentlemen' – Deposition of Martha Stacey.
26 'My mother remonstrated' – *ibid*.
27 'in drag' – Deposition of Amos Westropp Gibbings.
28 'laughing, chaffing' – Deposition of Martha Stacey.
28 'Slap-Bum Polka' – Jack Saul, *The Sins of the Cities of the Plain* (London, 1881).
29 'very effeminate' – *Reynolds's Newspaper*, 5 June 1870.
30 'handsomest frocks' – Trial testimony of Detective Officer Chamberlain.

4 In the Dock

31 'When first before' – 'The Funny He-She Ladies'.
33 'was crowded' – *Illustrated Police News*, 7 May 1870.
34 'crammed' – *Evening News*, 30 April 1870.
34 'great surprise' – *Daily Telegraph*, 30 April 1870.
35 'these two women' – *ibid*.
35 'did with each' – KB6/3, The National Archives.
37 'Both conducted' – *Daily Telegraph,* 30 April 1870.
37 'Last evening' – *ibid*.
38 'lasciviously ogling' – *Extraordinary Revelations*.
38 'I have been' – Deposition of Detective Officer Chamberlain.
38 'I found' – *Daily Telegraph*, 30 April 1870.
39 'for a year past' – *ibid*.
39 'seen both the prisoners' – Deposition of Police Constable Walker.
40 'Much of the evidence' – *Daily Telegraph*, 30 April 1870.
40 'The onus' – *ibid*.

5 *Foreign Bodies*

42 'EXAMINATION OF PEDERASTS' – Charles Vibert, *Précis de médicine légale* (Paris, 1893, translated by Dede Smith).

42 'I was in the street' – Trial testimony of Dr James Paul.

44 'Step inside' – Deposition of Dr Paul.

44 'Unfasten' – *ibid*.

44 'Without saying' – *ibid*.

44 'I did not use' – *ibid*.

44 'force' – *ibid*.

44 'I examined them' – *ibid*.

46 'a wheezing' – C. J. S. Thompson, *Ladies or Gentlemen? Women Who Posed as Men and Men Who Impersonated Women* (New York, 1993).

46 'doubtful repute' – *Observer*, 22 May 1870.

46 'Maria' – Thompson, *Ladies or Gentlemen?*

47 'no appearance of a beard' – Alfred Swaine Taylor, *The Principles and Practice of Medical Jurisprudence* (London, 1861).

47 'The state of the rectum' – *ibid*.

49 'abused by men' – Deposition of Dr Paul.

49 'special continental vice' – *The Leader*, 18 September 1858.

50 'I had never seen' – Trial testimony of Dr Paul.

50 'I examined Boulton' – Deposition of Dr Paul.

50 'Boulton was then removed' – *ibid*.

50 'The anus was *very*' – *ibid*.

51 'a foreign body' – Deposition of Dr Paul.

51 'an inordinate length' – *ibid*.

51 'Traction' – *ibid*.

51 'the dimensions' – Ambroise Tardieu, *Étude médico-légale sur les attentats aux mœurs* (Paris, 1857, and seventh edition, 1878, translated by Dede Smith).

6 *Wives and Daughters*

53 'Say Stella' – Jonathan Swift, 'To Stella, Visiting Me in My Sickness', 1720.

53 'independent means' – entry in the 1841 Census.

53 'And Ernest was' – Trial testimony of Mrs Mary Ann Boulton.

56 'Mamma' – *ibid*.

58 'everything' – *ibid*.

59 'reverses' – *ibid*.

59 'If he asked his father' – *ibid*.

60 'consumptive' – *ibid*.

61 'I was always' – *ibid*.

7 *Becoming Fanny*

65 'And all that's madly wild' – Thomas Parnell, *Poems upon Several Occasions* (London, 1773).

77 'sound in principles' – Sir James Park, *Some Account of Myself*, unpublished and undated MS, *c*.1835.

8 *A Tale of Two Sisters*

79 'A SISTER'S LOVE' – Jethro Jackson, *The Family Treasury of Western Literature, Science and Art* (London, 1854).

79 'sterner features' – *Evening Standard*, 2 May 1870.

85 'your mincing' – Louis Hurt to Ernest Boulton, 8 April 1870, Trial.

86 'They always said' – Trial testimony of Hugh Mundell.

9 *Monstrous Erections*

88 'At Wakefield Street' – 'The Funny He-She Ladies'.

88 'The crowd' – *Reynolds's Newspaper*, 15 May 1870.

89 'It is suspected' – *Daily Telegraph*, 30 April 1870.

89 'these foolish if not unnatural' – *Illustrated Police News*, 7 May 1870.

90 'Nothing' – *Extraordinary Revelations*.

90 'the filthy details' – *Reynolds's Newspaper*, 29 May 1870.

90 'noble lord' – *ibid*.

90 'allow seats' – *Evening Standard*, 6 May 1870.

91 'a most indecent' – *The Times*, 30 May 1870.

91 'such ebullitions' – *ibid*.

91 'The list' – *The Times*, 16 May 1870.

94 'a Theatrical' – Jim Davis, 'Androgynous Cliques and Epicene Colleges: Gender Transgression On and Off the Victorian Stage', *Nineteenth Century Theatre*, Vol. 26, No. 1 (Summer 1998).

95 '42 stamps' – *The Englishwoman's Domestic Magazine*, 1861.

96 'monstrous erections' – C. Willett Cunnington, *Feminine Attitudes in the Nineteenth Century* (London, 1935).

96 'a whopper' – *Curiosities of Street Literature, Comprising Cocks and Catchpennies* (London, 1871).

96 'hair-dressing establishments' – *Graphic*, 7 May 1870.

96 'The hairdresser' – Deposition of Maria Duffin.

97 'sterner features' – *Evening Standard*, 2 May 1870.

97 'great quantity' – *The Times*, 16 May 1870.

97 'evident defects' – Cunnington, *Feminine Attitudes*.

97 'One of the prostitutes' – Reay Tannahill, *Sex in History* (London, 1980).

98 'no one who goes' – *Godey's Lady's Book and Magazine*, 1871.

98 'If a girl' – Mrs H. R. Haweis, *The Art of Beauty* (London, 1878).

98 'one of the most innocent' – Edwin Creer, *A Popular Treatise on the Human Hair* (London, 1865).

99 'CAUTION TO LADIES' – *The Pearl*, April 1880.

10 *A Dirty Business*

102 '*Amenities of Leicester Square*' – *The Pearl*, 1880.

102 'considered' – *Daily Telegraph*, 10 May 1871.

103 'admirable' – in Alan Mackinnon, *The Oxford Amateurs: A Short History of Theatricals at the University* (London, 1910).

104 'well-known' – *Daily Telegraph*, 10 May 1871.

105 'Are you good-natured' – *The Times*, 24 September 1850.

106 'in a very mincing' – *The Times*, 25 October 1850.

106 'Did you see' – Willy Somerville to Stella Boulton, no date but *c*.1868, Letters.

106 'There is a considerable' – Evidence of Howard Vincent, 19 July 1881, *Minutes of Evidence of the Select Committee of the House of Lords on the Protection of Young Girls*, Parliamentary Papers, 1881.

106 'A great many' – *Flora Tristan's London Journal*, translated by Denis Palmer and Giselle Pincetl (London, 1980).

107 'army' – 'Xavier Mayne', *The Intersexes: A History of Simisexualism as a Problem in Social Life* (Rome, 1908).

107 'seven or eight' – 'Evidence of Silas Rendell Anniss, 27 February 1871', in *Analysis of the Evidence Given Before the Contagious Diseases Commission*, prepared by J. Salusbury Trelawny (London, 1872).

107 'such types' – 'Xavier Mayne', *The Intersexes*.

107 'oftentimes' – Statements of Jack Saul to Inspector Abberline of the Metropolitan Police, 10 and 12 August 1889, The National Archives.

108 'fancy woman' – 'H. Smith', *Yokel's Preceptor*.

108 'notorious' – *ibid*.

108 'spooney boy' – Statements of Jack Saul to Inspector Abberline.

108 'One man's prick' – 'Walter', *My Secret Life*.

109 'If you'll let us go' – Deposition of Detective Sergeant Kerley/*Reynolds's Newspaper*, 14 May 1871.

109 'I have been in the hands' – Letter from Malcolm Johnston, Dublin Commission Court – The Queen v Cornwall and Others, August 1884.

109 'Nearly all ' – *ibid*.

110 'Camp' – Statement of Malcolm Johnston, Dublin Commission Court.

111 'in a very extraordinary' – *Morning Post*, 23 June 1868.

111 'a charge' – *ibid*.

112 'been specially employed' – *Birmingham Daily Post*, 10 March 1871.

112 'the system' – *Freeman's Journal*, 9 March 1871.

113 'the slightest doubt' – Alfred Swaine Taylor, *Medical Jurisprudence* (London, 1846).

11 *Getting Up Evidence*

114 'That if any witness' – *A Compendious Abstract of the Public General Acts of the United Kingdom of Great Britain and Ireland* (London, 1823).

114 'literally inundated' – *Reynolds's Newspaper*, 15 May 1870.

114 'I have had a great deal' – *Daily Telegraph*, 30 May 1870.

116 'I have known Park' – Deposition of John Reeve.

117 'They were walking' – *ibid*.

118 'I have seen about twenty' – *ibid*.

118 'frequent complaints' – *ibid*.

120 'I noticed' – Deposition of George Smith.

120 'I saw him *wink*' – Trial testimony of George Smith.

120 'I dare say' – *Daily Telegraph*, 14 May 1870.

120 'Oh, you sweet little dear!' – Deposition of George Smith.

121 'I saw Boulton' – *ibid*.

121 'I've received' – *ibid*.

121 'Take no notice' – *ibid*.

121 'You're as bad' – *ibid*.

121 'They used to walk' – Trial testimony of George Smith.

122 'I've cautioned' – Deposition of George Smith.

123 'I don't think' – *The Times*, 14 May 1870.

123 'Have you been drinking' – *Daily Telegraph*, 14 May 1870.

123 'flippant' – *ibid*.

124 'getting up evidence' – Deposition of George Smith.

124 'a mistake as to the date' – *ibid*.

124 'at the Treasury-office' – *The Times*, 14 May 1870.

124 'I *may* be paid' – Deposition of George Smith/Trial testimony of George Smith/*The Times*, 14 May 1870.

124 'additions' – *The Times*, 14 May 1870.

12 *A Victorian Romance*

126 'At length I am a bride!' – *Letters from Laura and Eveline, Giving an Account of Their Mock-Marriage, Wedding Trip, Etc.*, (London, 1903).

128 'He laughed' – Trial testimony of Mary Ann Boulton.

129 'On one or two occasions' – *ibid*.

130 'nourish' – 1876 advertisement for Rowland's Macassar Oil.

131 'Rose of the garden' – Anne Fricker, 'Fading Away', 1854.

131 'ripened' – Trial testimony of Mary Ann Boulton.

133 'interfering' – *Daily Telegraph*, 10 May 1871.

133 'a man perfectly well-known' – Opening speech of the Attorney-General, Trial.

133 'apparently plying' – *ibid*.

134 'a marriage' – *The Times*, 6 June 1868.

135 'in all, five' – *The Times*, 10 November 1869.

135 'a chest' – *ibid*.

136 'My dear Mrs Boulton' – Lord Arthur Clinton to Mrs Boulton, 11 December 1868, Letters.

136 'said he would be very pleased' – Trial testimony of Mary Ann Boulton.

136 'My answer' – *ibid*.

137 'When I was dressing' – *ibid*.

137 'I fear I offended' – Lord Arthur Clinton to Mrs Boulton, 12

October 1868, Trial.

13 *Lord Arthur's Wife*

138 'MARRY!' – *The Ladies' Treasury*, March 1867.

140 'I thought Boulton' – Deposition of Eliza Clark.

141 'I have been' – *ibid*.

141 'I used to accuse' – *ibid*.

141 'I never could satisfy myself' – *Evening Standard*, 30 May 1870.

141 'Boulton generally dressed' – Deposition of Maria Duffin.

142 'When Boulton was there' – *ibid*.

143 'I beg your pardon' – Trial testimony of Maria George (*née* Duffin).

14 *The Toast of the Town*

148 'Oh! the dresses' – 'Cantab', 'The Spa at Scarborough: A Reminiscence' in *The Lovers' Dictionary: A Poetical Treasury of Lovers' Thoughts, Fancies, Addresses and Dilemmas* (London, 1867).

151 'it strengthens' – *Theakston's Guide to Scarborough* (Scarborough, 1868).

152 'Lord Arthur Pelham-Clinton, M.P.' – *Scarborough Gazette and Weekly List of Visitors*, 15 October 1868.

152 'Oct. 20, 1868.' – *Daily Telegraph*, 13 May 1871.

153 'the oldest' – George Crosby, *Crosby's Guide to Scarborough* (Scarborough, *c*.1850).

155 'honoured' – *Scarborough Gazette and Weekly List of Visitors*, 22 October 1868.

156 'an establishment' – *Scarborough Gazette and Weekly List of Visitors*, 15 October 1868.

156 'a popular demand' – Trial testimony of Oliver Sarony.

157 'Lord Arthur had' – Wybert Reeve to the Editor of the *Daily Telegraph*, 3 June 1870.

15 'Yr Affectionate Fanny'

159 'Don't be too particular' – words and music by John Orlando
Parry, 1843.

162 'I am just off' – Ernest Boulton to Lord Arthur Clinton, 4
December 1868, Letters.

162 'We were very drunk' – Ernest Boulton to Lord Arthur Clinton,
late 1868, letters read in evidence, Trial.

162 'tired and seedy' – *ibid*.

162 'How *can* you' – *ibid*.

162 'I must of course trust' – *ibid*.

162 'Now no promises' – *ibid*.

162 'A game pie' – *ibid*.

162 'If you have any coin' – *ibid*.

162 'Send me some money' – Ernest Boulton to Lord Arthur Clinton,
4 December 1868, Letters.

162 'I wanted the money' – Ernest Boulton to Lord Arthur Clinton,
late 1868, letters read in evidence, Trial.

162 'I shall leave here' – *ibid*.

162 'Why *cannot* you' – *ibid*.

162 'It is now five o'clock' – *ibid*.

162 'When you write' – *ibid*.

162 'I have waited' – *ibid*.

162 'I do not like' – *ibid*.

163 'I am quite tired' – *ibid*.

163 'We cannot go on' – *ibid*.

163 'I am most annoyed' – *ibid*.

163 'I am consoling' – *ibid*.

163 'And now, dear' – *ibid*.

163 'My Dearest Arthur' – Frederick Park to Lord Arthur Clinton, 22
November 1868, Letters.

164 'How *very* kind' – Frederick Park to Lord Arthur Clinton, 21

November 1868, Letters.

165 'Is the handle' – Frederick Park to Lord Arthur Clinton, late 1868, Letters.

16 The Dragon of Davies Street

167 'Ann Empson' – *Reynolds's Newspaper*, 5 June 1870.

169 'Are you married?' – *Reynolds's Newspaper*, 5 June 1870.

170 'Have you been drinking' – *The Times*, 30 May 1870.

171 'a mutton chop' – Deposition of Ann Empson.

171 'I was surprised' – *ibid*.

171 'I saw Lord Arthur' – Deposition of Ann Empson/*The Times*, 30 May 1870.

171 'I complained' – Deposition of Ann Empson.

172 'as an abuse' – *ibid*.

172 'I said to them' – *ibid*.

173 'lady's wearing apparel' – Trial Testimony of Ann Empson.

173 'The prisoner nearest' – *ibid*.

17 'Come Love'

175 'Love is a pretty pedlar' – Robert Jones, 'The Muses Gardin for Delights', 1610.

175 'Mr Ernest Boulton' – John Safford Fiske to Ernest Boulton, March/April 1870, Letters.

176 'having indecently' – *Illustrated Police News*, 16 July 1870.

177 'arse-quim' – *Letters from Laura and Eveline*.

180 'playing weekday tunes' – Trial testimony of Agnes Dickson

180 'Nothing like him' – Trial testimony of John Doig.

180 'by drinking' – John Jameson Jim to Ernest Boulton, February or March 1870, Letters.

181 'Have you the same love' – John Jameson Jim to Ernest Boulton, 8 April 1870, Letters.

181 '*Will* you stay' – 'Jack', to Ernest Boulton, 4 April 1870, Letters.

182 'of unblemished character' – Joseph Mullin to William H. Seward, 26 August 1867, 'Letters of Application and Recommendation During the Administrations of Abraham Lincoln and Andrew Jackson, 1861 to 1869', Microfilm M650, US National Archives and Records Administration.

184 'After we were married' – John Safford Fiske to Ernest Boulton, 20 April 1870, Letters.

184 'adventures' – John Safford Fiske to Ernest Boulton, 18 April 1870, Letters.

185 'his smiling face' – *ibid*.

185 'Laïs and Antinous' – *ibid*.

185 'ravishing' – *ibid.*

185 'Come love' – John Safford Fiske to Ernest Boulton, March/April 1870, Letters.

18 Un Souvenir d'Amour

187 'All Cracks are so full of Ails' – John Dunton, *The He-Strumpets: A Satyr on the Sodomite Club*, 1707, in Rictor Norton, *Mother Clap's Molly House* (London, 2006).

188 'In France' – William Allingham, *Fistula, Haemorrhoids, Painful Ulcers, Stricture, Prolapsus, and Other Painful Diseases of the Rectum* (London, 1871).

188 'immense prevalence' – William Acton, *A Complete Practical Treatise on the Diseases of the Urinary and Generative Organs*, (London, 1860).

189 'running down' – *ibid*.

189 'frequently to be seen' – George Drysdale, *The Elements of Social Science; or, Physical, Sexual and Natural Religion* (London, 1867).

190 'infected' – attributed to Lord Byron, 'Don Leon', *c*.1830.

190 'abomination' – *Extraordinary Revelations*.

190 'G—' – Philippe Ricord, *Illustrations of Syphilitic Disease*, translated by T. F. Belton (Philadelphia, 1851).

190 'sodomy' – Drysdale, *Elements*.

191 'I saw one case' – Trial testimony of Dr Henry James Johnson.

192 'principally dowagers' – Deposition of Amos Westropp Gibbings.

193 'shabby plaid trousers' – Deposition of Dr Richard Barwell.

193 'He was walking' – Trial testimony of George Layton.

194 'He confessed' – Trial testimony of Dr Richard Barwell.

195 'a gonorrhoeal discharge' – *ibid*.

195 'rather common clothing' – *ibid*.

196 'I examined him' – *ibid*.

197 'insisted' – *Lancet*, 28 May 1870.

197 'And so' – *Lancet*, 28 May 1870.

19 *The Battle of the Bottoms*

198 'An Awkward Question' – *The Pearl*, 1880.

199 'in close prison' – Opening address by Mr Digby Seymour, Trial.

199 'We are of the opinion' – *Report From the Departmental Committee on Prisons*, Prisons Committee (London, 1895).

200 'eminent medical gentlemen' – *Daily Telegraph*, 15 May 1871.

200 'by the direction' – *Reynolds's Newspaper*, 19 June 1870.

202 'vaginal spasms' – Evidence of Dr David McLoughlin to the Skey Committee on Pathology and Treatment of Venereal Disease, 6 December 1864.

205 'a feeling' – *Lancet*, 25 June 1870.

205 'The two things' – D— S— , *Eighteen Months' Imprisonment* (London, 1883).

206 'dignified courtesy' – Obituary notice of Dr Frederick Le Gros Clark, *British Medical Journal*, 6 August 1892.

207 'characteristic signs' – Tardieu, *Étude médico-légale*.

207 'noticed by all present' – Taylor, *Medical Jurisprudence* (1873 edition).

208 'Beware' – Tardieu, *Étude médico-légale*.

208 'a small varix' – Trial testimony of Dr Johnson.

209 'It may be relied upon' – *Reynolds's Newspaper*, 19 June 1870.

20 *He, She or It*

210 'There is not the slightest doubt' – *The Englishwoman's Domestic Magazine*, 1871.

211 'the smallness of the anus' – *Trial Testimony of Dr Johnson*.

212 'the Hermaphrodite Clique' – *Reynolds's Newspaper*, 5 June 1870.

212 'the Hermaphrodite Gang' – *Reynolds's Newspaper*, 12 June 1870.

212 'By special request' – *Extraordinary Revelations*.

212 'During the piece' – *Essex Herald*, 2 January 1869, in *Daily Telegraph*, 9 May 1870.

213 'Listening' – anonymous newspaper report in *Extraordinary Revelations*.

213 'We agreed' – *Daily Telegraph*, 13 May 1871.

213 'We may add' – *Extraordinary Revelations*.

214 'On one evening' – *Daily Telegraph*, 13 May 1871.

214 'My darling Ernie' – Louis Hurt to Ernest Boulton, 4 April 1870, read in evidence, Trial.

215 'rustics' – Louis Hurt to Lord Arthur Clinton, 9 October 1868, read in evidence, Trial.

215 'I really thought' – *Daily Telegraph*, 21 May 1870.

216 'I pretended to resist' – Saul, *Sins of the Cities*.

217 'I resigned' – *Daily Telegraph*, 21 May 1870.

218 'It was from the manner' – Deposition of Francis Kegan Cox.

218 'Oh you City birds' – *Daily Telegraph*, 21 May 1870.

219 'I treated Boulton' – *ibid*.

220 'I afterwards heard' – *ibid*.

222 'a letter from Captain Cox' – '657 – December 1870', Treasury Solicitor's Account Books, TS 40 14, The National Archives.

21 *A Bitches' Ball*

223 'a bitches' ball' – Statement of Malcolm Johnston, Dublin Commission Court.

225 'the slang term "drag"' – Deposition of Amos Westropp Gibbings.

226 'chanced to see' – Arthur Munby's diary entry for 13 April 1864, in Derek Hudson, *Munby: Man of Two Worlds* (London, 1974).

227 'dressed in the pastoral garb' – *The Times*, 1 August 1854.

227 'a hundred persons' – *ibid.*

227 'a sort of dance' – *Illustrated Police News*, 2 October 1880, in H. G. Cocks, *Nameless Offences: Homosexual Desire in the Nineteenth Century* (London, 2003).

228 'Sister' – *ibid.*

228 'They changed partners' – Deposition of Edward Nelson Haxell.

229 'the best amateur actress' – *ibid.*

229 'I heard Boulton sing' – *ibid.*

230 'There seems to be' – Jack Saul, *Sins of the Cities.*

230 'No doubt the proprietor' – *ibid.*

231 'I sat for a while' – *ibid.*

231 'dancing with a gentleman from the City' – *ibid.*

231 'During the evening' – *ibid.*

231 'Lord Arthur and Boulton' – *ibid.*

232 'at once knelt down' – *ibid.*

232 'soon brought to light' – *ibid.*

232 'How excited I became' – *ibid.*

232 'postillioned her bottomhole' – *ibid.*

233 'Opening her drawers' – *ibid.*

22 *The Wheels of Justice*

235 'We hope and believe' – *Pall Mall Gazette*, 8 June 1870.

235 'I am rather sorry' – Louis Hurt to Ernest Boulton, 17 April 1870,

Letters.

236 'I suppose' – Louis Hurt to John Safford Fiske, 29 May 1870,
Trial.

236 'My darling Ernie' – Louis Hurt to Ernest Boulton, 8 April 1870,
Letters.

237 'Do you advise' – Louis Hurt to John Safford Fiske, 29 May 1870,
Trial.

238 'heartily glad' – Louis Hurt to John Safford Fiske, 18 May 1870,
Trial.

238 'I was in Court' – Louis Hurt to John Safford Fiske, 29 May 1870,
Trial.

238 'My dear John' – Louis Hurt to John Safford Fiske, 18 May 1870,
Trial.

239 *'un ange'* – John Safford Fiske to Ernest Boulton, 18 April 1870,
Letters.

239 'I have just seen' – Louis Hurt to John Safford Fiske, May 1870,
Trial.

241 'Mr Fiske called' – Confidential Memorandum No 353: John
Lothrop Motley to Hamilton Fisk, Secretary of State, London, 11
June 1870, in 'Despatches from U.S. Ministers to Great Britain,
1791–1906', US National Archives and Records Administration.

243 'I asked Mr Fiske' – Trial testimony of Detective Officer Gollan.

244 'Mr Fiske – Facts' – Confidential Memorandum No 357.

23 *Dead or Disappeared*

246 'We have it on the authority' – *Reynolds's Newspaper*, 26 June
1870.

247 'Peers' – *ibid.*

247 'resolution' – *Pall Mall Gazette*, 8 June 1870.

248 'I took up my fare' – *Reynolds's Newspaper*, 12 June 1870.

249 'We understand' – *Weekly Times*, 12 June 1870.

249 'there are people' – *Observer*, 26 June 1870.

249 'The rumour' – *Daily Telegraph*, 20 June 1870.

250 'We are in a position' – *Lancet*, 25 June 1870.

250 'utter prostration' – *Evening Standard*, 20 June 1870.

250 'bed of sickness' – *ibid.*

250 'Nothing' – *ibid.*

251 'sad and wasted' – *Daily Telegraph*, 21 June 1870.

251 'A MIS-SPENT LIFE' – *Reynolds's Newspaper*, 26 June 1870.

251 'Lord Arthur's' – *Porcupine*, 25 June 1870.

251 'Verily' – *ibid.*

251 'The funeral' – *Weekly Times*, 26 June 1870.

252 'He hath borne' – *Echo*, 24 June 1870.

252 'persons' – *Nottingham Daily Guardian*, 22 June 1870.

252 'Is Lord Arthur' – *Porcupine*, 25 June 1870.

253 'It is understood' – *Daily Telegraph*, 10 May 1871.

256 'nothing' – Mr Ouvry to William Gladstone, 29 June 1870, folio 3011, Glynne Gladstone MSS.

256 'It is impossible' – *ibid.*

24 *This Slippery Sod*

257 'The management' – *Reynolds's Newspaper*, 29 May 1870.

261 'a rather effeminate' – *Illustrated Police News*, 30 July 1870.

261 'I walked' – *The Times*, 2 April 1870.

261 'Oh! pray don't' – *ibid.*

262 'Come with me' – *The Times*, 26 July 1870.

262 'I am ashamed' – *ibid.*

264 'Dear Stella' – Harry Park to Stella Boulton, early 1871, Letters.

266 'Mr Edward Henry Park?' – *Illustrated Police News*, 30 July 1870.

267 'a tall, stylishly-dressed' – *ibid.*

267 'The bench and court' – *ibid.*

268 'I am here' – *The Times*, 26 July 1870.

25 'Pestiferous and Pestilential'

269 'What words can paint' – *Extraordinary Revelations*.

271 'venereal disease' – 'Evidence of William Henry Sloggett, 30 January 1871', *Analysis of the Evidence Given Before the Contagious Diseases Commission*.

271 'a grand movement' – *London Entr'acte*, 23 January 1871.

272 '*contra*' – Sir Edward Coke, *Third Part of the Institutes of the Laws of England* (London, 1797).

272 'things fearful' – William Bradford, *Of Plymouth Plantation*, written between 1620 and 1647, in Jonathan Katz, *Gay American History* (New York, 1978).

273 'pestiferous' – in Richard Davenport-Hines, *Sex, Death and Punishment: Attitudes to Sex and Sexuality in Britain since the Renaissance* (London, 1991).

273 'abominations' – in Alan Bray, *Homosexuality in Renaissance England* (London, 1982).

273 'Henceforth, Borastus' – John Wilmot, *Sodom, or The Quintessence of Debauchery* (Paris, 1957).

273 'hugger-mugger' – *ibid*.

274 'The unnatural Lewdness' – Thomas Sherlock, *A Letter from the Lord Bishop of London to the Clergy and People of London and Westminster; on Occasion of the Late Earthquakes* (London, 1750).

275 'great hulking ruffians' – James Greenwood, 'A Night in the Workhouse', *Pall Mall Gazette*, 13 January 1866.

275 'Facts' – Charles Dickens, *Hard Times* (London, 1854).

275 'classification' – George Roberts, *An Etymological and Explanatory Dictionary of the Terms and Language of Geology* (London, 1839).

275 'peripheral excitement' – Isaac Baker Brown, *On the Curability of Certain Forms of Insanity, Epilepsy, Catalepsy, and Hysteria in*

Females (London, 1866).

277 'Androgynism' – *Medical Times and Gazette*, 9 February 1868.

277 'the slightest doubt' – Cunnington, *Feminine Attitudes*.

277 'unsexed' – *Pall Mall Gazette*, 29 June 1870.

278 'respectable young men' – *The Times*, 25 September 1857.

278 'Smirking' – *ibid.*

278 'unnatural' – in Michael Mason, *The Making of Victorian Sexuality* (Oxford, 1995).

278 'The increase' – 'H. Smith', *Yokel's Preceptor* c.1850

279 'who is known' – *Daily Telegraph*, 31 May 1870.

279 'It is certain' – *Saturday Review*, 20 May 1871.

279 'A certain form of iniquity' – *Daily Telegraph*, 31 May 1870.

279 'a doubtful fellowship' – *Daily Telegraph*, 31 May 1870.

279 'clique' – *Reynolds's Newspaper*, 5 June 1870.

279 'Vice' – *Daily Telegraph*, 31 May 1870.

279 'There is no saying how far things might go' – *The Times*, 31 May 1870.

279 'This London of ours' – *Reynolds's Newspaper*, 5 June 1870.

280 'organisation and concert' – *The Pall Mall Gazette*, 8 June 1870.

26 *The Ship of State*

282 'Herald, read the accusation!' – Lewis Carroll, *Alice's Adventures in Wonderland* (1865).

282 'To judge' – *Daily Telegraph*, 10 May 1871.

283 'the public' – *Porcupine*, 9 July 1870.

283 'It is thought' – *Penny Illustrated*, 11 December 1870.

284 'a bouquet' – *Illustrated Police News*, 13 May 1871.

284 'tastily' – *Daily Telegraph*, 10 May 1871.

284 'scarcely altered' – *ibid.*

285 'campish' – Frederick Park to Lord Arthur Clinton, 21 November 1868, Letters.

286 'a spider's web' – in John Juxon, *Lewis and Lewis: The Life and*

Times of a Victorian Solicitor (London, 1983).

286 'conspiracy to solicit' – 9 May 1871, DPP 4/6, The National Archives.

288 'unlawfully' – *ibid*.

288 'openly and publicly' – *ibid*.

291 'This is a prosecution' – Opening speech of the Attorney-General, Trial.

291 'his bounden duty' – *ibid*.

293 'Perhaps I am not going' – *ibid*.

293 'But' – *ibid*.

27 *The Most Sensational Event*

295 'By sometimes dressing' – Opening speech of the Attorney-General, Trial.

296 'irregular affections' – Solomon to Swinburne, 1862, in Jean Overton Fuller, *Swinburne: A Critical Biography* (London, 1968).

296 'Dolomite' – Solomon to Swinburne, 10 May 1871, in John Y. LeBourgeois, 'Swinburne and Simeon Solomon', *Notes and Queries*, March 1973.

296 'Boulton is very remarkable' – Solomon to Swinburne, 15 May 1871, in LeBourgeois, 'Swinburne and Simeon Solomon'.

296 'a very revolting' – *Illustrated Police News*, 4 June 1870.

297 'Dear Stella' – Harry Park to Stella Boulton, Letters.

298 'Dearest Stella' – Willy Somerville to Stella Boulton, Letters.

300 'My cawfish' – Opening speech of Sir John Karslake, Trial.

300 'It is cawfish' – *ibid*.

301 'Whatever it may mean' – *ibid*.

301 'painting their faces' – Opening speech of the Attorney-General, Trial.

302 'If every *roué* ' – *Extraordinary Revelations*.

303 'crush and spoil' – Opening speech of Mr Digby Seymour, Trial.

303 'thoroughly' – Trial testimony of William Kay.

304 'A thrill' – *Daily Telegraph*, 13 May 1871.

306 'the most sensational' – *Daily Telegraph*, 10 May 1871.

306 'roars of laughter' – *ibid*.

307 'Do you think' – *ibid*.

308 'acquitted' – Solomon to Swinburne, 15 May 1871, in LeBourgeois, 'Swinburne and Simeon Solomon'.

28 A Rout

309 'The conception' – *The Times*, 25 July 1871.

311 'What is that book' – Trial testimony of Dr James Paul.

313 'Just attend to me' – *ibid*.

314 'any Magistrate's order' – *ibid*.

315 'You should be more careful' – *ibid*.

315 'getting up evidence' – Deposition of George Smith.

316 'pay him' – Trial testimony of George Smith.

316 'a situation' – *The Times*, 14 May 1870.

316 'I have watched them' – *Daily Telegraph*, 30 April 1870.

317 'the unemployed' – Letter Book of the Commissioner of the Metropolitan Police, MEPO 1/48, The National Archives.

317 'Maladministration' – *ibid*.

317 'Mr Bradlaugh' – *ibid*.

317 'young Mr Boulton' – Opening address of Mr Digby Seymour, Trial.

319 '679 – Dec 1870' – Treasury Solicitor's Account Books, TS 40 14, The National Archives.

319 '492 – Dec 1870' – *ibid*.

320 'rewards' – Opening speech of Mr Digby Seymour, Trial.

29 'This Terrible Drama of Vice'

321 'She watches' – Fanny Fales (Mrs Frances Elizabeth Swift), *Voices*

of the Heart (Boston, 1853).

322 'own beloved Child' – Mary Ann Boulton to Ernest Boulton, Letters.

322 'wanted strength' – *ibid*.

322 'Are you the mother' – Trial testimony of Mary Ann Boulton.

322 'Exactly so' – *ibid*.

324 'a retentive memory' – *ibid*.

326 'Ernest has been' – *ibid*.

328 'We know as a fact' – Closing speech of Mr Digby Seymour, Trial.

328 'a friend' – Trial testimony of Mary Ann Boulton.

330 'nothing indecent' – Closing speech of Mr Digby Seymour, Trial.

330 'My son sent me' – Trial testimony of Mary Ann Boulton.

331 'You would expect' – Closing speech of Mr Digby Seymour, Trial. 'Ernest Boulton' – *ibid*.

331 'vile and wicked' – *ibid*.

332 'Dr Paul' – *ibid*.

332 'morbidly sensible' – Opening address of Mr Digby Seymour, Trial.

332 'the most exquisite torture' – *ibid*.

332 'Surely, Gentlemen' – Closing speech of Mr Digby Seymour, Trial.

334 'capable of plunging' – *ibid*.

335 'Gentlemen' – *Lloyd's Weekly Newspaper*, 21 May 1871.

30 Clouds and Sunshine

336 'Rose of the garden' – Fricker, 'Fading Away'.

336 'MR ERNEST BOULTON' – *Reynolds's Newspaper*, 6 August 1871, quoting from the *Era*, late July 1871.

337 'his Drawing-Room Entertainment' – *Liverpool Mercury*, 14 November/21 November 1871.

337 'Mr Boulton displayed' – *Liverpool Mercury*, 9 September 1873.

338 'PORTLAND HALL' – *Hampshire Telegraph and Sussex Chronicle*, 29 May 1872.

338 'The beauty' – *Hampshire Telegraph and Sussex Chronicle*, 5 June 1872.

339 'This so-called' – *Hampshire Advertiser*, 15 June 1872.

339 'notoriety' – *Birmingham Daily Post*, 17 June 1872.

339 'Beams of the morning' – Fricker, 'Fading Away'.

340 'the impudence' – *Pall Mall Gazette*, 18 October 1873.

341 'comedian' – *New York Clipper*, 9 April 1881.

341 'Ernest Byne' – *New York Clipper*, 11 April 1874.

341 'Two gentlemen' – *ibid*.

342 'ERNEST BYNE, pronounced' – *New York Clipper*, 25 April 1874.

342 'Your airs' – quoted in Laurence Senelick, *The Changing Room: Sex, Drag and Theatre* (London, 2000).

343 'Lord Arthur Clinton' – *Reynolds's Newspaper*, 20 October 1872.

343 'at the Installation' – *Morning Post*, 30 January 1878.

343 'My Lord Arthur Clinton' – *Clarence and Richmond Examiner and New South Wales Advertiser*, 25 February 1879.

344 'Elegant Parisian Clothes' – *Era*, 24 June 1877.

344 'Songs, Eccentricities' – *Era*, 10 March 1878.

344 'a most marvellous' – *Era*, 24 June 1877.

344 'The Bynes are' – *Era*, 22 July 1877.

344 'AN INDIGNANT NONCONFORMIST' – *Western Mail*, 14 April 1879.

344 'actor' – Census of 1881.

344 'Spring's fairest blossoms' – Fricker, 'Fading Away'.

346 'How *dare* you' – *Evening Standard*, 2 May 1870.

346 '*N'importe*' – Frederick Park to Lord Arthur Clinton, 21 November 1868, Letters.

346 'I give, devise' – Last Will and Testament of Frederick William Park, 17 July 1878.

347 'Song of the wild-bird' – Fricker, 'Fading Away'.

347 'Society absurdity' – *Era*, 22 December 1891.

348 'The performer' – *Era*, 13 June 1891.

348 'The Brothers Blair' – *Belfast News-Letter*, 13 June 1896.

350 'Hope's fairy promise' – Fricker, 'Fading Away'.

350 'But there's a land' – *ibid*.

Epilogue

354 'a professional Mary-Ann' – Statements of Jack Saul to Inspector Abberline.

354 'Lord Euston' – *ibid*.

354 'uttering a fictitious cheque' – *Hampshire Telegraph and Sussex Chronicle*, 25 January 1873.

354 'congestion' – Death certificate of Amos Westropp Gibbings, 29 March 1890.

355 'I invented' – Oscar Wilde to the Editor of the *Pall Mall Gazette*, 1 October 1894, in Merlin Holland and Rupert Hart-Davis, *The Complete Letters of Oscar Wilde* (London, 2000).

357 'For I've got a Peep-Show' – C. J. Pavitt, 'I've Got a Peep-Show' (*c.*1875).

357 'allowed any cloud ' – Trial testimony of Mary Ann Boulton.

358 'large and beautiful garden' – unsigned autobiographical essay by John Safford Fiske, *History of the Class of 1863 Yale College* (New Haven, Connecticut, 1905), in Jonathan Ned Katz, *Love Stories: Sex Between Men Before Homosexuality* (Chicago, 2001).

358 'passed through his hands' – *Wirksworth Parish Magazine*, October 1936, in Derek Wain, *The Hurts of Derbyshire* (Ashbourne, Derbyshire, 2002).

359 'my uncle' – Will of the Most Noble Henry Pelham Archibald Douglas Duke of Newcastle, 1927.

359 'His charming manner' – *Hampshire Chronicle*, 19 February 1940.

Index

Abberline, Inspector, 354

Abbey Green, Lanarkshire, 257–60, 266

Abrams (solicitor): acts for Fanny and Stella, 40, 198, 205, 285; advises Hurt and Fiske, 237–8, 240–1

Acton, William, 188–9

Alhambra *see* Royal Alhambra Palace

Allingham, William, 188

anal sex *see* sodomy

Anniss, Inspector Silas, 107

Attenborough, Mr (pawnbroker), 135

Attorney-General *see* Collier, Sir Robert

Barker, Emily, 108

Barwell, Dr Richard: examines and treats Fanny for syphilis, 193–7, 199, 203–4, 208–9, 238, 310–11; gives evidence at trial, 309–10, 331; later career and death, 357

Batson, Mary, 66–8, 70, 75

Beeton, Isabella and Samuel, 95

Belfast News-Letter, 348

Betsey H— (male prostitute), 108

Blair, Ernest and Eden (stage names of Stella and Gerard Boulton), 347

Boulton, Gerard (Stella's brother): birth and childhood, 55, 58; and Lord Arthur Clinton, 133; partners Stella as leading man, 340, 344, 347; in America, 341–2; returns to England, 344; adopts name Eden Blair, 347, 360; marriage and son, 348; with

Stella at death, 350; manages theatre in Winchester and death (1940), 360

Boulton, Mary Ann (Stella's mother): character and qualities, 51; marriage, 54–5; and Stella's dressing up as child, 56–7; decline in fortunes, 58–9; and Stella's poor health, 60–1, 128, 332; encourages Louis Hurt's interest in Stella, 126, 179, 328; and Stella's friends, 128–9; and Stella's relations with Lord Arthur Clinton, 131–7, 325–6, 329; and Stella's arrests, 133–4, 235; Louis Hurt offers support to, 236; testifies at Stella's trial, 321–30, 332, 334; death, 358

Boulton, Ernest *see* Boulton, Stella

Boulton, Stella: appearance and dress, 4–6, 13, 129, 141, 284, 296; at Strand Theatre, 4–6; arrested (1870), 7–11; gives name as Ernest Boulton, 9; Mundell meets and falls for, 12–23; appears before Bow Street magistrate and charged, 34–7; remanded in custody, 40–1; examined by Dr Paul, 44, 50–1, 310; birth and childhood, 55–6; singing, 55–7, 59, 131, 212–13, 220, 224, 229, 338–9, 341–2; dressing up as girl, 56–7; acting ambitions and performances, 57–9, 61, 212–14, 325; banking career, 59–60; attractive to men,

61–4; friendship with Fanny, 76, 79, 84–7; second court appearance, 88–91; drag wardrobe and accoutrements, 92–8; operation for fistula, 100, 177–8, 201; earlier arrests, 102–5, 133; acts in Oxford with Cumming, 103; earnings from prostitution, 104; testimonies and evidence against, 114–25; Louis Hurt courts, 126–7, 178–9; relations with Lord Arthur Clinton, 130–7, 139, 142–6; coming-of-age party (1867), 135–6; shares lodgings with Lord Arthur, 139, 142; character and behaviour, 144–5, 159–60; stage appearance in Scarborough, 152, 155–8; writes notes to Lord Arthur, 160–3; stays with Lord Arthur at Miss Empson's in Davies Street, 169, 172; and Lord Arthur's infidelity with Fanny, 174, 176; letter from Fiske, 175–6, 186; reconciliation with Fanny, 178; in Edinburgh, 179–81, 185; in Newgate Gaol, 198–9, 205–6, 245; medically examined in prison, 199–200, 204, 206, 208–9, 238; feminine appearance of body, 210–11, 214; supposed hermaphroditism, 211–17; dalliance with Captain Cox, 218–20; attends Carlotta's ball, 224, 229, 231–3; released on bail, 267, 283; trial before Lord Chief Justice, 282, 284, 291–2, 308; charges of sodomy withdrawn, 283; grows moustache, 284–5; criminal charges, 288–9; under police surveillance, 316–17; mother testifies for at trial, 324–6, 328–9; found not guilty, 335; resumes theatrical career after acquittal, 336–44, 347–8; changes name to Ernest Byne and moves to America, 340–1; returns to England, 344; as Ernest Blair, 347; male admirers in later years, 348–50; final illness, death and burial, 350–1, 358

Boulton, Thomas (Stella's father): marriage, 54–5; business reverses, 59, 325; and Lord Arthur Clinton, 132–3; Stella's arrest, 235; Louis Hurt offers support to, 236; absent from Stella's trial, 322–3

Bow Street Magistrates' Court, 33–4, 90, 169, 173

Bow Street Police Station, 8, 32, 115

Bradford, William, Governor of New England, 272

Bradlaugh, Charles, 317

Britain: social problems and change, 269–72

brothels, male, 107

Brown, Isaac Baker, 277

Brown, Colonel T. Allston, 342

Bruce, Henry, 291

Bryan, Alfred, 3

buggery see sodomy

Burlington Arcade, Piccadilly, 116, 119, 121–2, 306–7

Byne, Ernest (stage name of Boulton, Stella) see Boulton, Stella

Byron, George Gordon, 6th Baron: 'Don Leon', 190

Byron, H.J.: *One Hundred Thousand Pounds* (play), 212

Index

Caminada, Detective Sergeant Jerome, 227–8

Campbell, George, 227

Campbell ('Lady Jane Grey'), 104–5, 133

Carden, Sir Robert, 227

Carlotta *see* Gibbings, Amos Westropp

Caroline, Madame, 108

Carroll, Lewis: *Alice's Adventures in Wonderland*, 289

Casper, Dr Johann Ludwig, 207, 276

Castlehaven, Mervin Touchet, 2nd Earl of, 273, 290

Challis, John, 227

Chamberlain, Detective Officer William: and arrest of Fanny and Stella, 8, 10–11, 45, 109, 346; calls at Martha Stacey's house, 25–6, 29, 91, 98; testifies against Fanny and Stella, 37–9, 125; and medical examination of Fanny and Stella, 43–4; admits to surveillance of Fanny and Stella, 316; payments to, 319; retires from Metropolitan police and becomes private detective, 354

Charing Cross Hospital: Fanny attends for anal syphilis, 193

chirruping, 3–4

chloroform, 99–100

Clarence and Richmond Examiner and New South Wales Advertiser, 343

Clark, Eliza, 140–1, 143, 304

Coldbath Fields, House of Correction, 346

Cleveland Street Scandal (1890), 354

Clinton, Lord Arthur *see* Pelham–Clinton, Lord Arthur

Clinton, Lord Thomas, 252

Clutterbuck, Dr, 47

Cockburn Sir Alexander (Lord Chief Justice), 284

Coke, Sir Edward, 272

Collette, Charles Hastings (The Society for the Suppression of Vice), 296

Collier, Sir Robert (Attorney–General): prosecutes Fanny and Stella, 290–3, 296–300, 307, 327; calls witnesses, 300–5; on Home Secretary's interest in trial, 319

Colton, Eleanor, 302

Cox, Captain Francis Kegan, 217–22, 319

Cox, Jane, 302

Creer, Edwin, 98

Cumming, Martin Luther ('the Comical Countess'): uses Wakefield Street house, 24, 29; friendship with Fanny, 76, 128; arrested with Stella, 102–3, 133, 302; acting, 103, 129; attends Carlotta's ball, 229; Inspector Thomas pursues, 263; tried in absence, 288; appearance, 289; last sighting in Brussels, 353

Daily Telegraph, 35, 89, 102, 249, 251, 253, 279, 282, 284, 304, 306

Daly, Anthony, 111

Darwin, Charles, 269

Davies Street, London, 167, 169, 176

Departmental Committee on Prisons, 199

D'Eyncourt, Mr (magistrate), 268

Dibdin, Acting Sergeant Edwin, 262, 267

Dickens, Charles: on Surrey Theatre, 12; *Hard Times*, 275

Dickson, Mrs Agnes, 180, 236, 302

Doig, John, 180

Druid's Hall, City of London, 227

Drag balls, 226–30

Drysdale, George, 189–90; *The Elements of Social Science*, 48

Dublin Castle Scandal (1884), 353–4

Duffin, Hannah, 357

Duffin, Maria (*later* George), 96, 141–3, 304, 319, 357–8

Dunton, John: *The He-Strumpets*, 190

Edinburgh, 176, 178–81, 183–5

Edward, Prince of Wales: at Strand Theatre, 3; visits Scarborough, 150; in Mordaunt divorce case, 286

Edwards, Eliza, 46–7, 201, 204, 207

Edwards, Maria, 46–7

Empson, Ann, 167–73, 264, 305–6, 356

Englishwoman's Domestic Magazine, The, 95, 277

Era (theatrical newspaper), 344, 348

Essex Herald, 212

Euston, Henry James FitzRoy, Earl of, 354

Evening News, 34

Extraordinary Revelations see Lives of Boulton and Park, The: Extraordinary Revelations (anonymous pamphlet), 190

Fair Eliza (male prostitute), 108

Fanny see Park, Fanny Winifred

Farrer, Mrs Thomasin, 151

Farrier, Police Constable, 112

Fenians, 269, 317

Fenton, Fred see Park, Fanny Winifred

Ferguson, Charles see Park, Harry

Fiske, John Safford: in Edinburgh, 176, 181, 184; background and career, 182–3; infatuation with Stella, 185–6; and Louis Hurt, 236–8; letters to Stella in police hands, 239–40; visits London to explain relations with Stella, 241–2; premises searched by police, 243–4, 302; arrested and held in Newgate, 244–5, 257; charges of sodomy withdrawn, 283; trial, 288, 290, 292; Simeon Solomon describes, 296; retirement to Italy and death, 358

Flowers, James, 33, 35, 38–40, 43, 91, 93, 170, 197, 215

France: cross-dressers, 97

George, Maria *see* Duffin, Maria

Gepp and Sons (Chelmsford solicitors), 74, 138

Gibbings, Amos Westropp ('Carlotta'): meets Mundell, 22; uses Martha Stacey's Wakefield Street house of accommodation, 24–5, 27, 299; removes incriminating matter from Wakefield Street, 29, 98, 299; takes men's clothes to police station for Fanny and Stella, 32; engages solicitor for Fanny and Stella, 40; friendship with Fanny, 76; hosts ball at Haxell's Hotel, 223–4, 226, 228–30, 299; relations with Fanny, 224–5; appearance, 225; friendship with Sissy Thomas, 299; supposedly finances Fanny and Stella's

defence, 305; tours with Louis
  Munro, 354; death, 354
Gibson, Dr John Rowland, 203–4,
  206
Gladstone, William Ewart: on
  Duchess of Manchester, 2; as
  godfather, guardian and political
  patron of Lord Arthur, 153; and
  settling of Mr Roberts's bill,
  256
Gladwell, Arthur, 305
Gollan, Detective Officer Roderick,
  243–4, 302, 358
gonorrhoea, 202
Graham, Fanny Winifred *see* Park,
  Fanny Winifred
Graphic (newspaper), 96
Greenwood, James, 274–5
Greenwood, John, 119, 318–19

H—, Betsey *see* Betsey H—
Hagen, Catherine, 345, 347
Hagen, Oliver, 345
hairstyles, 96
Hammond, Charles, 108
Hampshire Advertiser, 339
*Hampshire Telegraph and Sussex
  Chronicle*, 338–9
Harvey, Dr Alfred, 199–200, 202,
  241
Haweis, Mrs H.R.: *The Art of Beauty*,
  98
Haxell, Edward Nelson, 228–30, 357
Haxell's Hotel, West Strand: ball,
  223–4, 228–9; incorporated into
  Strand Palace Hotel, 357
Haymarket, London, 102
Heath, Sir Robert, 243, 290
Henry, Sir Thomas, 314–15
hermaphrodites, 211–12
Hewitt, Frank, 108

Highbury Barn *see* drag balls
homosexual: as term, 276
houses of accommodation, 26–7
House of Correction *see* Coldbath
  Fields, House of Correction
Hughes, Dr William, 177–8,
  199–203
Hulme, Manchester, 227
Hurt, Louis: on Stella's mincing walk,
  85; courts Stella, 126–7, 132,
  179; invites Stella to Edinburgh,
  178–9, 188; background and
  character, 179; on Stella's
  feminine appearance, 214–15,
  285; and arrest of Stella and
  Fanny, 235–6; devotion to Stella,
  236; visits police, 240; arrested
  and confined in Newgate, 245,
  257; charges of sodomy
  withdrawn, 283; trial, 288, 290;
  Mrs Boulton testifies about, 328;
  later career and death, 358–9

Illustrated London News, 35
Illustrated Police News, 34, 89, 249,
  267

Jim, John Jameson, 180, 237
Johnson, Dr Henry James, 191, 202,
  204, 208, 210–11; *Gonorrhoea
  and Its Consequences*, 202
Johnston, Betsy, 108
Johnston, Malcolm ('the Maid of
  Athens'), 109–10, 223, 3533
Jones, Lieutenant (friend of Lord
  Arthur Clinton), 135

Karslake, Sir John, 295
Kay, William, 303
Kean, James, 111
Kerley, Detective Sergeant Frederick,

8, 37, 43–5, 109, 319, 354–5

Kersey, Benjamin, 112

Lancet (journal), 197, 205–6, 250

Layton, George, 193

Le Gros Clark, Dr Frederick, 199–202, 206

Leopold, Prince: birth, 99

Lesmahagow, Lanarkshire *see* Abbey Green

Lewis, Mr George: acts for Fanny and Stella, 285–7; character and style, 286–7; and Martha Stacey, 305; advises Stella's mother as witness, 321–2; later career and knighthood, 355

Lewis, Mr (chief clerk in bank), 60–1

Littlechild, Inspector, 355

Liverpool Mercury, 337

Lives of Boulton and Park: Extraordinary Revelations (pamphlet), 90

London and County Bank, Islington, 60

London Lock Hospital, 202

Lord Chief Justice *see* Cockburn, Sir Alexander (Lord Chief Justice)

Lyceum Theatre, London, 15

Martin, Bennett, 105

masturbation, 276–7

Mayne, Sir Richard (Metropolitan Police Commissioner), 316

Medical Times and Gazette, 276

Metropolitan Police: special branch and surveillance, 317–18

Motley, John Lothrop, 241, 244

Mullin, Judge Joseph, 182–3

Munby, Arthur, 226

Mundell, Hugh: at Strand Theatre, 1, 4, 6; accompanies Fanny and Stella to police station, 10–11, 23, 32; meets Fanny and Stella, 12–23; appears in Bow Street Magistrates' Court, 33–4, 90; on bond between Fanny and Stella, 86; as chief prosecution witness, 237, 301, 308; later career as chiropodist, 356

Munro, Louis: as Stella's leading man, 337–9; takes up with Carlotta Gibbings, 354

New York, 341

New York Clipper (newspaper), 342

Newcastle, Henry Pelham Alexander Pelham-Clinton, 6th Duke of, 252

Newcastle, Henry Pelham Archibald Pelham-Clinton, 7th Duke of, 359

Newgate Gaol, 198–9, 205–6, 245

Newlyn, Sambrooke, 254

Norris, Isabella, 70

Northern Echo, 343

Nottingham Daily Guardian, 252

Observer (newspaper), 249

Ortner, Houle & Co., Messrs, 135

Ouvry, Mr (solicitor), 255–6

Pall Mall Gazette, 247, 274, 277, 280, 340

Paris: cross-dressers, 97

Park, Judge Alexander (Fanny's father), 74–7, 263, 268, 340

Park, Lieut. Atherton Allan (Fanny's brother), 65, 67

Park, Fanny Winifred: at Strand Theatre, 1, 3, 6; appearance and dress, 5, 13, 74, 80–2, 129, 141–2, 284; arrested, 7–11, 31; gives name as Frederick William Park, 9; Mundell meets, 12–23;

appears before Bow Street
magistrate and charged, 34–7;
remanded in custody, 40–1;
examined by Dr Paul, 50–1, 310;
family background and
upbringing, 65–6; character and
looks, 67–70, 79–82, 345–6;
effeminacy, 68–70, 74; home
schooled, 70; liking for men,
71–3; articled to solicitor, 75,
138; behaviour and manner,
75–6; acting, 76–7, 82–3, 212;
Stella's view of, 79; early sexual
experience, 80–1; pretends to
widowhood, 83–4; friendship
with Stella, 84–7, 128; second
court appearance, 88–91; drag
wardrobe and accoutrements,
92–8; hair care, 96–7; beard
problem, 97–8; testimonies and
evidence against, 114–18, 121–5;
absences from Gepp & Sons
(solicitors), 138–9, 148–9; at
Stella's Southampton Street
lodgings with Lord Arthur,
139–40, 142; and Stella's
relations with Lord Arthur,
144–6; hopes for marriage to
Lord Arthur, 146–7;
correspondence and confidences
with Lord Arthur, 163–6; at Miss
Empson's in Davies Street, 169,
172, 174; Lord Arthur sleeps
with, 174, 176; reconciliation
with Stella, 178; treated for
syphilis, 187–8, 191–3, 196–7,
203, 238, 309–11, 345; trial
before Lord Chief Justice, 191–2,
282, 284, 308; in Newgate Gaol,
198–9, 205–6, 245; medically
examined in prison, 199–200,

204, 206, 208–9, 238; femininity
of body, 210–11; supposed
hermaphroditism, 211–12, 215;
relations with Carlotta Gibbings,
224–5; attends Carlotta's ball,
224, 228–31; released on bail,
267, 283; charges of sodomy
withdrawn, 283; grows beard,
284–5; criminal charges, 288;
letters to Lord Arthur read out in
court, 299–300; under police
surveillance, 316–17; in Mrs
Boulton's testimony, 328; and
father's death, 340–1; acting in
America as 'Fred Fenton', 341;
death from syphilis, 345; estate
and will, 347

Park, Harry (Fanny's brother): and
Fanny's home life, 66–70; sexual
relations with men, 71–2, 77;
arrested and absconds to
Scotland, 73–4, 82, 113, 187–8,
261–3; bond with Fanny, 74; in
Edinburgh, 176; propensity for
working men, 192; prospective
arrest, 237; lies low (as Charles
Ferguson) in Abbey Green,
Lanarkshire, 257–60, 266; sexual
adventures in London, 260–2;
letter to Stella, 264–5, 297–8;
rearrested by Thompson, 267–8;
and sentenced to twelve months'
hard labour, 267–8, 298; and
father's death, 341

Park, Frederick William *see* Park,
Fanny Winifred

Park, Lucy (Fanny's sister), 66–8, 70,
72

Parry, Mr Sergeant, 268, 300, 307,
313–14

Paul, Dr James Thomas: duties as

police surgeon, 42–3; examines
Fanny and Stella, 44–5, 50–1,
199, 238, 310, 315; interest in
sodomy, 46, 48–50, 201, 276;
studies under Alfred Swaine
Taylor, 201; gives evidence and
cross-examined at trial, 309,
311–15, 327, 331–2; later career
and death, 353
Pavitt, Charles, 76, 128, 212–14,
325, 357
*Pearl, The: a Monthly Journal of
Facetiae and Voluptuous Reading*,
99
Peck, Louisa, 139–40, 161, 180, 305,
308
Peel, Percival, 229
Pelham-Clinton, Lord Arthur: Stella's
relations with, 129–37, 139,
142–6, 218; theatrical interests,
132–3; engagement to Miss
Matthews collapses, 134; financial
difficulties, 134–6, 144, 155;
offers to provide catering for
Stella's coming-of-age party,
136–7; comes between Stella and
Fanny, 143; Fanny hopes to
marry, 146–7; visits Scarborough
with Stella, 152–4, 156–8, 325–6;
and Stella's moods and demands,
160–3; correspondence and
confidences with Fanny, 163–6;
lodges at Miss Empson's in
Davies Street, 168–9, 171–3;
sleeps with Fanny, 174, 176;
confirms Stella is a man, 215; and
Stella's dalliance with Captain
Cox, 218–21; with Stella at
Carlotta's ball, 231–3; arrest
delayed, 246–7; disappearance
and reported death and burial,

247–56, 287, 337; letters from
Fanny read out in court, 299–300;
Mrs Boulton approves of, 329;
reported reappearances in New
York and Australia, 343–4;
question of death unsolved, 359
Penny Illustrated, 283
Poland, Mr (prosecuting attorney),
91–2, 241–2, 297
Pollard, William (Assistant Treasury
Solicitor), 221, 287, 316, 318
Porcupine (journal), 251–2, 283
prostitutes, male: prevalence, 104–7;
payments for, 107–8; marry, 108;
relations with police, 109–13;
blackmailed, 110–11
prostitution: in Britain, 270

Queensberry, John Sholto Douglas,
8th Marquis of, 355

Reeve, John, 116–19, 304, 357
Reeve, Wybert, 157–8
Reynolds's Newspaper, 88, 114, 209,
247, 251, 279, 343
Richards, Mr & Mrs (of Dulwich),
129–30, 329
Ricord, Philippe, 190, 205
Rimmel, Eugene, 2
Roberts, George, 355
Roberts, W.H., 218, 221, 250–2, 255
Rochester, John Wilmot, 2nd Earl of:
Sodom, 273
Royal Alhambra Palace, Leicester
Square, 116–18, 304

Sarah (whore), 108–9
Sarony, Napoleon, 342
Sarony, Oliver, 156
Saturday Review, 81, 279
Saul, Jack: earnings as prostitute,

107–8; on attraction to men of cross-dressers, 230; observes Stella and Lord Arthur at Carlotta's ball, 231–3; in Cleveland Street scandal (1890), 354; *The Sins of the Cities of the Plain*, 216, 356

Scarborough: social life, 148–52; Stella and Lord Arthur visit, 162–7

Scarborough Gazette and Weekly List of Visitors, 148–9, 151–3

Scott, Eliza (or Elijah), 106

Seward, William H., 182

Seymour, William Digby: defends Stella at trial, 303, 311, 314–15, 317, 320, 322, 326–7, 329–34

Shelly, Mr (manager of Surrey Theatre), 13–14

Sherlock, Thomas, Bishop of London, 274

Shillingford, Police Constable Thomas, 103, 302

Sidebottom, Alexander, 356

Sinclair, Donald, 175–6, 184, 237

Sinclair, Robbie, 184, 237

'Sissy' *see* Thomas, Cecil

Sloggett, William Henry, 271

Smith, George, 116, 119–25, 306–8, 316, 319

Sneaking Regard, A (burlesque farce), 94

Sodomy (buggery): as criminal offence, 36–7; medical evidence and experience of, 47–9, 204–5, 207, 238; between men and women, 49; penalty for, 78; and syphilis, 189–90, 193–7; defined, 198, 276; seen as social evil, 272–6, 278–81; as issue in Fanny and Stella trial, 292–4, 320

Solomon, Simeon, 296, 308, 355

Somerville, Dr, 47

Somerville, William, 106, 288, 298

Sothern, Edward Askew, 91

Southampton Street, London: Stella and Lord Arthur lodge in, 139–41; Stella and Lord Arthur leave, 161

Stacey, Frances (Martha's niece), 27, 29

Stacey, Martha, 24–9, 93, 304–5, 308, 316

Stacey, Mrs (Martha's mother), 25, 27

Stella *see* Boulton, Stella

Stock, Essex *see* Theatre Royal

Straight, Mr (defence lawyer), 170–1, 217, 219, 300

Strand Theatre, London, 1–3, 15, 22, 38

Surrey Theatre, London, 12–13, 15–16

Swinburne, Algernon Charles, 296

syphilis, 188–9, 193–5; feared, 271

Talbot, James Beard, 106

Tardieu, Ambroise, 205, 207–8; *Étude médico-légale sur les attentats aux moeurs*, 48, 276, 311–12

Taylor, Dr Alfred Swaine, 46–8, 200–1, 204, 207; *A Manual of Medical Jurisprudence*, 200

Teague, Inspector, 227

Theakston, Solomon Wilkinson, 148, 151, 154

Theakston's Guide to Scarborough, 151

Theatre Royal, Stock, Essex, 212

Thomas, Cecil ('Sissy'): at Strand Theatre, 1, 4, 7; friendship with

Stella, 128; Inspector Thomas pursues, 263; tried *in absentia*, 288, 298; later career, 356

Thompson, Inspector James: and arrest of Fanny and Stella, 8–9, 37, 42–3, 45, 88; overwhelmed with testimonies, 114–15, 118–19, 124; and Fiske's status as Consul, 240; requests search of Fiske's premises in Edinburgh, 243; and disappearance of Lord Arthur, 248, 253–5, 263; travels to Scotland to apprehend Harry Park, 263–4, 266–7; and Fanny and Stella's lying-low on bail, 283; payments to George Smith, 307; meets Dr Paul before arrest of Fanny and Stella, 313–14; conspires to bring charges, 316, 318–19; retirement and death, 354

Times, The, 278–9

Toole, J.L. (actor), 91

Tottenham, 54

Treasury: payments to witnesses and police officers, 319–20

Tristan, Flora, 107

Tyrwhitt, Mr (magistrate), 112

Vane-Tempest, Lady Susan, 343

Veyne, Dr François-Auguste, 97

Victoria, Queen, 99

Vincent, Howard, 106

Wakefield Street: house investigated by police, 24–5, 29–30, 38–9, 91, 299, 304

Walker, Police Constable Charles, 39, 125, 316

'Walter': *My Secret Life*, 108

Warner, Henry B., 347

Weekly Times, 249, 252

Western Mail, 344

Westminster Hall, 282

White, Police Constable George, 77, 113, 261–2, 264, 267, 298

White, Mr (of Gresham Street), 97

Wight, Albert, 128

Wilde, Oscar, 355; *Lady Windermere's Fan*, 355–6

Wimpole Street, 65, 67

Yardley, Mr (magistrate), 262

Yokel's Preceptor, The, 15, 279